Metamodernism

Radical Cultural Studies

Series editors: Fay Brauer, Maggie Humm, Tim Lawrence, Stephen Maddison, Ashwani Sharma and Debra Benita Shaw (Centre for Cultural Studies Research, University of East London, UK)

The Radical Cultural Studies series publishes monographs and edited collections to provide new and radical analyses of the culturopolitics, sociopolitics, aesthetics and ethics of contemporary cultures. The series is designed to stimulate debates across and within disciplines, foster new approaches to Cultural Studies and assess the radical potential of key ideas and theories.

Sewing, Fighting and Writing: Radical Practices in Work, Politics and Culture, Maria Tamboukou

Radical Space: Exploring Politics and Practice, edited by Debra Benita Shaw and Maggie Humm

Science Fiction, Fantasy and Politics: Transmedia World-Building Beyond Capitalism, Dan Hassler-Forest

EU, Europe Unfinished: Europe and the Balkans in a Time of Crisis, edited by Zlatan Krajina and Nebojša Blanuša

Postcolonial Interruptions, Unauthorised Modernities, Iain Chambers

Austerity as Public Mood: Social Anxieties and Social Struggles, Kirsten Forkert

Metamodernism: Historicity, Affect, Depth, after Postmodernism, edited by Robin van den Akker, Alison Gibbons and Timotheus Vermeulen

Pornography, Materiality and Cultural Politics, Stephen Maddison (forthcoming)

Affect and Social Media: Emotion, New Materialism, Anxiety and Contagion, edited by Tony Sampson, Stephen Maddison and Darren Ellis (forthcoming)

Writing the Modern Family: Contemporary Literature, Motherhood and Neoliberal Culture, Roberta Garrett (forthcoming)

The Male Body in Digital Culture, Jamie Hakim (forthcoming)

Metamodernism

Historicity, Affect, and Depth After Postmodernism

Edited by Robin van den Akker,
Alison Gibbons and Timotheus Vermeulen

ROWMAN &
LITTLEFIELD
──────INTERNATIONAL
London • New York

Published by Rowman & Littlefield International Ltd
Unit A, Whitacre Mews, 26–34 Stannary Street, London SE11 4AB
www.rowmaninternational.com

Rowman & Littlefield International Ltd. is an affiliate of Rowman & Littlefield
4501 Forbes Boulevard, Suite 200, Lanham, Maryland 20706, USA
With additional offices in Boulder, New York, Toronto (Canada), and Plymouth (UK)
www.rowman.com

British Library Cataloguing in Publication Data
A catalogue record for this book is available from the British Library

ISBN: HB 978-1-7834-8960-2
           PB 978-1-7834-8961-9

Library of Congress Cataloging-in-Publication Data
Names: Van den Akker, Robin, 1982– editor. | Gibbons, Alison, editor. | Vermeulen,
    Timotheus, editor.
Title: Metamodernism : historicity, affect and depth after postmodernism / edited by
    Robin van den Akker, Alison Gibbons and Timotheus Vermeulen.
Description: London ; New York : Rowman & Littlefield International, [2017] |
    Series: Radical cultural studies | Includes bibliographical references and index.
Identifiers: LCCN 2017031627 (print) | LCCN 2017041820 (ebook) | ISBN
    9781783489626 (electronic) | ISBN 9781783489602 (cloth : alk. paper) | ISBN
    9781783489619 (pbk. : alk. paper)
Subjects: LCSH: Post-postmodernism (Literature) | Postmodernism (Literature) |
    Literature—Aesthetics.
Classification: LCC PN98.P67 (ebook) | LCC PN98.P67 M49 2017 (print) | DDC
    809/.9113—dc23
LC record available at https://lccn.loc.gov/2017031627

∞™ The paper used in this publication meets the minimum requirements of American
National Standard for Information Sciences – Permanence of Paper for Printed Library
Materials, ANSI/NISO Z39.48–1992.

Printed in the United States of America

For Julie; for Nick; for Ines.

Contents

List of Figures and Table

FIGURES

TABLE

Acknowledgements

This book has benefited from many stimulating discussions, sharp debates and critical interventions. We are particularly grateful to the many contributors to the research platform *Notes on Metamodernism* that was founded in 2009 and that we have been editing with a great editorial team ever since.

The aim of the research platform was, and still is, to make a start with mapping, transcoding and situating contemporary aesthetics and culture by way of the arts. Today it features countless contributions from – mostly young – writers across the globe, all of whom have sought to document and conceptualise developments in arts, aesthetics and culture that are symptomatic of the post-postmodern or, rather, metamodern condition. Without these contributions, our research project on metamodernism – to which we hope this volume will contribute – would have been more daunting, if not to say impossible, as well as too single-minded to say anything meaningful about the recent reconfigurations of Western capitalist societies at large. If we have to name anything that has given us the satisfaction that comes – is supposed to come – with intellectual collaboration and exploring new lines of inquiry, it has been *NoM*.

We especially have to thank Nadine Feßler, Luke Turner and Hila Shachar (in the order of appearance in our editorial life) for their co-explorations of metamodernism and their much-needed interventions in the editorial course of *NoM*. Nadine and Hila were both unable to contribute an undoubtedly very valuable chapter to this volume – and their voices will be missed. Luke's ongoing artistic practice, alongside Nastja Säde Rönkkö and Shia LaBeouf, has been both fascinating to observe from afar and thought-provoking in its ambitions.

Our respective departments have been supportive of our research – the Faculty of Philosophy at Erasmus University Rotterdam and the Humanities

Department at Erasmus University College Rotterdam, the Department of Cultural Studies at the University of Nijmegen, the Institute for Media and Communication at the University of Oslo and the Humanities Research Centre at Sheffield Hallam University who also provided financial support for us to meet during the process of editing this book.

We have been fortunate to be invited to various symposiums and conferences on the post-postmodern contemporary. Raoul Eshelman's Thinking in Unity After Postmodernism (Munchen, 2010) has been the first in a series of forums in which our intuitions and conceptualisations have been rigorously tested and accordingly adjusted. Another notable litmus-test of our ideas has been Danuta Fjellestad's and David Watson's The Future of Futures Symposium (Uppsala 2013), an event filled with fierce debates (and for that we are more than thankful) with, especially, Jennifer Ashton, Walter Benn Michaels, Marie-Laure Ryan, Pieter Vermeulen and Phillip E. Wegner. We very much enjoyed Oscillate! Metamodernism and the Humanities, a symposium at the University of Strathclyde. Thank you to the organisers for inviting us, and for the great conversations: Biserka Anderson, Fateha Aziz, Sara Helen Binney, Andrew Campbell, Brendan Dempsey, Fiona McKay, Craig Pollard, Emma Sullivan and Andrew Woods, among others.

We had the pleasure of co-organising the symposium Metamodernism: The Return of History at Stedelijk Museum in Amsterdam (2014). The event added countless new coordinates, alternative itineraries and uncharted spaces to our map of the contemporary. For this, we would like to thank our co-organisers Hendrik Folkerts and Britte Sloothaak. Hang in there, chaps! We also would like to thank the participants for their invaluable cartographic efforts: Michel Bauwens, Hassnae Bouazza, Jelle Brandt Corstius, Francis Fukuyama, Ewald Engelen, Jörg Heiser, Birgitta Jónsdóttir, Shia LaBeouf, Zihni Ozdil, Nina Power, Sarah Rifky, Nastja Säde Rönkkö, Cally Spooner, Jonas Staal, Adam Thirlwell, Camille de Toledo, Luke Turner and Sjoerd van Tuinen.

We definitely must thank Christian Moraru for his ongoing support and encouragement, for his own inspiring work on the contemporary and for including us in *American Book Review*'s (2013) issue on metamodernism. We indeed still have our work cut out for us, Christian!

We are in debt to many friends and colleagues with whom we have discussed postmodernism and post-postmodernism (whether under the name of metamodernism or otherwise) – so many thanks to Ross Abbinnett, Jan Alber, Bassam el Baroni, Alice Bell, Jonathan Bignell, Antoon van den Braembussche, Rosi Braidotti, Joe Bray, Kieran Connell, Ben Cranfield, Allard van den Dulk, Amy Elias, Tarek El-Ariss, Mark Fisher, Matthew Hart, Maria Hlavajova, Brian McHale, Simone Knox, Stephen Knudsen, Jos de Mul, Niels van Poecke, Wendy Knepper, Milica Tomic, Anselm Wagner, Tanja Wagner, James Whitfield and countless others.

We must, of course, thank the editorial team at Rowman and Littlefield International who have been enthusiastic about the project since we first discussed it with them: Martina O'Sullivan, Michael Watson and the Radical Cultural Studies series editors: Fay (Fae) Brauer, Maggie Humm, Tim Lawrence, Stephen Maddison, Ashwani Sharma and Debra Benita Shaw.

Finally, our greatest thanks go to our partners to whom we dedicate this book.

Chapter 1

Periodising the 2000s, or, the Emergence of Metamodernism

Robin van den Akker and Timotheus Vermeulen

> Thinking at once negatively and positively about it is a beginning, but what we need is a new vocabulary. The languages that have been useful in talking about culture and politics in the past don't really seem adequate to this historical moment. (Jameson on postmodernism quoted in Stephanson 1988, 12–13)

In 1989, the social theorist Francis Fukuyama wrote a controversial article in the *National Interest* under the title 'The End of History?' In the article, he argued that with the pending demise of the communist empire, History with a capital H – that is, not simply the chronology of time passing, but the chronicle of mankind's evolutionary process – had ended. With the 'unabashed victory of liberal democracy', he suggested in his subsequent book *The End of History and the Last Man* (1992, xii):

> mankind had achieved a form of society that satisfied its deepest and most fundamental longings. . . . This did not mean that the natural cycle of birth, life, and death would end, that important events would no longer happen, or that newspapers reporting them would cease to be published. It meant, rather, that there would be no further progress in the development of underlying principles and institutions, because all of the really big questions had been settled.

Some twenty years later, in 2012, Fukuyama wrote another article broaching the subject of History. Published in *Foreign Affairs*, it was entitled 'The Future of History'. Here, Fukuyama wrote that calling the End of History may, in retrospect, have been just a bit premature, for the alleged 'unabashed victory of liberal democracy', he conceded, had since come under some scrutiny. Democratic governments all over the world increasingly failed to deliver on its promises: most national economies have not proliferated but have stagnated or gone into long-term recessions; political extremism – left and right, liberal and conservative, secular and religious – is on the rise; the middle classes, the traditional stronghold of twentieth-century liberal democracy, are shrinking; and social media have problematised twentieth-century notions of freedom of speech and the free press. In addition, a serious contender for geopolitical hegemony has emerged: China's state-regulated market system. There are, in other words, plenty of 'big questions' left to answer.

Since the turn of the millennium, it has become increasingly commonplace to declare that History has not halted and has not come to a standstill. Various authors from across the political spectrum have, for instance, written about the remarkable 'return' (Kagan 2008), 'revenge' (Milne 2012) or 'rebirth' (Badiou 2012) of History after the End of History. These authors all agree, as a premise, that History has been rebooted by recent world historical crises of an ecological, economic or (geo-)political nature. Arquilla perhaps most aptly summarises the current historical moment with his notion of a 'bend of History' (2011). A bending of History may simultaneously imply forcing History into a different direction or shape as well as causing History to deflect from the more or less straight line of teleological narrative. It also captures the increasing awareness across culture that there is something at stake, yet we are still very much unsure what this something – hidden around the bend, as it were – might be (and we will only really know in hindsight).

To an extent, this book is about the bend of History and its associated 'senses of a bend' that have come to define contemporary cultural production and political discourse. Our use of the phrase 'senses of a bend' is, of course, both a wink and a homage to Fredric Jameson's canonical essay 'Postmodernism, or the Cultural Logic of Late Capitalism' in which he tried to come to terms with all of the – by then very dominant – 'senses of the end of this or that' (1991 [1984], 1) in postmodern art, culture and politics. For Jameson, the main casualties of all of these postmodern 'senses of the end' might have very well been History and the historical imagination.

Now that History appears to have, once more, been kick-started, the postmodern vernacular has proven increasingly inapt and inept in coming to terms with our changed social situation. This goes for discussions of History as much as it goes for debates about the arts. We can think, here, of the waning of a host of different postmodern impulses, which nonetheless share some kind of family resemblance (Jameson's 'senses of the end', if you will): pop art and deconstructive conceptual art (from Warhol to Hirst, by way of Koons); punk, new wave and grunge's cynicism in popular music; disaffected minimalism in cinema; spectacular formalism in architecture; metafictional irony in literature, as well as the whole emphasis on a dehumanising cyberspace in science fictions of all kinds. Moreover, since the turn of the millennium, we have seen the emergence of various 'new', often overlapping, aesthetic phenomena such as the New Romanticism in the arts (Vermeulen and van den Akker 2010), the New Mannerism in crafts (van Tuinen, this volume), the New Aesthetic in design (Sterling 2012), the New Sincerity in literature (Konstantinou 2009, 2016a), the New Weird or Nu-Folk in music (Poecke 2014), Quirky Cinema and Quality Television (MacDowell 2012; Vermeulen and Rustad 2013), as well as the discovery of a new terrain for architecture (Allen and McQuade 2011), each of them characterised by an attempt to incorporate postmodern stylistic and formal conventions while moving beyond them. Meanwhile, we witness the return of realist and modernist forms, techniques and aspirations (to which the metamodern has a decidedly different relation than the postmodern).

Metamodernism: Historicity, Affect and Depth after Postmodernism seeks to map and conceptualise the artistic and cultural phenomena related to the various senses of a bend and the return – in critical discourse and the popular imagination – of History (as the sum total of our objective conditions as well as the narrative that ties our present to a distant past and a distant future). In the seventies and eighties, critics like Linda Hutcheon, Charles Jencks, Hal Foster and Brian McHale began speaking of postmodernism (regardless of what they meant by it) because they believed the modernist ideals, methods and sensibilities had been superseded by something else entirely. Alongside other contemporary scholars (such as Lipovetsky 2005; Eshelman 2008; Bourriaud 2009; Kirby 2009; Moraru 2011), we feel that the postmodern discourses have lost their critical value when it comes to understanding contemporary arts, culture, aesthetics and politics. As Searle, writing about altermodernism, noted: 'Postmodernism is dead, but something altogether weirder has taken its place' (2009). Thus, what is needed is a new language to put into words this altogether weirder reality and its still stranger cultural landscape.

This book is an attempt to create such a language, or at least series of linked dialects, to come to an understanding of our current historical moment, a language that allows us to come to terms with the gap between what we thought we knew and the things we experience in our daily lives. For us, this language is metamodernism. There, we've said it. Admittedly, the hubris of delineating a historical moment and describing a social situation in terms of yet another '-ism' opens us up for Homeric laughter at best and fierce scorn at worst. Indeed, as Barker and Jane suggest in the most recent edition of their handbook *Cultural Studies*, such attempts are 'easy to mock' (2016, 251). This may be so – and we are happy to take the flak – but let us explain why we think our attempt deserves more than an easy laugh.

This book is part of an ongoing research project in which we – alongside many others – seek to: (1) map today's dominant cultural developments by way of the arts; (2) develop an adequate language to discuss these dominant ways of feeling, doing and thinking; and (3) relate these contemporary concepts, percepts and affects to recent reconfigurations of Western capitalist societies. These exercises in mapping, translating and situating are necessary to be able to discuss the ground tones in contemporary culture and, by extension, its undertones and overtones. It enables, in other words, discussing the dominant patterns in contemporary culture by means of a shared language, while allowing for the 'presence and coexistence of a range of very different, yet subordinate, features' (Jameson 1991 [1984], 4). Doing so leads to an understanding of what can and what cannot be done and thought – and, hence, what may *still* remain to be done and thought – in light of the most recent reconfigurations of Western capitalist societies and global capitalism.

METAMODERNISM

As we have defined it, metamodernism is a structure of feeling that emerged in the 2000s and has become the dominant cultural logic of Western capitalist societies. We use the term metamodernism both as a heuristic label to come to terms with a range of aesthetic and cultural predilections and as a notion to periodise these preferences. In other words, this book is neither a Greenbergian plea for a specific kind of art nor a Jencksian pigeonholing of individual architects. It is an attempt to chart – in much the same way Jameson has done for postmodernism – the dominant cultural logic of a specific stage in the development of Western capitalist societies, in all its many forms and disguises. It is an attempt, however flawed, to come to terms with today's condition as well as its culture, aesthetics and politics, by way of the arts.

The term metamodernism is by no means a new one. It has been used in geographical contexts as diverse as South America, Asia and Western Europe and has been used in disciplines as varied as experimental poetry and technology studies, physics, economics, mathematics and Eastern spirituality. The term has, in other words, a long and scattered history, the full lineage of which still has to be traced. Abramson (2015b) uncovered some of its prior uses, pinpointing its first articulation in the 1970s when it was used by Zavarzadeh to describe a tendency in literature to 'move beyond the interpretive modernist novel' (1975, 69). This tendency, Zavarzadeh argued, is exemplified by tropes (black humour, parody, metafiction, the abandonment of depth-models) and authors (Robbe-Grillet, Barth, Barthelme, Wolfe) that make apparent that his use of the term 'metamodern' indicates what is today generally considered (a variant of) postmodernism. This book is not the place for such a full-blown archaeology. Still, a few observations regarding the ways in which we use the term, and how this usage differs from others with similar interests in the post-postmodern, are in order.

When we wrote our initial essay 'Notes on Metamodernism' (2010) in 2008, our notion of the metamodern was constructed on foundations as diverse as Raymond William's notion of a structure of feeling (and its function in Fredric Jameson's (1991 [1984]) and David Harvey's (1990) studies of the interrelation between late capitalism and postmodern culture), Jos de Mul's (1999 [1990]) canonical study of the Romantic roots of modernism and postmodernism, and the recent neo-romantic turn in the visual arts of the early 2000s. In researching the term, we were aware of at least two other relevant uses of metamodernism. The first was Furlani's (2007) thorough, evocative study *Postmodernism and After: Guy Davenport* in which he discusses the oeuvre of writer Guy Davenport in terms of complementarity and 'contrasts absorbed into harmony' that aspire to transcend postmodern disorder (2007, 158). Second, in her essay 'Interconnections in Blakean and Metamodern Space' (2007), Dumitrescu describes metamodernism as a 'budding cultural paradigm' (2007) that is characterised by holism, connectionism and integration. Studying work by two very different authors – Blake and Houellebecq – Dumitrescu puts the emphasis on three particular strategies that for her defy postmodernism: 'connectionism (as a mode of thinking), bootstrapping (as a way of identifying connections) and the principle of theory overlapping' which, she argues, 'are but aspects of metamodernism' (2007). Both Furlani and Dumitrescu seek to develop an alternative – solution, even – to what they perceive to be the artistic dead ends and cultural failures of postmodernism; both look for these alternatives in dated and/or isolated forms of art, and both propose some kind of synthesis or harmony between modern and postmodern modes. Given the shared use of nomenclature, there are – unsurprisingly – some overlaps between their use and ours. Nevertheless, our employment of 'metamodernism' is different on at least three counts: (1) the aim and line of inquiry; (2) the selection of cultural texts and practices, and, inevitably given these differences; (3) the (preliminary) findings.

First of all, the cultural texts and practices we would describe as metamodern do, in our view, not offer a solution to the problematic of postmodernism (however the postmodern is perceived). Despite suggestions to the contrary (see Turner 2011; Eve 2012; Abramson 2015a), our conceptualisation of metamodernism is *neither* a manifesto, *nor* a social movement, stylistic register, or philosophy – even though it takes into account a number of developments that may well be regarded as social movements (Occupy, the Tea Party), stylistic registers (the New Sincerity, Freak Folk) and philosophies (Speculative Realism, OOO). Metamodernism is a structure of feeling that emerges from, and reacts to, the postmodern as much as it is a cultural logic that corresponds to today's stage of global capitalism. As such, it is shot through with productive contradictions, simmering tensions, ideological formations and – to be frank – frightening developments (our incapacity to effectively combat xenophobic populism comes to mind). In some ways, there is reason for optimism; in many ways we think we are even worse off than before. Thus, we wish to state very clearly that we are not celebrating the waning of the postmodern – nor, indeed, are we pushing a metamodern agenda.

Second, and crucially, metamodernism – as a structure of feeling or cultural logic – is developed through a systematic reading of dominant tendencies in contemporary artistic and cultural production rather than isolated or dated phenomena. These tendencies, moreover, are – in their insistence on the impossibility of reconciliation, their slipperiness, their adherence to postmodern tropes – markedly different from those discussed by Furlani and Dumitrescu (or indeed the many others we do not mention here). Our study of the romantic turn in the visual arts of the early 2000s is a case in point (Vermeulen and van den Akker 2010). This study comprised of dozens of contemporary cultural texts – from individual works to whole oeuvres to group exhibitions to museum shows. It is a flawed essay, for sure. We failed, for instance, to recognise and include the emergent nationalist, if not fascist, tendencies in contemporary culture as mediated through, say, the overtly neoromantic work of Dennis Rudolph. A consistent feature, though, of both our work and the chapters included in this volume is the textual analysis of culturally dominant phenomena as a starting point for any critique of the current historical moment.

Third, metamodernism – as a heuristic label and a periodising term – is characterised by oscillation rather than synthesis, harmony, reconciliation and so on (Vermeulen and van den Akker 2010). This oscillation could be said to be shorthand for the dominant way in which the various senses of a bend are manifest in today's artistic representations, cultural mediations and political discourses. Whereas the postmodern 'Holiday from History' (Will 2001; Krauthammer 2003) amounted to the sensibility that the dialectic came to a standstill in the mediatised and commoditised comfort zones of the Global North, the current historical moment evokes the sense that the dialectic is once more in motion or, indeed, as is its unstable nature, in constant oscillation, continuously overcoming and undermining hitherto fixed or consolidated positions.

A STRUCTURE OF FEELING

It should be clear from our discussion earlier that we understand metamodernism first and foremost as what Raymond Williams called a 'structure of feeling': a sensibility, a sentiment that is so pervasive as to call it structural. 'Structure of feeling' is, in some ways, a confusing concept. As O'Connor writes, scholars have used it in all kinds of ways, not all of them compatible (2006, 79). Some treat it as a cultural superstructure in the classical Marxian sense or as cultural hegemonic following a more Gramscian notion; at times, it features as a sensibility, then as a literary strategy. Part of the blame must be placed on the shoulders of Williams himself (see Simpson 1995; Filmer 2003; O'Connor 2006). Surprisingly, considering how central the concept was to his thinking, Williams never systematically developed it. He fleshed it out in fits and starts, across essays and books years apart, more often than not while pursuing other lines of thought. Consequently, as Simpson has noted, the 'key formulation' of the structure of feeling was used 'at times quite loosely', with 'some fundamental problems and unsolved ambiguities in the exposition' (Simpson 1995, 36).

Williams first introduced the notion of the structure of feeling in a thin volume of film criticism that he co-authored with Michael Orrom in 1954. *A Preface to Film* is, perhaps because of its theoretical slightness, often over-looked in accounts of the concept, yet it offers a keen insight in the intuition that spurred Williams on to propose it. A structure of feeling, Williams wrote, 'lies deeply embedded in our lives; it cannot be merely extracted and summa-rized; it is perhaps only in art – and this is the importance of art – that it can be realized, and communicated, as a whole experience' (Williams 1954, 40). In other words, a structure of feeling is a sentiment, or rather still a sensibility that everyone shares, that everyone is aware of, but which cannot easily, if at all, be pinned down. Its tenor, however, can be traced in art, which has the capability to express a common experience of a time and place. If this today, after decades of (post)structuralism and the quantification of the humanities, sounds vague, it is precisely what Williams intended (2001 [1954], 33):

> While we may, in the study of a past period, separate out particular aspects of life, and treat them as if they were self-contained, it is obvious that this is only how they may be studied, not how they were experienced. We examine each element as a precipitate, but in the living experience of the time every element was in solution, an inseparable part of a complex while. And it seems to be true, from the nature of art, that it is from such a totality that the artist draws; it is in art, primarily, that the effect of the totality, the dominant structure of feeling, is expressed and embodied. To relate a work of art to any part of that observed totality may, in varying degrees, be useful; but it is a common experience, in analysis, to realize that when one has measured the work against the separable parts, there yet remains some element for which there is no external counterpart. This element, I believe, is what I have named the structure of feeling of a period.

As drinkers of Scotch whiskey will know, single malt island and coastal whiskeys tend to be characterised by a saline savour. None of these whiskeys count salt among their ingredients, however. Like all single malts, the spirits only contain malted grain – often barley, occasionally rye – yeast and water. Their distinct saltiness, presumably, is blown into the brew via the sea winds. In *A Preface to Film*, Williams describes the concept of the structure of feeling in much the same way: it is that element of culture that circumscribes it but nonetheless cannot be traced back to any one of its individual ingredients. It can be ascribed, instead, to the particular experience of time or place. Subsequently, the dominant structure of feeling expressed by the art of one period or generation – ironic, anxious – may differ radically from that of another – sincere, hopeful. Indeed, Williams is at pains to explain that artistic conventions are malleable depending on the context: 'As the structure changes, new means are perceived and realized, while old means come to appear empty and artificial' (2001 [1954], 33).

A structure of feeling is, in this sense, 'a particular quality of social experience . . . historically distinct from other particular qualities, which gives the sense of a generation or of a period' (Williams 1977, 131). It is present in movements and styles and other phenomena without being reducible to any of them in particular. For example, Obama's 'Yes we can', the cinematic tradition of 'Quirky' associated with the films of Wes Anderson and Miranda July, the 'Freak Folk' of Coco Rosie and Devendra Banhart and the literary trend emanating from the writings of David Foster Wallace known as the 'New Sincerity' are each characterised by a sense of earnestness and hope, however much their context, genre, rhetorical logic, stylistic register and/ or intention may vary from one another. In contrast, the politics and culture of the nineties – ranging from the third way to grunge, from tradition of the 'smart' film to the oeuvre of Bret Easton Ellis – were typified by a rather cynical attitude towards reality.

Just as the prefix 'post-' related directly to the structure of feeling postmodernism addressed – to what Jameson called the 'senses of an end' – the prefix 'meta-' too establishes a particular understanding of the current sensibility. *Meta* in Greek means three things: with or among, between and after. We will deal with the consequence of each of these in turn.

With or *Among*

First, the metamodern structure of feeling is situated *with or among* older and newer structures of feeling. As indicated, this first and foremost entails that metamodernism is today's dominant structure of feeling among a host of subordinate structures of feeling that Williams dubbed residuals and emergents. Yet it also entails that metamodern culture has a distinctively different relation to the past and the future than postmodern culture. The prefix 'post-' indicated, among other things, a disconnected present that 'bracketed the past' and foreclosed utopian desires (Jameson 1991 [1984]) – being, as it were, beyond such petty concerns as already tested or yet to be realised ways of living, succumbing instead to a credit-fuelled moment of euphoria, induced by free-floating signifiers on surface level. In contrast, the prefix 'meta-' evokes a moment in which the past and the future are seen as alternative credit issuers – say, a local credit union or global peer-to-peer lender – that may enable us to be taken out of post-postmodern bankruptcy into the realms of a renewed pathos, ethos and logos, albeit in a rather post-collective or, at best, loosely networked manner.

This corresponds, for instance, to the many Western European and Northern American literatures that both incorporate and move beyond postmodern authorial strategies by harking back, paradoxically, to modernist, realist or even earlier forms (e.g. see James 2012; van den Akker 2013; James and Seshagiri 2014; Pressman 2014). In the introduction to their edited collection *Reconsidering the Postmodern*, Vaessen and van Dijk, for instance, argue that the various contemporary European literatures search for 'a new position that tries to reconcile postmodern and pre-postmodern, humanistic elements' (2011, 23). Yet, as we previously argued (2010), there is some kind of cultural predilection, among all of the now–newly available 'pre-postmodern' elements, for modernism. James and Seshagiri, in their article 'Metamodernism: Narrative of Continuity and Revolution', have since made a similar point (2014, 87):

> a growing number of contemporary novelists – amongst them Julian Barnes, Ian McEwan, Cynthia Ozick, Will Self, and Zadie Smith – place a conception of modernism as revolution at the heart of their fictions, styling their twenty-first-century literary innovations as explicit engagements with the innovations of the early-twentieth century writing.

Mary Holland likewise reconnects twenty-first-century American fiction to the modern in 'Metamodernism', the closing chapter of *Succeeding Postmodernism* (2013, 199–202). Holland sees in contemporary fiction a 'truthful tension', the encapsulation of 'the twenty-first century mood of possibility for connection within self-conscious acts of language' (2013, 201). This, she argues, 'is also a kind of post-structural, metafictional version of modernism. But it is a modernism that is crucially self-aware, literature that is aware of being literature operating in a modernist vein, through postmodernist literary techniques turned towards modernist goals: metamodernism' (2013, 201). In this sense, here Holland's words, as well as James and Seshagiri's, in spite of the many differences between our arguments, echo our own formulation of metamodernism, by highlighting the tension, a being with or among, of postmodernist and modernist – and even realist and earlier – strategies and sensibilities across the contemporary metamodern structure of feeling.

These trends in contemporary literature point towards that what might be understood as the 'upcycling' of past styles, conventions and techniques. Whereas the postmoderns 'recycled' popular culture, canonised works and dead Masters by means of parody or pastiche, metamodern artists – from writers to artists in a broader sense – increasingly pick out from the scrapheap of history those elements that allow them to resignify the present and reimagine a future. We borrow these environmentalist notions (see, for example, McDonough and Braungart 2002) to emphasise the similarities and differences between postmodern and metamodern practices. Whereas both recycling and upcycling are forms of re-using waste products, the former results in a product with less purity and use value than the original, while the latter aims to approach – or do justice – to the original's style and substance while purportedly adding value. Metamodern artists often employ similar strategies to their postmodern predecessors in the way that they eclectically quote past styles, freely use older techniques and playfully adopt traditional conventions. Indeed, they, too, recycle the scrapheap of history. Yet, in doing so, metamodern artists attempt to move beyond the worn-out sensibilities and emptied practices of the postmodernists – not by radically parting with their attitudes and techniques but by incorporating and redirecting them towards new positions and horizons (however effective or politically sound these may be).

Between

The metamodern structure of feeling is also characterised by an oscillating in-betweenness or, rather, a dialectical movement that identifies with and negates – and hence, overcomes and undermines – conflicting positions, while being never congruent with these positions (keeping being *with or among* in check).[1] We would describe this oscillation as a both-neither dynamic (2010). The prefix 'meta' here refers to the Platonic notion of *metaxy* (μεταξὺ). As Voegelin (1989) has documented, Plato uses *metaxy* in *Symposium* to describe a sense of in-betweenness, as illustrated by the experience of the Eros and the *heros*, the demi-gods of Greek antiquity, more generally. 'What Is Love (*Eros*)?', Socrates asks his teacher Diotima. 'Is he mortal?' No, Diotima answers:

> he is neither mortal nor immortal, but in a *mean* (*metaxy*) between the two . . . an *intermediate* (*metaxy*) between the divine and the mortal. . . . He interprets . . . between gods and men, conveying and taking across to the gods the prayers and sacrifices of men, and to men the commands and replies of the gods; he is the mediator who spans the chasm which divides them.

---

[1] Boeve, Lieven. 2014. *Lyotard and Theology*. London, New York: Bloomsbury.

Because these *heros* are, impossibly, both god and man, they are also neither man nor god. Being mortal, after all, suggests that you will one day die, whereas divine immortality implies that death does not apply to you. Indeed, the Greek *heros*, as Voegelin has noted, oscillate continuously between 'life and death, immortality and mortality, perfection and imperfection, time and timelessness, between order and disorder, truth and untruth, sense and senselessness of existence' (1989, 119–20). To speak of metaxy, thus, is to speak of a movement between (opposite) poles: not a binary so much as a continuum that stretches from one to the other, not a balance but a pendulum swinging between various extremes.

We infer the notion of metaxy not to in order describe the human condition, let alone prescribe a model for artistic production, but to try to grasp the sensibility of the metamodern condition, to comprehend what it means to experience and live in the twenty-first century. Metamodernism oscillates between what we may call – but what of course cannot be reduced to – postmodern and pre-postmodern (and often modern) predilections: between irony and enthusiasm, between sarcasm and sincerity, between eclecticism and purity, between deconstruction and construction and so forth. Yet ultimately, it points to a sensibility that should be situated beyond the postmodern, one that is related to recent metamorphoses or qualitative changes in Western capitalist societies. Importantly, in moving back and forth between positions (modern and postmodern, say), metamodernism does *not* combine the 'best of both worlds' so to speak. A structure of feeling may amount to a 'world' or realm, but it is not better or worse. It is a discourse that gives meaning to our experience, such as what is good and what is bad in the first place. It, for instance, enables Bernie Sanders or Jeremy Corbyn to evoke the longevity of their principles while also enabling Donald Trump and Geert Wilders to shift daily between ideological positions while getting away with it.

After

Historically, metamodernism is tied to a moment after postmodernism in the sense that it has developed from and displaces postmodernism as the dominant cultural logic of Western capitalist societies. We argue that this shift from postmodernism to metamodernism should be situated in the 2000s, lest those years are not considered as a temporal decade but conceived as a historical period (roughly lasting, as we shortly illustrate, from 1999 to 2011) in which its various preconditions – gradually set in place in preceding decades – all emerged, converged and coagulated. It was in the 2000s, after all, that the millennial generation came of age; the maturity and availability of digital technologies and renewable technologies reached a critical threshold; the BRICs rose to geopolitical prominence; the era of 'facile fossils' and fantasies of nuclear abundance gave way to 'extreme oil' and dreams of fracking-induced energy independence; the so-called fourth wave of terrorism hit Western shores; the Iraq War destabilised the region and bankrupted the US treasury and war chest; 'Project Europe' got de-railed with the Dutch and French 'no' to the European Constitution; immigration policies and multicultural ideals backlashed in the midst of a revival of nationalist populism; US hegemony declined; the Arab Spring toppled many a dictator that had long served as a puppet for foreign vested interests; bad debts became, finally and inevitably, as much a problem for the Global North as it always has been for the Global South; and the financial crises inaugurated yet another round of neoliberalisation (this time by means of austerity measures of all sorts), exposing and deepening the institutionalised drive towards financial instability, economic inequality, labour precarity and ecological disaster.

Each in its own way, these developments gathered momentum and 'jelled and combined' – to use Jameson's (1991 [1984], xix) apt expression – to form the conditions in which the metamodern structure of feeling could become dominant. Thus, we attribute a similar historical importance to the '2000s' (as a transitional period) when it comes to the crystallisation of metamodernism into today's dominant cultural logic, as Jameson attributed to the '1960s' (as a transitional period) in relation to the emergence of postmodernism (Jameson 1984).

PERIODISING THE 2000s

Our claim that the 2000s should be conceived as a period entails that the previously listed developments should not be seen as a series of unrelated events but rather should be conceptualised as interlocking dialectical movements across spatial scales, temporal cycles and techno-economic, cultural and institutional levels. In this section, we attempt to think the present historically by means of various necessarily brief and incomplete sketches that together intimate a rough outline of the contemporary metamodern condition.

Let's start in a more or less classic Marxist vein by highlighting the various protests that neatly bookend the 2000s as a period and constitute a cycle of struggles consisting of so-called networked social movements that coalesced around economic inequalities and democratic deficits (Castells 2012). This cycle started at the turn of the millennium with the alterglobalist protests – in Seattle (1999) and Genua (2001) – and ended, for now, with the various movements-cum-encampments protesting inequality and austerity such as 'Syntagma Square' (Greece, 2010), the Indignados (Spain, 2011) and Occupy (US, EU and many other countries, 2011–2012). However different these protests might have been, they shared networked modes of organisation, grievances over global and, increasingly, national economic inequalities and a dissatisfaction with a political elite who foreclosed any democratic means to address these frustrations as they clung to the neoliberal consensus in the aftermath of the 2008 crisis (see Hardt and Negri 2011; Castells, Caraça and Cardoso 2012).

It would be a mistake, however, to ignore – or dismiss, as some kind of progressive reflex – another form of political mobilisation that runs more or less parallel to this cycle. We are thinking, here, of the rise of right-wing populist movements across Europe and the Unites States built on a platform of identitarian, anti-immigrant, anti-Islam, anti-establishment and, lest we forget, in the final instance, economic issues. This wave, too, became much more pronounced at the end of the 1990s and swelled during the first decade of the new millennium (often in very visible niches or utterly dark corners of the Internet), culminating in the substantial political clout of, say, the *Tea Party* (post-2009), *UKIP* under Nigel Farage's leadership (re-elected as leader in 2010) and *National Front*'s Marine Le Pen (elected as leader in 2011) (see, for instance, Caiani and Parenti 2016 [2013]; Greven, 2016).

Both of these political groundswells originated in a growing group of people disaffected with neoliberal globalisation, disenfranchised with representative democracy and at ease with the Internet as a means to discuss, cultivate and rally around shared frustrations (however disparate). In a sense, then, these political positions could be seen as the dialectical inversion of the centrist – and mass mediatised (see Browse, this volume) – politics that came to dominate the postmodern years, culminating in the 'thirdway' of, say, Bill Clinton, Tony Blair and Gerhard Schröder. Summarised, this centrism entailed a liberal consensus – across the political spectrum, yet to varying degrees depending on the national context – that consisted of economic neoliberalism and (multi-)cultural liberalism with its promises of trickle-down economics, careless consumerism, frictionless diversity and eternal growth in a global village.

Meanwhile, '9/11' inaugurated a series of terrorist attacks on US and European soil perpetrated or inspired by the global terrorist network Al Qaida that brought the jihadist violence of a once-relatively distant 'fourth wave of terrorism' (Rapoport 2002) to Western cities such as New York and Washington (2001), Madrid (2004), Amsterdam (2004), London (2005), Stockholm (2010) and Toulouse (2012). The origins of this fourth wave of terrorism (after the anarchist wave beginning in the 1880s, the anti-colonial wave beginning in the 1920s and the new left wave beginning in the 1960s) are manifold (see Rapoport 2002). For our purposes, however, we would like to highlight that those involved in perpetrating these attacks were increasingly recruited from among a growing group of young men and women born – or living – in Western societies. Their radicalisation was caused, more often than not, by the perceived injustices of the Second Intifida (2000–2006), the

Iraq War (2003–2011) and the death of Al-Qaida's Osama bin Laden (2011), the persisting inequalities – and lack of social and economic mobility – in their home countries, and the exposure to Salafist-Jihadist doctrines through radical imams, local networks and – increasingly – the Internet.

The Iraq War (2003–2011) is in itself a pivotal moment in this periodising narrative. Started on the back of the Afghan War (2001) by a US-led coalition under the false pretences of a 'Global War on Terror' and 'Freedom', it culminated in a series of unintended consequences (in a dialectical sense). The invasion plunged Iraq into a bloody civil war and created a context in which terrorist networks proliferated, most prominently the various groups that would ultimately result – by means of Al Qaida – in Daesh (1999–present). By the time American troops withdrew from Iraq, the Arab Spring was well under way with mass street protests resulting in regime changes in Tunisia (2010) and Egypt (2011) and all-out civil wars in Yemen (2011), Libya (2011) and Syria (2011) characterised by multi-sided foreign interference motivated by geopolitical interests.

Concurrently, Gore's 'inconvenient truth' (2006) of human-induced climate change sunk in (if you allow us to momentarily regress to a 'Great Man Theory' of history), alongside a refuelling and changing of gears of the so-called Denial Machine (Sasaki 2006). Perhaps the clearest indication of this heightened awareness about climate change (and the sharpest rebuttal of the deniers) has been the increased usage of the notion of the Anthropocene. Since the turn of the millennium, the term has increasingly gained traction across the humanities, social- and natural sciences, as well popular discourse, to indicate that humans have left significant traces in the planet's geology and continue to have a devastating impact on its ecosystems. The rapid and widespread adoption of one single concept across academia, with its increasingly patrolled disciplinary boundaries and highly specialised jargonised niches, is a rare intellectual event in itself; it may very well point towards humankind's becoming conscious of its destructive behaviour.

Simultaneously, the 2000s have been bracketed by the collapse of a 'double bubble' consisting of the dot-com crash (1999–2001) and the global financial crisis (2007–2008) (Perez 2009). This twofold crash implied, as Perez argued in the midst of the crisis, 'that what we are facing is not just a financial crisis but rather the end of a period' (2009, 803). This entailed, in fact, two ends. Perez's first end, the dot-com crash, spelled the end of the 'instalment period' (1971–1999) and the beginning of the 'deployment period' (2001–present) of the revolution in computer technologies that began in the 1970s (see also 2003). In the current deployment period the diffusion, if not to say, omnipresence, of digital tools and skills formed the conditions for two interrelated sets of qualitative changes (by way of the dialectical transformation of quantity into quality).

First, we can observe a qualitative change on a cultural level structured around the social affordances of networked computers. This reconfiguration can be characterised by a 'shared logic', which emerged after the dotcom-crash, across 'investment decisions' and 'consumer choices' (Perez 2009, 14). This logic can be described as a shift towards social media platforms and 'Web 2.0' business models (O'Reilly 2005), such as Google (1998; IPO 2004), Skype (2003), Facebook (2004), Twitter (2006), Tumblr (2007), AirBnB (2008), TaskRabbit (2008), Uber (2009), WhatsApp (2010) and Instagram (2010). Seen from this vantage point, the 2000s have been marked by the waning of the logic of television (or mass media) culture and the emergence of the logic of network (or social media) culture (for better and for worse).

Second, and on the level of the forces of production, we can observe that the digital tools and skills, and the immaterial or creative forms of labour associated with network culture, are not any longer predominantly confined to the sites of businesses or governments but now also increasingly spill over into society at large, resulting in a fourth technological leap in the productive powers of capitalism. We argue, in line with Jameson and by way of Mandel (cited in Jameson (1991 [1984], 120), that this leap can be likened to the shift from the steam engines – essentially external combustion engines – that powered the first 'quantum leap' of capitalism from the 1840s onwards to the internal combustion engines that powered its second leap from the 1890s onwards (alongside electricity). Similarly, we now see a shift from the workplace-specific computers (because they were relatively costly and large) that powered the third 'quantum leap' into late capitalism from the 1940s onwards (alongside nuclear energy) to the personal computers (which are instead relatively cheap and small) that began to provide the impetus for a fourth, not yet fully crystallised, leap of capitalism from the late 1990s onwards (alongside, potentially, renewables).

Perez's second 'end', the end of financial liberalisation in a narrow sense and neoliberalism in a broad sense, was much anticipated yet never quite – or, perhaps, has not yet – materialised in the aftermath of the global financial crisis (2007–2008) and, later, the European sovereign debt crisis (2010–2011). The global financial crisis amounted to the fourth structural or systemic crisis of capitalism since the nineteenth century – following the crises of the 1890s, the 1930s and the 1970s (Duménil and Lévy 2011, 14–19; see also Kaletsky 2011 [2010] who traces the first systemic crisis to 1815 rather than the 1890s). Neoliberalism can be best described as 'a variegated form of regulatory restructuring' (Brenner, Peck and Theodore 2011, 9) – with a basic logic and a variety of local manifestations – that amounts to inverted class war. The basic aim of its regulatory framework was, and still is, to restore and further the economic interests of 'the highest income brackets, capitalist owners, and the upper fractions of management' in the face of declining compound growth (Duménil and Lévy 2011, 8; see also Duménil and Lévy 2004 and Harvey 2005). Since the 1970s, its default policy outcomes included removed trade barriers on the world market and increased worker competition across the globe, outsourced production and frictionless financial flows, privatised public assets and cut welfare provisions, flexible labour markets and stagnating – even precarious – living wages (except for the economic elite). Its main results have been staggering levels of income and wealth inequality, as well as catastrophic amounts of burnt fossils and discarded rubbish.

Up until the global financial crisis, these rising levels of inequality were papered over – or veiled by – increasingly booming levels of economic growth and increasingly unsustainable levels of consumer debt, epitomised by the proliferation of sub-prime mortgages in the 2000s. With the crash of the financial system, banks fell over toxic assets, business defaulted on bad debts and economies sharply contracted in fear. In Europe, meanwhile, the crisis spiralled into a full-blown sovereign debt crisis (2010–2011) taking several nations on to – or over – the brink of bankruptcy. In an unprecedented series of government bailouts, these colossal losses were socialised while previously privatised gains remained intact. As homes were foreclosed, jobs rapidly vanished and economies entered a slump despite stimulation packages, it became abundantly clear that the neoliberal doctrine had failed the large majority in Western societies (as it had consequently done elsewhere in the world) – except, of course, the 1 per cent. In addition, many European countries imposed 'austerity measures' in exchange for, or to avoid, supranational bailouts by both the EU and the IMF (an unnecessarily cruel and highly unproductive act, the IMF recently conceded, as the plight of the many unemployed young people in, especially, Greece and Spain underlines).

Many commentators therefore expected that, as has historically been the case, such a crisis would lead to a drastic restructuration, and clear change in direction, of regulatory frameworks and policy settings. The Great Depression of the 1930s (to which the most recent crisis has been widely compared), after all, resulted in a regulated financial sector and the social democratic or Keynesian compromise of the welfare state. Similarly, the crisis of the 1970s resulted in a deregulated financial sector, flexible forms of accumulation and drastic cuts in welfare provisions (see Harvey 1990, 121–97; Duménil and Lévy 2011, 14–19). The global financial crisis would surely steer capitalism in a radically different direction. This has not happened. As Brenner, Peck and Theodore aptly summarised in 'Neoliberalism Resurgent?' (2010, 266):

It soon became clear that the global crisis had set the stage for another neoliberal counteroffensive. The promised round of financial regulatory reforms was quickly diffused; emergency spending programs were phased out, as profitability was restored, but as unemployment and home foreclosures continued to rise; social state restructuring and public service cutbacks were (re)presented as overriding imperatives for fiscal restoration and debt recovery; and risks and responsibilities were again being off-loaded by central governments – to state and local administrations, to school boards and health authorities, to charities and voluntary groups, and ultimately to households. The United States and the United Kingdom, in particular, witnessed dramatic conservative resurgencies, affirmed by electoral victories and promptly followed by new rounds of righteous budget slashing. Meanwhile, as the eurozone economies diverged dramatically, between German growth and collapsing 'PIGS' (Portugal, Ireland, Greece, and Spain), policy settings ranged from fiscal restraint to enforced austerity.

This apparent resurgence of neoliberalism in the aftermath of the crisis does not entail that we are *not* witnessing a fourth update of capitalism – a 'capitalism 4.0' (Kaletsky 2011 [2010]) as it were. We most certainly are. As Duménil and Lévy (2011, 22) argued, 'The establishment of a new . . . course of events will be a long and painstaking process' in which only class struggle can determine the course we take, as societies, along the bifurcating paths – to the left an ecosocialist path, to the right yet another neoliberal path (with, possibly, fascist overtones) – that opened up in the aftermath of the crises at the close of the period.

Thus far, writing from today's perspective, we appear to have been too rapidly moving along the neoliberal path leading – in twenty, thirty years or so – to a clusterfuck of world-historical proportions (as good a politicising phrase as any in our social situation) in which wealth is concentrated at the top 1 per cent of the pyramid, while rising sea levels and super storms crumble its base, where the rest of us reside in highly precarious conditions.

OUTLINE OF THE BOOK

A period, Jameson once wrote (1984, 178), should be understood as 'a common objective condition to which a whole range of varied responses and creative innovations is then possible, but always within that situation's structural limits'. This book aims to map, translate and situate the dominant artistic responses and aesthetic innovations that emerged in, and reacted to, the 'common objective condition' (including, that is, the metamodern structure of feeling) of contemporary Western capitalist societies. The various contributions, each in its own way, set out from ways of thinking, feeling and doing that cannot any longer be understood in terms of the postmodern. In doing so, they begin to formulate a metamodern vernacular that enables us to adequately address the cultural politics and political cultures of global capitalism as seen from the perspective of Western societies (predominantly, however, the US and the EU).

The list of artistic practices under consideration is long and varied. It includes neo-romanticism, quirky, queer utopianism (MacDowell), historioplasticity (Toth), super-hybridity (Heiser), the 'artisanal turn' by way of mannerism (van Tuinen), four post-ironic authorial strategies (Konstantinou), post-solipsistic defencelessness (Timmer), affective autofiction (Gibbons), tonal warmth and heart (Rustad and Schwind), re-construction (Huber and Funk), curated authenticity (Browse) and performatism (Eshelman). The list ranges, too, across many media – including film, television, literature, visual arts, photography, crafts and the Internet. Despite this variety in strategies and media, we believe that they are all expressions of a decidedly metamodern cultural logic. This cultural logic comes into better focus as soon as we cut transversally across these various examples along the axes of historicity, affect and depth. Each of these axes has its own section in this volume in which we introduce the notions of metamodern historicity, affect and depth in more detail. It should be emphasised, however, that the chapters included in each of these respective sections do resonate with and across the other axes (indeed, this is what we mean by transversal cuts).

We have chosen the axes of historicity, affect and depth as structural logic for the volume because they are the very same axes that Jameson used to conceptualise the postmodern cultural logic. In highlighting the forms of historicity, affective modalities and depth levels that together (partly) constitute the metamodern cultural logic, we are, in other words, capable of teasing out the similarities and, especially, the differences with postmodernism (as conceptualised by Jameson). This, to be sure, is not to criticise Jameson's work on postmodernism – far from it. Rather, we attempt to think *with* Jameson in order to be able to grasp today's perplexing reality and changing cultural landscape. This, to be sure, does not entail a mere reconstruction of the Jamesonian edifice (as some kind of Vegas-style replica of the Taj Mahal). As Wegner argues in *Periodizing Jameson* (by quoting Borsteels in Wegner 2014, xix):

> rather than remaining at the level of exegesis, which always means somewhat desperately trying to stabilize the correct reading of a thinker, it is a question of taking up a transformative and critical sort of reading by way of a separate and localized – theoretical – intervention in the present that attempts to think of our actuality in the terms provided.

In doing so, we make the case – together with the other contributors to this book – that we can observe a new dominant cultural logic corresponding to a fourth reconfiguration of Western capitalist societies: metamodernism.

NOTE

1. To be sure, the difference between connectionism and oscillation might best be explained by drawing on the island metaphor that both Dumitrescu and ourselves have used. At the end of her essay, Dumitrescu (2007) argues:

> To use a metaphor employed by Jünger in *Eumeswil*: late modernity and postmodernism have revealed the inherent insularity of individuals, the intrinsic fragmentarism of any meaning one can find in an ocean of seeming meaninglessness. However, between these islands, between these fragments that should by their very broken nature be parts of something, there can be interconnections that make them all parts of a network or of several networks, connections that redeem the forgotten nature of these islands as places of meaning, wonder and delight.

If Dumitrescu's argument is that contemporary culture's attitude towards irreconcilable opposites is to interconnect them in the way a network is connected, is a captain on a ship sailing between the various islands of the archipelago, our response is that this is a spot-on description of the postmodern Lyotard proposed in *The Differend* (1983; translation 1988, especially 130–45), which he indeed envisaged as an admiral a 'travelling judge' navigating islands, negotiating discourses. (That Dumitrescu's captain constantly rebuilds his ship, modifying this then that is an interesting addendum but also rather similar to Lyotard's classification of postmodern architecture as an architecture of 'minor modifications'.) As Lyotard's interpreter Lieven Boeve has perceptively argued: Lyotard's focus lies with the 'linkage' of a 'heteregenuous plurality' of discourses (2014, 81–82), that is to say with the admiral as much as the sea. What Dumitrescu speaks about when she speaks about 'interconnections', it seems to us, she is talking about linkage; networks: the sea, the milieu. Indeed, her reference to Houellebecq, a postmodern author if there ever was one, suggests as much. Our argument, by contrast – which to be sure we do not wish to suggest is a more accurate description of the phenomenon Dumitrescu refers to but instead a description of a rather different structure of feeling – would be, as we have said elsewhere, that contemporary culture imagines a scenario in which the ship sinks and the sailor, the judge, has to set sail for one island while understanding that each island has its value. For us metamodernism is this moment of radical doubt, of constantly, at times desperately, repositioning between the islands, finally choosing one. The terms we chose early on were, with a nod to our former mentor Jos de Mul's description of Romanticism, oscillation and metaxy.

Section I

HISTORICITY

i. Metamodern Historicity

Robin van den Akker

The past few years have been marked by repeated evocations of a concept that had for a long time been repressed: History (with a capital 'H'). In the 2000s, as we noted in the introduction, theorists across the political spectrum claimed a return – or rather, bend (Arquilla 2011) – of History after the End of History. This is, for me, but one of the many signs that our current historical moment – or, rather, social situation (in a more spatial sense) – has seen the emergence of a new 'regime of historicity' in culture, to borrow Hartog's (2016) insightful notion. A regime of historicity can be defined as the specific modality in which 'man is present to himself as a being in history' (Ricoeur, cited in Hartog 2016, 53). This entails, in other words, that there are various modalities in which one can relate past, present, and future (or be in history) and that these modalities vary over time and across cultures.

It by now should not come as a surprise that the key to deciphering the postmodern regime of historicity can be found in Fukuyama's notion of the End of History – yet only indirectly and by means of a detour along one of Jameson's most elegant dialectical turns. 'Fukuyama's "end of history"', Jameson once wrote (1998, 90), 'is not really about Time at all but rather about Space'. For Jameson, the historical significance of all those discussions about the End of History does not lie in their accuracy (although the thesis nicely encapsulated the euphoria of the neoconservative right and the defeatism of the progressive left under postmodernism) but is rather to be found in its material conditions and ideological implications. This is to say that the general sense of an end – that is, the fact that such an end is conceivable and had become more or less common sense – stemmed from two mutations in capitalism itself (1998).

The first mutation relates to the emergence of a truly globalised world market under US hegemony. Under late capitalism, and with the inclusion of

the hitherto disconnected regions of, say, a reforming China and a disintegrat-
ing Soviet Union, an even further extension of the world market had become
impossible. Capital had simply reached its spatial limits. Seen from a Western perspective, moreover, this seemingly translated into a period of relative
stability and affluence. The second mutation pertains to the completed incor-
poration of culture by the commodity logic. Everyday life increasingly took
place in a mass-mediatised, credit-driven consumer bubble that hatched each
bored moment against so many variations on a theme park, to borrow the title
of Sorkin's (1992) great book. As a result, Jameson (1991 [1984]) conceptualised everyday experience as merely consisting of a series of 'impersonal'
and 'free-floating' intensities amounting to the euphoric immediacy of so
many disconnected presents. (This euphoric, a-historical present has its corol-
laries in the waning of affect and the vanishing of depth under postmodernism, as Gibbons and Vermeulen show in their respective introductions to the
other sections of this book.)

Through this classic Jamesonian analysis, which plays itself out, as it were,
on two chessboards simultaneously, the global and the local, it becomes clear
that the 'end' must be seen as a cipher for the 'blocking of the historical
imagination' in a postmodern comfort zone. Under postmodernism, in other
words, it became increasingly impossible – or seemingly unnecessary – to
imagine a historical moment before or after an unchecked capitalism (and, by
implication, liberal democracies and neoliberal economics), an ideological
disposition that perhaps can best be described in terms of 'capitalist realism'
in its both artistic and political sense (Lueg and Richter 1963; Fisher 2009).
This resulted in 'sheer historical amnesia and the stifling of the sense of history itself' (Jameson 1998, 90).

In the introduction we argued that the 2000s should be seen as a period
(lasting, roughly, from 1999 to 2011) in which the conditions emerged and
coagulated for (1) the becoming dominant of the metamodern structure
of feeling and (2) a fourth reconfiguration of Western capitalist societies
and global capitalism (playing, too, on two chessboards simultaneously).
In this social situation, we can observe a new metamodern regime of
historicity that has, as a defining trait, that its present opens onto – in an
attempt to bring within its fold – pasts possibilities and possible futures
(defined as being *with* or *among* residual and emergent structures of feeling). This regime can perhaps best be characterised as multi-tensed, an
admittedly less catchy phrase than the 'presentism' of the postmodern
regime and the 'futurism' of the modern regime – as illustrated by, say,
the avant-gardist imperative of the new (Hartog 2016). Put simply: the
moderns determinedly walked through a front door that opened onto a
future *Ville Radieuse*; the postmoderns looked out a back window into a
glossy past while doing some interior decoration (Hamilton's 'Just What
is it. . . . ' (1956) comes to mind, here) and the metamoderns open a back

door while walking through a front door as if re-enacting an M.C. Escher drawing.

In the various contributions to this section, MacDowell, Toth, Heiser and Van Tuinen make, each in their own way, a start with mapping and conceptualising the metamodern regime of historicity and, importantly, its narrative structures, tenses and sensibilities. As James MacDowell emphasises, such cartographic exercises should set out from meticulous 'cultural criticism' at the level of 'specific textual detail'. This 'dogged preoccupation with detail' is 'necessary to ensure that we do not misrepresent or oversimplify those texts or aesthetic strategies that we wish to dub metamodern'. Writing as a film critic, MacDowell then proceeds by comparing 'notes' on three 'cinematic sensibilities stemming from a shared metamodern structure of feeling': quirky, queer utopianism and neo-romanticism.

In chapter 3, literary critic Josh Toth brings this dogged preoccupation with detail to bear on Morrison's *Beloved* (1987). By reading the novel in conjunction with Malabou's 'Hegelian concept of plasticity', Toth introduces 'the subtle difference' between the historio*graphic* metafiction characterising many a postmodern novel and the historio*plastic* metafiction of a more recent body of work. *Beloved*, he argues, should be read as an 'exemplary (if not inaugural) text' of such historioplastic metafiction and, hence, 'marks the beginning of a movement out of postmodernism'.

In chapter 4, the art critic Jörg Heiser revisits a set of recent aesthetic strategies labelled 'super-hybridity' in order to cast critical light on a 'dark truth' residing within network culture in times of multipolar geopolitical conflicts. While reconceptualising Bloch's (1985 [1935]) temporal notion of 'non-simultaneity' and drawing from cultural texts from today's conflict zones, he demonstrates that 'cultural confluences occurring rapidly in one given place and time are not only corrupted from the outside'; they may, Heiser argues, also 'rot from the inside' as many of today's most frightening fantasies 'seek justification in the mythical past while embracing the techno-cultural now'.

In chapter 5, the cultural philosopher Sjoerd van Tuinen provides a speculative art history of the 'artisanal turn' in contemporary art, design and cultural theory by means of 'a mannerist genealogy for metamodern crafts and craftsmanship'. In doing so, he turns 'to the sixteenth century to find in it not only a model for the present but a futuricity that is already included in it'. Contemporary artisanal practices, he argues, inhabit an "a-synchronous" present' wherein 'a heterogeneity of (material, technical, social, political, digital, etc.) practices which, in their hybrid togetherness, express and construct the contemporary'.

Taken together, these chapters provide an analysis of the multi-tensed narrative structures that constitute the metamodern regime of historicity in a contemporary culture that harks back to its past futures to make the present into the future's past.

Chapter 2

The Metamodern, the Quirky
and Film Criticism

James MacDowell

Categories like modernism and postmodernism are, after all, only heuristic labels that we create in our attempts to chart cultural changes and continuities. Post-postmodernism needs a new label of its own. (Hutcheon 2002 [1995], 165–66)

One of the most striking features of our criticism is the casual way in which we allow ourselves to reduce . . . variety, thoughtlessly, carelessly, to simple categories, the impoverishment of which is evident whenever we look at any existing novel. (Booth 1961, 62)

This chapter addresses tensions resulting from my sympathy for both of the preceding quotations. In solidarity with Vermeulen and van den Akker's (2010) response to Hutcheon's call, I consider the metamodern to be a useful category for understanding a host of contemporary phenomena which, taken together, suggest a cultural logic that seems to be modifying logics long associated with the postmodern. If it is to demonstrate its pertinence and robustness, though, the heuristic label 'metamodernism' needs to be able to withstand criticisms and challenges from a variety of perspectives (see Eve 2012). This fact is hardly lost on Vermeulen and van den Akker themselves, who state that their definition of metamodernism 'should be read as an invitation for debate rather than an extending of a dogma' (2010, 2). This chapter thus raises a potential challenge that stems from my intuition that Booth's warning in the quotation above neatly expresses an important quandary for those of us who consider ourselves first and foremost *critics* – rather, perhaps, than theorists, philosophers, sociologists or historians – of the arts.

METAMODERNISM, THEORY AND CRITICISM

While naming many individual artists, aesthetic practices and texts in their influential article 'Notes on Metamodernism', it should not be surprising that Vermeulen and van den Akker offer only the briefest overview of the phenomena to which they refer. Though proposing metamodernism as a category to help explain (among other things) an array of contemporary cultural forms and aesthetic strategies, the chapter is not firstly concerned to offer in-depth critical accounts of those forms or strategies, but instead to outline a broader overarching logic under which they might be grouped. Unsurprisingly then, artists, architects and filmmakers are mentioned in the chapter only in passing, their work synopsised in one or two evocative phrases. Forming part of a single explorative and self-professedly 'essayistic' (Vermeulen and van den Akker 2010, 2) work of cultural theory, this is all the article's references to actual works need to do – indeed, what they *must* do – in order to serve the argument. In fact, this inaugural piece was able to be so ambitious and provocative an intervention partly thanks to its fleet-footedness, granting it freedom to cover so much textual (as well as theoretical) ground so lightly. In order for the concept of metamodernism to possess explanatory power for not just the theorist but also the critic of culture, however, the usefulness of the category must be able to be demonstrated at a deeper level than synopsis alone – that is: at the level of specific textual detail which is the proper realm of criticism. While this is something that has begun for literature (e.g. Moraru 2013; Gibbons 2015) and the visual arts (e.g. Vermeulen 2013; the blog www.metamodernism.com), there has not yet been a comparable thrust towards detailed criticism concerning what we might wish to call cinematic metamodernism. This chapter addresses that neglect.

Whether attempting to categorise cultural phenomena according to something as grand as a sociohistorical epoch, or as localised as an aesthetic trend, a responsible critic is likely to experience conflicting desires: (1) to argue that the phenomena in question share similarities such that they may fruitfully be considered as a group and (2) to acknowledge variety across and within these phenomena such that it would be misplaced, unhelpful or dishonest to view them simply as interchangeable. This double-bind may be felt especially keenly by the critic wishing to deploy any new '-ism': the necessity of arguing for the existence of significant connections, and the simultaneous need not to use too blunt an instrument for the task. A more discrete concept than metamodernism, which both Vermeulen and van den Akker and I have nonetheless elsewhere associated with the term, is the 'quirky'. The quirky is an aesthetic sensibility that I argue provides a useful lens through which to view strands of contemporary culture – particularly in American cinema – that share suggestively related approaches to style, thematic interests, comic address and tone (MacDowell 2010, 2012). It is observable across other cultural forms too: in television (*Pushing Daisies*, *New Girl* and *Flight of the Conchords*, etc.), indie music (e.g. Sufjan Stevens, Jeffrey Lewis, Moldy Peaches, Jon Brion), 'alternative' stand-up comedy (Demitri Martin, Josie Long, etc.), aspects of contemporary fiction (especially clustered around the McSweeney's publishing house), public radio/podcasts (*This American Life*, the Maximum Fun network, etc.) and so on (see MacDowell 2016). But it is in the realm of contemporary filmmaking that the quirky sensibility is represented most clearly, especially in the kinds of millennial and post-millennial American indie comedies and comedy dramas brought to mind by names and titles such as Wes Anderson, Michel Gondry, Spike Jonze, Miranda July, Charlie Kaufman, Jared Hess, Mike Mills, *Buffalo '66* (1998), *Punch-Drunk Love* (2002), *I Heart Huckabees* (2004), *Lars and the Real Girl* (2007), *Paper Heart* (2009), *Safety Not Guaranteed* (2012), *The Secret Life of Walter Mitty* (2013), or *Welcome to Me* (2015).

Despite my desire to employ the terms metamodern and quirky, I am forever mindful of the fact that, as categories and heuristic labels, both risk impoverishing the phenomena they describe if defined carelessly or applied indiscriminately. Thus writing firstly from the perspective of a (film) critic, I aim here to take that risk seriously as well as propose some potential responses. On one hand, I am suggesting that criticism's characteristically dogged preoccupation with detail will be necessary to ensure that we do not misrepresent or oversimplify those texts or aesthetic strategies that we wish to dub 'metamodern'. Another benefit of granting a central place to critical close reading in the intellectual work of defining metamodernism, however, is that doing so will improve not only our accounts of 'metamodern' texts, but also our theorising of the metamodern itself.

As Andrew Britton notes, the danger in a kind of theorising which overlooks the importance of criticism is that it 'reduces the objects it purports to theorise to mere pretexts for rationalising the validity of its own premises' (2009, 373); as such, there can be no valuable theory of culture 'which does not stay close to the concrete and which does not strive continually to check its own assumptions and procedures in relation to producible texts' (2009, 373). This could be said to be particularly true, in fact, for theories of the metamodern – a concept associated so intimately with categories such as 'sensibility' and, most consistently, 'structure of feeling'. A term coined by Raymond Williams to help identify the tenor of sociohistorical moments in terms of 'feeling much more than of thought – a pattern of impulses, restraints, tones' (1979, 159), a structure of feeling is observable in 'the most delicate and least tangible parts of our activity', and expressed aesthetically in a period's 'characteristic approaches and tones' (1965, 64). Accurately isolating, describing and engaging with intangible and delicate phenomena such as approaches and tones requires methods of analysis committed (in theory!) to precision and attentiveness. In this sense, the intellectual labour required to define and delineate the metamodern seems especially apt to remind us once more that 'the business of theory and the business of criticism cannot, in practice, be hived off from each other' (Britton 2009, 376).

Clarifying how we might most usefully employ the terms 'metamodern' and 'quirky' also, however, requires reflection on the kinds of categories we see them as constituting. Before actually attempting the sorts of textual criticism I am proposing, then, it is necessary for me to be explicit about this matter.

THE QUIRKY AND THE METAMODERN: SENSIBILITIES AND STRUCTURES OF FEELING

In the process of questioning certain over-ambitious accounts of the post-modern, Terry Eagleton once suggested that, rather than conceptualising postmodernism as 'the dominant culture of our age', it may be more accurate to think of it as 'a good deal more sectoral and specific than that. Is postmodernity the appropriate philosophy for our time', he asked, or is it simply 'the world view of . . . erstwhile revolutionary Western intellectuals who, with typical intellectual arrogance, have projected it upon contemporary history as a whole?' (2008 [1983], 202). To my mind, one thing that makes metamodernism the most persuasive concept to have emerged from the theoretical rush to name the 'post-postmodern' is Vermeulen and van den Akker's relatively modest characterisation of it as an 'emerging structure of feeling' (2010, 2). I say this because this characterisation helps deflect some of the more troubling implications of Eagleton's undeniably valid line of questioning.

To argue that we have recently seen the emergence of a new structure of feeling is to lay claim to naming something far more plausible than, say, a new sociohistorical or philosophical epoch, since it is a far more delimited phenomenon. First of all, a structure of feeling will be only one of many such localised 'structures' at work in a particular time and place; as the anthropologist Angela Garcia reminds us, 'At any given time, there are multiple structures of feeling in operation' (2008, 724). Second, as Williams suggested, a structure of feeling will not be 'possessed in the same way by the many individuals in the community' (1965, 65). In the case of the metamodern, it is unsurprising, for instance, that a key 'post-ironic' (Konstantinou 2009 and this volume) novel such as Dave Eggers's *A Heartbreaking Work of Staggering Genius* (2001) should strike one *Amazon* reviewer as an expression of 'exactly how "our" (current twenty somethings) generation feels: both desensitised, seen-it-all before, alert to cliché and knowing cultural references – and idealistic, hopeful'

('R_Byass', 1), while also causing another to respond to the effect that 'I am part of the MTV generation, and found every character in this book completely unrelatable' ('A. Nelson', 1). A structure of feeling will obviously not be 'felt' by all within – nor will it 'structure' all the culture of – a sociohistorical moment. Just as the postmodern might itself be best conceptualised not as an 'age' but rather as simply one structure of feeling belonging to certain outposts *of* an age (see Pfeil 1988 for a discussion of postmodernism as a structure of feeling), so does it seem plausible to view the metamodern as one structure of feeling circulating within the contemporary moment.

Another good reason for conceptualising the metamodern as a structure of feeling is to acknowledge that – in keeping with this phrase's final word, 'feeling' – this structure will be expressed culturally in terms of an affective and tonal logic as much as through any other means. Specifically, a structure of feeling is liable to manifest itself in the form of numerous aesthetic *sensibilities* – a term used repeatedly in 'Notes on Metamodernism'; and here, again, the function of criticism for responsibly defining the metamodern becomes key.

I see the quirky as one sensibility prompted by the metamodern structure of feeling. The quirky, as I define it in relation to film, often features a number of conventions: a modal combination of the melodramatic with the comedic; a mixing of comic styles such as bathetic deadpan, comedy-of-embarrassment and slapstick; a visual and aural style that frequently courts a fastidious and simplified sense of artificiality; and a thematic interest in childhood and 'innocence'. Most pervasive, however, is a tone that balances ironic detachment from, and sincere engagement with, films' fictional worlds and their characters (MacDowell 2010). One example, for instance, is the way that the tone of a quirky film frequently both lampoons *and* celebrates misguided or shortsighted protagonists on quixotic quests: say, the disturbingly-yet-touchingly narcissistic protagonist of *Welcome to Me*, who spends her lottery winnings on creating a bizarre *Oprah*-like television show dedicated to dramatising her life story and philosophy. The sensibility's characteristic tone ensures that such central characters' statuses as 'heroes' are to an extent qualified via their being treated in something like what Northrop Frye defined as the 'ironic mode', wherein protagonists are suggested to be in some sense 'inferior in power or intelligence to ourselves' (1957, 33–34); yet, at the same time, their utter commitment and dedication is nonetheless implicitly positioned as somehow praiseworthy, resulting in a continually conflicted tonal register of simultaneous amused distance and affectionate sympathy.

The quirky, though, may be only one among *several* cinematic sensibilities prompted by a metamodern structure of feeling. This much is suggested by the number of trends in recent filmmaking that have been similarly discussed in terms of the way they keep sincerity and irony in tension. For instance, 'New Punk Cinema' has been characterised as 'navigating the terrain between sincerity and irony' (Rombes 2005, 85); Gorfinkel has noted a contemporary approach to historical 'anachronism' in American film that produces 'a current of sincerity specifically tempered by an ironic detachment' (2005, 166); Mayshark describes 'post-pop' cinema as moving beyond a 'stand-off between irony and sentiment, [and] toward a sort of self-conscious *meaningfulness*' (2007, 5); Dogme 95 was claimed by its creators to exist 'in the area between a very solemn thing and deep irony' (MacKenzie 2003, 81); Guy Maddin's self-conscious pastiches of silent movie melodrama have been described as 'attempts to rediscover and rehabilitate innocence and belief in the face of a ruling sentiment of incredulity and cynicism' (Beard 2005, 11), and so on. Add to this disparate list, say, Vermeulen and van den Akker's definition of David Lynch as a metamodern director (2010, 10), Warwick's (2012) piece on 'the metamodernism of Terry Gilliam's *Tideland*', as well as additional films or television programmes discussed in such terms by commentators on the blog *Notes on Metamodernism* (see Loader 2010; Shachar 2011; Rustad 2012), and it quickly becomes clear that, if searching for cinematic expressions of this structure of feeling, we are both spoiled for choice and in need of some clarification. (And this is even before acknowledging that tensions between irony and sincerity are hardly, of course, something new to cinema; c.f. Pye 2007.)

One way of offering some clarification will be to acknowledge the existence of some distinct metamodern cinematic sensibilities. Just as those films or filmmaking approaches deemed postmodern could hardly be viewed as interchangeable or homogeneous, so do we need to discriminate between different ways in which a film might be said to 'be' metamodern. In the space that remains, then, I shall briefly compare and contrast moments from three recent American films that may productively be viewed as expressing a metamodern structure of feeling, yet which – importantly – find very different means of doing so. The first, Wes Anderson's animated *Fantastic Mr. Fox* (2009), I would consider a characteristic instance of the quirky sensibility; the second, Benh Zeitlin's short film *Glory at Sea* (2008), I view as conveying a distinctly contemporary strain of neo-romanticism; the third, John Cameron Mitchell's *Shortbus* (2006), offers a riotous, uplifting queer utopianism. All these films share a characteristically metamodern logic of 'oscillating between a modern enthusiasm and a postmodern irony', 'between modern commitment and markedly postmodern detachment', 'between naïveté and knowingness' (Vermeulen and van den Akker 2010, 5–6). Yet, at the same time, none of them could ever rightly be confused with each other. This is to say, then, that they suggest three different cinematic sensibilities stemming from a shared metamodern structure of feeling.

NOTES ON THREE METAMODERN CINEMATIC MOMENTS

First, a moment from *Fantastic Mr. Fox*. This scene comes towards the end of the film and begins with the wily Mr. Fox (voiced by George Clooney) speeding away on motorbike-and-sidecar from a successful rescue mission with his partners-in-crime Kylie, Kristofferson and his son Ash. Alerted by Kylie to something noteworthy on the horizon near the road down which they are racing, Fox screeches the bike to a halt, removes his goggles and looks across the landscape to see, perched on the top of a hill, the distant silhouette of a large black wolf – a type of animal of which we know Fox to be deathly afraid. Seemingly forgetting his fear, and lifting his balaclava over his head, Fox stares enraptured, then shouts towards the animal: 'Where'd you come from? What are you doing here?' After trying unsuccessfully to communicate in English, then Latin ('Canis Lupus – Volpes Volpes . . .'), he now offers French: 'Pensez-vous que l'hiver sera rude?' he yells, before translating to his compatriots, 'I'm asking if he thinks we're in for a hard winter'; but again he receives no answer. '. . . I have a phobia of wolves!' he tries. At this the wolf seems to stir in the distance, raising up its body slightly to attention; we now abruptly cut in to an extreme close-up of Fox's eyes, which we discover to be suddenly brimming with tears that he tenses his cheeks to keep from falling. Now cutting to a medium-long shot, with nervous uncertainty Fox half-raises his right hand to his side then pauses, before steeling his nerves, lifting his arm and committing to the gesture: a raised-fist salute that he lifts aloft and holds (Figure 2.1). After a couple of seconds the wolf reciprocates, raising

Figure 2.1. *Fantastic Mr. Fox*: Fox's raised-fist salute to the wolf.

its silhouetted fist up to mirror Fox's. When the wolf then disappears off into a nearby thicket of trees, Fox marvels, 'what a beautiful creature. Wish him luck, boys'. They do so, and he starts the bike off back down the road and towards home.

Next, a snapshot from the epic climax of *Glory at Sea* – a twenty-five-minute New Orleans–set short film about a rag-tag group of survivors of a terrible storm who together build a rickety boat from the wreckage of their destroyed homes and town, and sail out to sea in search of the loved ones they have lost (Figure 2.2). By the end of this movie it is still unclear why these townspeople think their children, husbands, wives and friends could still be alive out there under the waves. They have simply followed the lead of a mysterious stranger (Geremy Jasper), who began the film in some indeterminate underwater kingdom being hauled cruelly away from his lover (Meggy Tucker), and – once deposited ashore – has vowed to return to her. We, though, have had the benefit of having the film narrated to us by a young girl (Chantise Colon), who we understand has somehow survived, and is now speaking to us in the past tense from the watery depths, telling us of how her father helped the stranger build his boat. The makeshift rescue vessel the inhabitants of the film's post-apocalyptic shantytown construct is simultaneously grand and woefully inadequate to the task of sea travel, yet sail it intrepidly into the sea they do.

In the film's last act, the boat gives up the ghost, coming to a halt in the middle of the sea and splintering apart, sending our quixotic characters into the water. This, however, is before the film's final twist. Exploring the underwater world, one by one the members of the search party seek out and find

Figure 2.2. *Glory at Sea*: **The community's rickety boat sets sail.**

their loved ones – grabbing them in ecstatic gratitude, hugging them close and kissing as the film's grand, joyous orchestral score swells. The first discovery sees the mystery man find his lover; the last sees our narrator's father finding his daughter, staring into her eyes, drawing her into an embrace and swimming with her for the surface. As they move above us towards the sunlight streaming down through the sea, she utters the film's final words: 'I'm always asking my dad how that boat knew to go down right there, right over us', she tells us: 'He laughs and says, "God did it"'. We fade slowly to white, then cut suddenly to black.

Finally, a sketch of the last scene of *Shortbus* – a multi-protagonist film following regulars of the titular queer-and-straight-inclusive sex club/cabaret/salon in a 2006 New York City. The film has been focused particularly on the relationships between two long-term couples: Sofia (Sook-Yin Lee) and her husband Rob (Raphael Barker), and former hustler James (Paul Dawson) and his boyfriend Jamie (P. J. DeBoy). Both couples have had problems: Sofia has been incapable of reaching orgasm and has been deceiving Rob about this, leading to bitter arguments but no progress; James, meanwhile, has been suicidally depressed and caused Jamie some pain by introducing a third man, Ceth (Jay Brannan), into their relationship. The film's final sequence takes place during a city-wide electrical blackout. All our protagonists show up to an event at Shortbus where they settle in to watch the club's transgender mistress (Justin Bond) holding a concert by candlelight, singing a tender song called 'In the End'. Beginning quietly with an arrangement for solo voice and string quartet, the mood set by the song facilitates, first, a softening of

Figure 2.3. *Shortbus*: **Sofia's threesome with the club regulars.**

the previously tense mood between Jamie and James, with the couple starting to make out on the floor while Ceth looks on contentedly. Sitting across
the room from her husband, Sofia is cautiously approached and begins to be
kissed, by a particular swinging couple – club regulars she has previously
admired from afar (Figure 2.3); she looks to Rob who offers her an assenting
nod, which Sofia returns before starting to kiss the couple's female member.

Now, though, as the mistress's song winds down, the salon's patrons start
to crane their necks to locate the source of an offscreen sound – the flourish-
ing trombones and trumpets of a marching brass band, who suddenly burst
from nowhere into the club to everyone's surprise and delight. The band picks
up the song where it was left off, providing a triumphal lift to a final repeated
burst of the chorus, causing the concert to escalate into a group singalong
(and quasi-orgy) involving all present. As the handheld camera frantically
pans and zooms around the room's various communal musical and sexual
activities, James and Jamie's make-out session is joined by Ceth; Rob begins
kissing a female stranger on the couch next to him; and the caresses of Sofia's
threesome escalate until we cut into an extreme close-up on Sofia's face as
she experiences her first orgasm. At this moment, power immediately returns
to the city, spreading out across a colourful CGI image of the skyline, and the
camera recedes and spins into space.

Although even these brief critical descriptions begin to suggest the
moments' diversity, one thing binding them and their films together is their
expression of various logics common to the metamodern. Those logics are
affective, and to that extent tonal in character. An under-theorised but crucial
concept, the tone of a film 'cannot be reduced to story, style or authorial disposition in isolation' (Sconce 2002, 352), but should rather be thought of as
a result of 'the ways in which the film addresses its spectator and implicitly
invites us to understand its attitude to its material and the stylistic register it
employs' (Pye 2007, 7). The broad tonal trait shared by all three scenes is
something like an attitude of emotional and intellectual commitment (or affirmation, hopefulness, sentiment) in the face of a nonetheless-present potential
for skepticism (or irony, consciousness of absurdity, affected distance) – a
quality heightened by all three scenes taking place at or near their films' con-
clusions. Yet, despite this very general similarity, they nonetheless achieve
very different things in very different ways. Thus, although all are perhaps
describable as cinematic expressions of a metamodern structure of feeling,
they are also expressions of distinct cinematic sensibilities.

In Anderson's film, it is important that Fox might momentarily hesitate
before raising his fist, but even more important that he raises it nonetheless.
Equally, his words to the wolf might begin with a brief precocious romp
through different languages, but only when wry dialogue ceases can bodily
gesture take over to communicate the desired solidarity between one wild

and another nominally civilised animal. The whole scene is made to feel rather narratively incongruous (it is a deeply jarring capper to a preceding high-spirited action rescue sequence); yet its peculiar power stems partly from the paradoxical sense of it constituting an *almost* 'naturalistic' pause, an aside, within the film's otherwise-tight and propulsive children's film storytelling. Our ability to take the moment's emotional appeals seriously may be somewhat qualified by a constant awareness of the animation style's juddering artificiality (perhaps especially when the wolf's spindly arm shoots up so suddenly in the distance); but the emphatic cut-in to an extreme close-up of Fox's eyes and their promise of tears remains a bold and stirring way of inviting us to share his vulnerability – its power undiminished even if we note the self-conscious stylistic nod to Sergio Leone (who himself never used this strategy to such specifically tender effect).

What makes this film's tone so characteristically *quirky* is its intensification of something common to the sensibility, and Anderson's work especially. His films typically combine strategies that encourage ironic emotional distance (e.g. deadpan comedy, highly self-conscious tableau framings, pointedly artificial décor) with a disarmingly beautiful 'childlike' aesthetic. Overly precise and overtly un-naturalistic, yet inviting associations with objects that might be addressed to children (e.g. the toy theatres of *The Royal Tenenbaums*, the children's book covers in *Moonrise Kingdom*), Anderson's style often permits both a detachment from a naïve investment in the fiction and a sense of wide-eyed wonder at an aesthetic of the orderly and the miniature (see Mac-Dowell 2014). In terms of visual style, distilled orderliness is obviously central to *Fantastic Mr. Fox* and its animation generally, as well as this moment

Figure 2.4. *Fantastic Mr. Fox*: The tear that gathers but does not fall.

specifically (static shots, symmetrical and flat framings). But this quality also resonates tonally: there is the sense of intense emotion being somewhat restrained by the great distance between Fox and the wolf; the contained neatness of the reciprocated affirmative gesture; the tear that gathers but does not fall (Figure 2.4), and so on. Offering through its controlled and constrained aesthetic a characteristically quirky expression of a metamodern affective logic, this film's approach is very different from that of *Glory at Sea*.

The central unexplained supernatural (or metaphysical) conceit of Zeitlin's film is patently whimsical, almost ridiculous. These qualities are made to clash against its location and subject matter, which emphatically evoke one of the most tragic events to befall the United States in this century: Hurricane Katrina and its shameful aftermath. Yet the film's rhetorical and affective commitment to its fantastical premise is so intense that the utopian wish-fulfillment seems less a naïve retreat from, and more a radical refusal of, the requirements of despair. Like *Fantastic Mr. Fox*, the film moves into a realm beyond language – here an underwater realm of body and gesture – in order to achieve its moment of greatest transcendence. The style uses an insistent over-emphasis on an established cinematic cliché – the editing piling-up one close-up of ecstatic embracing bodies upon another, upon another, as the resolutely triumphant score rises and soars (Figure 2.5). While our narrator's words that close the film ('. . . He laughs and says, "God did it"') certainly act in some way to acknowledge the absurdity of what we have just experienced (it has the potential to invoke mocking laughter), the exuberance with which that experience has been rendered – and the wresting of exuberance from a backdrop of true tragedy – ensures that, if we laugh in disbelief, it is likely to be a laugh augmented by tears.

Figure 2.5.   *Glory at Sea*: The narrator is found by her father beneath the waves.

I take *Glory at Sea* to be a filmic embodiment of what Vermeulen and van den Akker refer to as 'an emergent neoromantic sensibility' in contemporary aesthetics – a sensibility in which, they claim, 'metamodernism appears to find its clearest expression' (2010, 8). This is most obvious in its central premise. Like the 'Romantic Conceptualist' (Heiser 2007) Bas Jan Ader's fateful journey to sea while *In Search of the Miraculous* (1975), Zeitlin's characters' voyage seems a doomed act of misplaced heroism – initially conveying pathos because we acknowledge the likelihood of its failure; unlike that earlier journey, however, this quest actually achieves the eventual moment of Romantic sublimity that was its purpose to seek. And yet, formally, the film seems to me to offer a contemporary cinematic take on a characteristically Romantic impossibility: the 'attempt to turn the finite into the infinite' (Vermeulen and van den Akker 2010, 8). In contrast to the quirky's exquisitely controlled style, here we have the film's camera seeming in a perpetual headlong rush to try to capture all the excitement going on in the world around it – seldom static, often shaking, being bumped into by actors – and a comparatively frantic editing style that makes the whole film feel almost like one huge, inclusive montage sequence. Moreover – in a sense echoing the aspirations of its ambitious-yet-doomed boat – this low-budget short film behaves as if it believed itself to be a multi-million-dollar Hollywood epic: the almost excessively grand score, the large cast, the action set-pieces – these are not the usual stock-in-trade of American independent short-filmmaking. Its incongruous valiant optimism causes it to feel as if it is always straining against its boundaries, throwing itself against the finite confines of its form in a manner that feels Romantic, where an equivalent high-budget full-length feature telling the same story would surely feel more straightforwardly mythic.

Like *Glory at Sea*, the ending of *Shortbus* is similarly in part about snatching (a moment of) joy from the jaws of anguish, but it again expresses its own distinct sensibility. The film has been careful to place its action firmly within a history of New York City that includes 9/11 (one of the first scenes prominently shows the gaping hole of Ground Zero) and the AIDS crisis (an imagined version of former mayor Ed Koch [Alan Mandell] has appeared at the salon, here depicted as an ex-closet-case begging penance for not better serving the gay community in the 1980s); equally, prior to the conclusion we have witnessed both Jamie's failed suicide attempt, and Sofia and Rob's marriage reaching crisis point. The song sung by Justin Bond, and joined in by everyone else, spins uplift from the chanted refrain that '*we all get it in the end . . .*', so that the communal candlelit sing-along and inclusive sexual activity of the closing moments create the sense of a community binding together to temporarily celebrate the warding off of darkness – here literalised by the blackout. Going one step further, though, the final seconds take the film into a more lyrical and magical mode when the power of this community first achieves what was previously impossible, giving Sofia her first orgasm, then metaphorically seems to achieve the *actually* impossible by restoring electricity to the city – Shortbus' window being the first to illuminate, before lights begin to snap on all around it, spreading out across the skyline (Figure 2.6). This New York is rendered by iridescent CGI animation so as to resemble a toy-model illuminated by multicoloured Christmas light–like bulbs, and in this sense it offers a clear reminder of the film's artificial nature. However, like Anderson's stop-motion and Zeitlin's fantastical storyline, this reminder of the constructed quality of what we're seeing nonetheless isn't able – indeed, isn't desiring – to undercut the emotional impact of this implausible but hugely energising moment of joyous affirmation.

What is actually *being* affirmed here, moreover, definitively distinguishes this film's particular metamodern sensibility from those of both *Fantastic Mr. Fox* and *Glory at Sea* (despite faintly recalling the former in its final aesthetic recourse to childlike artificiality, and the latter in the frantic energy of its camerawork and focus on communal intimacy). Unlike the touchingly executed but undeniably conventional focus upon heterosexual lovers and familial reunion in Zeitlin's movie, or a *pater familias'* thrilling but fleeting encounter with 'the wild' in Anderson's, *Shortbus'* climax is clearly concerned rhetorically to champion the altogether more lively and 'transgressive' values of shared, non-monogamous queer sexual expression. Indeed, it is the film's utter commitment to what it implies to be the almost transcendental powers of queer sociality that I would argue makes this a specifically metamodern (as opposed to postmodern) vision of queerness. As noted by queer feminist Lynne Huffer, a common thread in postmodern queer theory has been an embrace of radical, anti-social negativity that defines the subject as finally 'fractured, unstable, and permanently dislodged not only from its

Figure 2.6. *Shortbus*: **The final image of electricity returning to the city.**

humanist foundations . . . but also, and more significantly, from any sense of the interdependency and connectedness with others that lie at the heart of the social realm' (2013, 62). By contrast, far from succumbing to or championing radical isolation, *Shortbus* concludes instead with a welcoming extension of queer inclusivity (e.g. the nominally straight Sofia finally cumming with a man *and* woman, surrounded by a room filled with a wide range of gendered and sexual subjects); a positive embracing of what we all as humans irreducibly *do* share ('we *all* get it in the end'); and a metaphorical suggestion of the power precisely of radical togetherness (the apparently impossible regeneration of the city's electricity recalling an earlier playful metaphor spun by Bond to the effect that there exists 'a magical circuit board, a motherboard, filled with desire, that travels all over the world – that touches you, that touches me, that connects everybody'). As Leopold Lippert has written of the film, its conclusion's implicit answer to 'the challenges of late postmodernity' for queer subjects seems to be that 'the mere celebration of social instability, diffusion and negativity no longer holds', and that there must also be a place for the possibility of collective 'queer utopianism' (2010, 205). I would suggest that this is as good a term as any for the particular form of metamodern cinematic sensibility expressed in *Shortbus*.

It is thus an overarching tone of defiant affirmation, commitment and sincere engagement in the face of an implicitly acknowledged potential for despair, disillusionment or ironic detachment that I see as connecting these moments and their films, and which connects them in turn to a metamodern structure of feeling. 'It's like the 60s, only with less hope', Justin Bond has said of the salon at one point in *Shortbus*; but end on a moment of hopeful celebration this film does. 'That supposed to be some type of boat?' a child has asked of the vessel being constructed by the stranger in *Glory at Sea* – 'You gonna die!'; yet this film nevertheless concludes with an unbelievable but glorious triumph over death. 'They say our tree may never grow back', Fox says of his family's home that was destroyed by their corporate enemies in the final scene of Anderson's film, 'but one day *something* will.' All in some sense constituting expressions of the metamodern, their particular approaches nonetheless cannot be accounted for by this designation alone – or, rather, merely to describe them as 'metamodern' will take us only a certain distance towards understanding their workings and achievements. This latter task is best attempted through a criticism concerned in part to articulate where instances of 'metamodern' cinema both converge and differ.

CONCLUSION

This chapter has been concerned to deepen our understanding of metamodern filmmaking by proposing the existence of two further distinct metamodern cinematic sensibilities in addition to the quirky: a filmic neo-romanticism and a queer utopianism. One pressing question to address will clearly be whether there are other contemporary films that seem to express similar sensibilities to *Glory at Sea* and *Shortbus*. Zeitlin's own first feature-length film *Beasts of the Southern Wild* (2012), for instance, is another candidate for a filmic neo-romanticism, while Mitchell's earlier *Hedwig and the Angry Inch* (2001) is certainly discussable in relation to queer utopianism. Outside these directors' other work, I would also provisionally align many of the films of the Polish brothers (e.g. *Northfork* 2003 or *The Astronaut Farmer* 2006) with the former, and those of Jamie Babbit (e.g. *But I'm a Cheerleader* 1999 or *Itty Bitty Titty Committee* 2007) with the latter. As in the case of the term 'metamodern' itself, whether these additional categories will ultimately prove valuable is a question that can be answered only by further criticism attentive to the material particulars of individual texts. Yet, given metamodernism's nature as a structure of feeling – a phenomenon sensed in 'the most delicate and least tangible parts' of a culture (Williams 1965, 64) – the findings of this criticism will undoubtedly be relevant not only for how we discuss specific metamodern texts but also for how we theorise the metamodern more broadly.

Chapter 3

Toni Morrison's *Beloved* and the Rise of Historioplastic Metafiction

Josh Toth

Spirit necessarily appears in Time, and it appears in Time just so long as it has not *grasped* its pure Notion, i.e. has not annulled Time. (Hegel 1977, §801)

In his seminar on 30 March 1955, Jacques Lacan asks his participants to play a game of 'odds and evens', the very same game Dupin describes in Poe's 'The Purloined Letter' (1998 [1844]). The session of play begins (as the seminar proper ends) with one of Lacan's more striking commandments: 'Do it at random. Show us your symbolic inertia' (1991, 190). The participants are thus commanded to act randomly so as to confirm the impossibility of doing so. And, indeed, the ensuing demonstration of 'symbolic inertia' opens up the possibility that 'the human subject doesn't foment this game, he takes his place in it. . . . He is himself an element in this chain which, as soon as it is unwound, organises itself in accordance with laws. Hence the subject is always . . . caught up in crisscrossing networks' (192–93). Lacan's point of emphasis is clearly the inescapable 'play' of a constructed (or artificial) reality, a 'symbolic order' that precedes and defines our involvement *in* it. For this reason, he repeatedly stresses (in the seminar that follows the session of 'play') the metafictional implications of Poe's story, the fact that each character 'plays [a] role' (194), that each role has a 'destiny' (195), that the story stages and reduplicates a 'human drama . . . founded on the existence of established bonds, ties, pacts' (197).

However, in his essay on David Lynch's *Lost Highway* (2000), the pre-eminently Lacanian (yet adamantly post-postmodern) Slajov Žižek explains that 'the pervert's universe is the universe of the pure symbolic order, of the signifier's game running its course . . . a universe without closure, unencumbered by *the inertia of the Real*' (2000, 36, my emphasis). This obvious inversion of Lacan's imperative is certainly remarkable; yet we must avoid the temptation to view it as a repudiation. While Lacan places the emphasis on the inescapable nature (or inertia) of the symbolic, Žižek places it on the fact that the symbolic order never exists independent of a Real it both defines and disfigures. Žižek's critique of a perverse (or postmodern) ideology is, in other words, already implicit in Lacan's seminar. For confirmation we need to only consider Lacan's repudiation of the Minister in Poe's story, a pervert who exposes *just to revel in* the impossibility of any foundation that might justify moral law, who 'dares all things, those unbecoming as well as those becoming a man' (Poe 1998 [1844], 251). My point is this: Žižek articulates a shift in emphasis, not a rejection of a past model (see also Toth 2010, 2013). By cautiously redeploying Catherine Malabou's recent reread-ing of Hegel, we might better understand this shift in focus as a reminder that the Real – that history itself – is necessarily and essentially 'plastic'; it has 'a capacity to receive form and a capacity to produce form' (2005, 9). Viewed in this way, Žižek's shift in focus returns us to the fact that the symbolic – as an inescapable narrative in which we all play our 'parts' – is no less restricted than the hand of a sculptor before a piece of clay.

But this is surely less of a revelation than it is a shift in perspective. If it is possible to map Žižek's 'shift' onto the aesthetic shift that became appar-ent in the late 1980s and early 1990s, then it is hardly surprising that it is often very difficult to distinguish the cultural artifacts of postmodernism from the cultural artifacts of – what Vermeulen and van den Akker (2010) call – metamodernism. After all, and in retrospect, it is difficult (if not sim-ply impossible) to accept the now-canonical reification of postmodernism as irresponsibly solipsistic or corrosively self-reflexive. And yet, postmodern-ism's tendency to fixate on the signifier's game running its course (via its predominant interest in play, irony, groundlessness, whatever) certainly risks sanctioning the affectation of a certain problematic irresponsibility, perverts playing at pointless games. Much of the fiction that has been produced in the past twenty or so years attempts to distance itself from postmodernism for precisely this reason. The fiction and criticism of both Jonathan Franzen (e.g. 'Mr. Difficult') and David Foster Wallace (e.g. 'E Unibus Pluram') are obvi-ous examples. Moreover, as Robert McLaughlin (2007) notes, the very rhe-torical strategies we typically associate with postmodernism are now being redeployed by the political right. Increasingly, in fact, alt-right populists like Donald Trump (in America) and Marine and Marion Le Pen (in France) tend to revel in a 'pervert's universe', willfully distorting any number of 'facts' so as to 'say to it like it is'. There is, in other words, good reason to endorse and indeed celebrate the effort to move beyond postmodernism. Yet this move beyond postmodernism rarely (if ever) denies the inescapabilty of the sym-bolic, of reality, as construct. It simply insists upon, or shifts the emphasis to, a ground that, while impossible to know (in full, or finally), necessarily effects the contours of its own disfiguration. At its best, then – or at its most efficacious – the contemporary critique of postmodernism exposes the danger of perversely and irresponsibly forgetting our responsibility to (the truth of) the past; at precisely the same time, though, it returns us to a particularly postmodern insistence that the past (as Real) is nothing to be known. How else might we account for both the end of postmodernism *and* the continued persistence of its quintessential genre: metafiction?

This brings me to Morrison's *Beloved* (1987), which I'd like to position here as an exemplary (if not inaugural) text, one that marks the beginning of a movement out of postmodernism. While numerous 'metafictional' texts have since precipitated this shift in emphasis – for example, the work of David Foster Wallace, Mark Z. Danielewski, Mark Leyner, Charlie Kaufman, Quentin Tarantino, Sophia Coppola, Wes Anderson – *Beloved* introduces the subtle difference between the historiographic metafiction Linda Hutcheon associates with postmodernism proper and the more recent (yet still historically charged) metafiction that seems to eschew and even critique the specific interests of those earlier texts. Read alongside Malabou's recovery of a distinctly Hegelian concept of plasticity – a recovery that goes hand-in-hand with her pronouncement that the 'deconstruction of presence is now a completed procedure' (2007, 36) – we might articulate this difference as the difference between historiographic metafiction (which emphasises the inescapability of the graphic construct) and historio*plastic* metafiction (which shifts our attention to the infinite yet bound pliability of the past). Like any other example of historiographic metafiction, Morrison's novel exposes and embraces the past's pliability in the face of its symbolic construction; yet it insists (also) that we can neither deny that pliability nor abandon our responsibility to its limitations, to the *forms* that yield history.

NARRATIVE CASTS

Without question, and regardless of the ways in which it has been labelled by critics, Toni Morrison's *Beloved* re-deploys a series of stylistic devices that can be identified with postmodernism. The novel reimagines the life of Margaret Garner: her escape from enslavement in 1856, her eventual capture and her subsequent decision to protect *by killing* her daughter. In Morrison's hands, though, 'Margaret' becomes 'Sethe'; and, unlike Margaret, Sethe remains in Ohio (the state to which Margaret/Sethe escaped), living to see the Civil War begin and end. Indeed, *Beloved* is set in the years following the Civil War, but it approaches its central animating event – Sethe's brutal slaughter of her child, Beloved – again and again via a spiral-like series of narrative returns, or casts. The event is recounted several times and from a series of different perspectives.

The first seemingly 'full' account of the event comes from the perspective of a 'schoolteacher, one nephew, one slave catcher and a sheriff' (1988 [1987], 148). Although this account is extremely detailed, the fact that it comes from the perspective of white slave holders forces us to question its veracity. Morrison goes out of her way to stress the fact that this event is not narrated by a simply omniscient, or objective, narrator. We are told that 'a crazy old nigger was standing in the woodpile with an axe' and that 'about twelve yards beyond that nigger was another one – a woman with a flower in her hat' (1988 [1987], 149). This narrative voice (which employs the derogatory 'nigger') is in striking contrast to the voice that narrates the majority of the novel. By creating this contrast, Morrison reminds us that all narrative perspectives are skewed and that we can never assume any one account is finally accurate, or without bias. This fact is further highlighted when Stamp Paid, the community's moral patriarch and former agent of the Underground Railroad, attempts to show (and explain) an article about Sethe to Paul D, a former slave from Sethe's plantation and Sethe's eventual lover. As Davis notes, 'When Paul D is confronted by the newspaper account of Sethe's deed, the reader is made aware that textual documents invariably fail to capture life exactly as it is experienced. Although he can't read, Paul D finds the representation of Sethe's face to be inauthentic': 'That ain't her mouth' (1998, 248). As with the shift in narrative perspective, this stress on the impossibility of accurate representation forces the reader to accept the contingent and unstable nature of all narrative acts, including those that constitute the novel itself. In these moments, we are reminded that *Beloved* is a series of narrative castings, various attempts to provide accurate (narrative) forms for a host of real traumatic events (i.e. the middle passage, Margaret Garner's decision to kill her daughter, slavery in general) that exceed the possibility of symbolisation, remediation or re-formation. Yet these various narrative casts cannot be aligned (neatly or evenly) with the often circular (or regressive) nature of postmodern metafiction.

Rather than folding in on itself – as, say, a high postmodern text like Barth's 'Title' (1988 [1968]) does – and eventually collapsing in a state of infinite, self-reflexive regress (designed primarily to expose the inescapability of symbolic constructs), *Beloved*'s various narrative castings denote a clear ethical commitment to an essential narrative paradox: the fact that the impossibility of a certainly right narrative act allows for the very possibility of such acts. We see this most obviously in Sethe's circular attempts to tell her story to Paul D: 'Sethe knew that the circle she was making around the room, him, the subject, would remain one. That she could never close in, pin it down for anybody who had to ask' (Morrison 1988 [1987], 163). In those moments when Sethe's stories are clearly induced by a struggle to close in on her 'subject' – to form, that is, its essence into being – we see that the very promise of complete narrative apprehension is made possible by the Real's continual resistance to that apprehension. Moreover, while it is clear that the inability to achieve closure animates their various (re)castings, neither Sethe nor Morrison abandons the possibility of 'getting it right'. The novel is always sincere in its efforts to (re)form the past accurately.

Put differently, the novel enacts a series of temporal (or momentary) 'deployments'. Such deployments are, if we follow Malabou, distinctly Hegelian. Consider, as Malabou does, the following passage from Hegel's *Philosophy of Mind*: 'And so in [spirit] every character under which it appears is a stage in a process of specification and development, a step forward towards its goal, in order to make itself into, and to realize in itself, what it implicitly is' (Hegel 1971, §387). Likewise, in Morrison's novel, the deployment of narrative towards its end – which is, by implication, the very possibility of a temporalisation that maintains a future to come (a future, for instance, when the trauma of the past is finally cast aside) – is made possible by the plasticity of that end (which is always also the point of its origin). Since Hegel's 'God "transplants (*verstzt*) himself into the world of time" . . . and thus appears in time before himself' (Malabou 2005, 119), temporalisation is the very possibility of representation, 'the becoming accidental of essence' (119). Representation is thus the articulation (or re-casting) of what 'sees (itself) coming' (118) – 'the process through which individual subjectivity repeats the moments of the divine alienation' (112). Even if we shift Malabou's (and/or Hegel's) focus from the individual subject (and from God) to the past as subject, the implication is largely the same: the past as plastic, as 'the giver and recipient of its own form' (2005, 118), makes possible the articulation of its truth in the form of what is (always still) to come. In other words, the past is grasped when the shape it is given signals (also) its potential for future reformation. For Malabou (and, I'm suggesting, Morrison) this coming into being of what 'sees (itself) coming' promises but never entails 'the final banishment of all temporality and the advent of spirit's unchanging and indifferent present' (2005, 128). The Hegelian *Aufhebung* (in Malabou's hands) must be understood and embraced as always and perpetually '[the] "time which lies ahead"' (2005, 128), the plasticity of which results in (or makes possible) a perpetual series of momentary casts: for 'this possibility of *seeing in advance* (*voir d'avance*) is exactly what opens up for the subject the horizon of a pure and absolute future' (2005, 126).

Malabou's radical re-reading of the Hegalian *Aufhebung* clearly resonates with Derrida's discussion of the specter in *Hamlet* (1994, 3–48) – that is, as that which beckons from the past to promise the future – and thus the ordeal of the undecidable. But it resonates also, I am suggesting, with the function of

the ghost in *Beloved*. That the presence of the ghost signals the very 'possibility of *seeing in advance*' (Malabou 2005, 126) becomes apparent if we consider the way in which Sethe (at least in the beginning) employs her stories
and her words to apprehend and understand (via representation) the traumas
of her past. These 'rememories' (as Sethe terms them) are never 'stable' or
absolute, but (for that very reason) they provide her with a certain amount of
control over and responsibility for her past:

> Before Paul D came and sat on her porch steps, words whispered in the keeping
> room had kept her going. Helped her endure the chastising ghost; refurbished
> the baby faces of [her sons] Howard and Buglar and kept them whole in the
> world because in her dreams she saw only their parts in trees; and kept her hus-
> band shadowy but *there* – somewhere. (1988 [1987], 86)

This ability to 'refurbish' the past, or to keep certain aspects of it whole via
a reliance on fragmentation (on an ability to focus, only, on 'parts'), is intimately tied to the essential and ultimately empowering plasticity of the past,
and thus the perpetual promise (implied by that plasticity) that the trauma
of the past can be healed, or known – reformed at last. By employing techniques we might associate with a traditional oral storyteller (see Bergthaller
2006/2007), Sethe is able to make narrative decisions about her past because
the promise of apprehending that past remains deferred, an inherently and
necessarily impossible promise. Thus, before the arrival of Paul D and the
subsequent manifestation of her daughter's ghost, Sethe willingly, repeatedly
and to positive effect endures the undecidablity of the ghostly (or plastic),
the possibility and the impossibility of reforming the past in its essence, of
remembering (finally).

The novel's apparent endorsement of this ordeal is further stressed by the
central trauma around which the entire novel is structured: Sethe's decision
to murder her children. (She is, of course, prevented from killing anyone
other than Beloved.) The fact that, while caught between two equally horrific options – abandon her children to slavery or kill them before they can
be taken – Sethe makes a decision at all confirms the text's overriding ethics; we must permit the infinite pliability of a single moment to inform our
decision-making process while simultaneously imposing upon that pliability
the static form of a (single) decision. In other words, a decision must be
made – even if it can never 'provide itself with the infinite information and
the unlimited knowledge that could justify it' (Derrida 2002, 255). And just
as Sethe is compelled to make an 'impossible' decision (at the moment of
Beloved's murder and then again and again each time she attempts to recast
that moment in narrative), the reader is repeatedly forced to make an impossible judgement, or interpretive casting, about that decision and about the

meaning of the text itself. Such a judgement and/or final interpretation always seems both necessary and possible (or visible in advance) even though the novel refuses to provide the means to legitimate it. Not only are we forced, as Cutter notes, to make an ultimately untenable decision about Beloved's status as a ghost (2000, 63), we repeatedly find ourselves judging the morality of Sethe's behavior. Is she ultimately a protective mother who sacrifices her own conscience and sanity for the sake of her child and the possibility of subverting an inescapable economy of slavery? Or, does she simply confuse her own fears and history with those of her children, robbing Beloved of any future options or alternative means of escape? As Wu (2003) suggests, the novel constantly frustrates our ability to decide (finally) between these two alternatives. No reader is ever in possession of all the facts, all the angles, all the possible forms; any judgement of Sethe, like any interpretation of the novel, must necessarily be informed by yet imposed upon the infinitely pliable. Like Sethe, we find ourselves faced with the spectre of a certainly correct decision yet forced to concede that our ability to make a final interpretation is necessarily contingent upon both the possibility and the impossibility of that spectre, a spectre that implies, while perpetually doing without, a fixed or final form.

FROM PLASTIC GHOST TO OSSIFIED MEMORY

The very first paragraph of the novel informs us that the house Sethe and Denver (the daughter Sethe was ultimately prevented from killing) live in is haunted: '124 was spiteful. Full of a baby's venom' (Morrison 1988 [1987], 3). This ghost that haunts (the murdered baby, Beloved) is powerful enough and angry enough to slam a dog 'into the wall hard enough to break two of his legs and dislocate his eye' (1988 [1987], 12), yet it is, also, as Sethe assures Paul D, 'just a baby' (13). This ghost is, while troublesome, manageable, even (at times) reassuring, a fluid and amorphous revenant of past trauma. However, the troublesome – or rather, the unstable and unpredictable – nature of this baby ghost (and/as the past) compels Sethe's sons to 'run away' (3) and, finally, forces Sethe and Denver to perform a type of exorcism, 'to end the persecution by calling forth the ghost that tried them so' (4). This exorcism is intimately tied to both Sethe's and Denver's (and, by extension, Howard and Buglar's) desire to 'get over' the past, to leave it behind once and for all, to forget. For this reason, the exorcism Sethe and Denver perform is less an exorcism than a conjuration, for the novel clearly ties the promise of forgetting to the possibility of reforming the past once and for all, of remembering finally and with certainty: 'a conversation, they thought, an exchange of views or something would help' (4). Or, as Sethe asserts, 'If [Beloved]'d only come, I could make it clear to her' (4).

What compels Sethe in the beginning is the promise that, if she can remember and, in turn, cast her past *just right*, if she can (re)form her trauma (in its essence) and lay it out for Beloved (and, perhaps, all others, including herself) to see and understand, she will cease to be haunted. This is the central irony, or paradox, of the novel: what haunts us is the promise of a future without ghosts. As long as a ghost persists, as long as it continues to haunt, it leaves open the possibility (as Derrida demonstrates [1994, 40–48]) that it can be exorcised and/or conjured, that its ghostly nature can be formed into this *or* that, presence *or* absence (and, of course, either will do). This paradox of a promise that motivates because it is impossible, or endlessly deferred, clearly frustrates Sethe; and yet, at the same time, it provides her with strength, a power over her own past. Indeed, in Denver's view, Sethe has always been a 'queenly woman', a woman who 'never looked away', a woman who had 'the presence of mind to repair a dog gone savage' (Morrison 1988 [1987], 12). However, Paul D's arrival (and Beloved's soon after) effects a clear change in Sethe. She becomes increasingly irresponsible and weak, a woman who (for the first time) begins 'looking away' (1988 [1987], 12) from Denver and, we are led to assume, the past in general. This change in Sethe is clearly linked to the fact that Paul D's arrival initiates a final, and finally effective, exorcism. It is, after all, impossible to disassociate Sethe's newfound assurance that 'the responsibility for her breasts, at last, was in somebody else's hands' from Paul D's violent attack on 124 Bluestone, an attack seemingly *inspired* by his own need to exorcise and forget the past, to force all ghosts to leave, to 'get the hell out!' (18). Via his intrusive arrival at 124, Paul D – a man who, we should note, keeps his memories safely stored in 'the tobacco tin lodged in his chest' (113) – exorcises the trauma of Sethe's past, compelling her to 'leave it to [him]' (46), to forget (finally).

And for a short time after Paul D's arrival and exorcism – the time, more specifically, it takes to spend a carefree day at the fair – life does seem better. The promise haunting Sethe is fulfilled. She no longer needs to make decisions about her past, about the stories she once felt compelled to tell and tell again. But when Sethe and Denver return from their first day out in eighteen years, they find Beloved on their doorstep, fully formed and in the flesh. The suggestion is that the ultimate effect of Paul D's exorcism – that is, his rejection of the ghost's ambiguous presence – is an equally effective conjuration, the arrival of the ghost as a fully material and undeniably present woman. What was once a fluid, negotiable (or plastic) baby ghost becomes, because of Paul D's utter rejection of all things that haunt, a fixed and undeniable reality: the end of the promise of a future to come, the end (for Sethe) of time itself. Beloved walks 'fully dressed . . . *out of the water*' (Morrison 1988 [1987], 50, my emphasis); and, upon first encountering her, Sethe is compelled to empty her bladder of 'endless' water (51). Beloved's emergence from the water (and Sethe's concurrent evacuation of bodily fluid) highlights the fact that Beloved's ostensible transformation from ghost to concrete woman can be read, much more simply, as the ossification of the past's plasticity. The absolute absence of the past as ghost is presented as no different from its absolute presence, for either marks the end of a certain pliability that can inform while being formed, a certain fluidity and doubt that makes 'negotiation' (and, thus, decisions, stories, the future) possible.

But Denver is quick to acknowledge the dangerous and disconcerting effects of Beloved's presence. While Denver does not deny the fact that all her and Sethe's attempts to 'reason with the baby ghost . . . got nowhere' (1988 [1987], 104), she remains certain that 'Paul D messed them up for good' (37). At first, of course, Denver's rejection of Paul D (as well as her refusal to see the effects of his exorcism as positive) speaks to her own desire to dwell in the past and thus cling to the pariah-like identity that the past provided. For a time, in fact, Denver becomes quite enamoured with Beloved. However, her distrust of Paul D's insistence on forgetting (paralleled as it is by Beloved's increasingly imperious demands on Sethe) leads to her realisation that the ghost of Beloved provided her and Sethe with something essential, something the material Beloved threatens to destroy altogether. Beloved as ghost represented the possibility and the impossibility of remembering and/or forgetting, of reforming. The space of doubt left open by the ghost was a space in which claims could be made, stories told, histories (re)cast. Beloved's presence refuses anything but the ossified truth, the event itself (now and forever). As the actual manifestation of past trauma, Beloved's presence leaves no room for negotiations, for the ordeal of 'the undecidable': 'Denver thought she understood the connection between her mother and Beloved: Sethe was trying to make up for the handsaw; Beloved was making her pay for it. But there would never be any end to that, and seeing her mother diminished shamed and infuriated her. Yet she knew Sethe's greatest fear was the same one Denver had in the beginning – that Beloved might leave' (251). Because Beloved, the 'one and only person [Sethe] felt she had to convince', cannot be persuaded to accept the possibility that 'what [Sethe] had done was right' (251), Sethe no longer has the ability (or the faith) to persuade herself.

As Sethe herself 'gidd[ily]' realises soon after her arrival, Beloved's presence effectively closes off the need for (or possibility of) storytelling, representation, narrative decision making: 'I don't have to remember nothing. I don't even have to explain. She understands it all' (1988 [1987], 183). Sethe thus becomes the very antithesis of Žižek's postmodern pervert, utterly relinquishing (as she does) participation in 'the signifier's game' (1988 [1987], 36) and succumbing to an illusory (yet hegemonic) Real. And without the ability or reason to tell (and therefore construct) her own past, Sethe is left without control, or power: 'The mood changed and the arguments began. Slowly at first. A complaint from Beloved, an apology from Sethe . . . She took the best of everything . . . and the more she took, the more Sethe began to talk, to explain, . . . Beloved wasn't interested . . . Sethe pleaded for for-giveness, counting, listing again and again her reasons' (241–42). Sethe is lit-erarily immobilised by Beloved's presence, by the apparent ossification of a traumatic past. We see this ossification expressed most clearly via Morrison's use of a type of pathetic fallacy that directly echoes Beloved's transforma-tion from a state of plasticity to a state of fixity. Immediately after Beloved claims to recognise Sethe's song – and Sethe decides that Beloved is, with-out a doubt, her daughter returned from the dead – we are told that 'outside, snow solidified itself into graceful forms. The peace of winter stars seemed permanent' (176). At this point, the desire to fix the plasticity of the past (by exorcising the spectral) clearly results in a stifling state of timelessness, a state in which temporal movement (narrative, interpretive, ethical) is simply impossible; Sethe is 'wrapped in a timeless present' (184). The absence of the ghost – or rather, the fact of its undeniable presence – entails the end of all decisions or forward movement.

    In the end, the dangerous nature of Beloved's presence mobilises Ella (a woman with her own profound traumas and another former agent of the underground railway): 'As long as the ghost showed out from its ghostly place . . . Ella respected it. But if it took flesh and came in her world, well, the shoe was on the other foot. She didn't mind a little communication between the two worlds, but this was an invasion' (1988 [1987], 257). As Luckhurst puts it, Ella and the community react to the fact that 'the impossible Real, the materializing of "actual history", [has] force[d] itself into the Symbolic' (1996, 249). This intrusion results in the dangerous conflation of the Real and the symbolic, the radically unethical ossification of the past *as Real*. Unless we accept and endure its inherent plasticity, the past cannot inform its perpetual re-formation as what 'sees (itself) coming'. All we are left with is, literally (in the case of *Beloved*), 'the final banishment of all temporality and the advent of the [ghost's] unchanging and indifferent present' (Malabou 2005, 128). Without the *possibility* of Beloved's manifestation, Sethe (along with the community) is threatened with a type of melancholic paralysis, an inability to change the past via the perpetuation of stories and conflicting interpretations. Or, as a number of critics (including Luckhurst) suggest, Beloved's presence forbids the possibility of mourning (or perhaps healing), of perpetually and ethically recasting the past.

COMING AND GOING (AGAIN)

When, in the end, Ella finally brings the community of women together to find 'the right combination, the key, the code, the sound that broke the back of words' (1988 [1987], 261), a second and final exorcism ostensibly ensues. Beloved magically disappears. However, we need to remember that the Beloved who stands before the thirty chanting women is not the baby ghost that haunted 124 Bluestone all those years before Paul D's arrival. This Beloved is, instead, 'a pregnant woman, naked and smiling in the heat of the afternoon sun' (261). This Beloved is a woman of flesh. As a representative of the past, she no longer exists as a paradoxically impossible possibility, a thing always yet to be apprehended, understood, (re)formed. She is here and now: the past made present, unavoidable, paralysing. For this reason, the apparent exorcism at the end is anything but an exorcism. The thirty women who come to sing before 124 Bluestone do not come to expel a ghost; they come to insist that the ghost return *as ghost*, that the past return once again to the (plastic) realm of the Real. The women work together so as to dismiss Beloved as a material presence and, in turn, reopen the possibility of a community that finds strength in the sharing and re-forming of past traumas. And yet there is a sense (also) that the women go too far, that this 'anti-exorcism' is actually a call to forget absolutely, a call demanding the final expulsion of Beloved as both woman and ghost. We are told, after all, that after Beloved's mysterious disappearance, the community 'forgot her like a bad dream' (274). At this point in the novel, we should certainly understand that absolute forgetfulness is no less dangerous than absolute remembrance. The former denies the informing restrictions of the plastic (and/or the specter's materiality), merely running a course that is 'unencumbered by the inertia of the Real' (Žižek 2000, 36). The latter succumbs to the illusion of an absolute that is anterior to the very possibility of re-formation.

While the women may indeed wish to forget (finally) the traumatic past Beloved represents, the novel insists that the ghost of Beloved will (or must) remain. The anti-exorcism renews a certain vital sense of uncertainty, or (again) plasticity. After the women manage to subdue Sethe (who, during Beloved's expulsion, comes to relive the moment when Schoolteacher came to collect her and her children), Beloved is mysteriously 'gone'. However, 'a little boy put it out how he had been looking for bait back of 124, down by the stream, and saw, cutting through the woods, a naked woman with fish for hair' (1988 [1987], 267). From that point on, we are told, 'her footprints come and go, come and go' (275). The anti-exorcism with which the women expel Beloved thus effects her return to the water from which she emerged. It effects the past's return to a state of spectral plasticity. Perhaps not surprisingly, then, this return of uncertainty corresponds with Sethe's renewed ability to reimagine (or 'rememory') her past. At the very moment Beloved's concrete presence is expelled, Sethe begins to re-enact the very day she decided to murder her baby daughter. But, instead of running to the shed to begin her mercy killing (once again), she decides (this time) to attack the slave master directly (who Sethe, in a state of delusion, sees in the place of her white neighbor, Edward Bodwin). More simply, the expulsion of a past made present and absolute – and, in turn, the corresponding return of the impossible possibility of re-forming that past – returns to Sethe the power to remember her traumas.

While the novel ends with Sethe a clearly broken woman, we are given the suggestion that, in the wake of Beloved's return to that which must be negotiated via rumor and storytelling, Sethe (along with the community at large) once again has the opportunity to make narrative decisions – to take, that is, responsibility for and control over a past that must continue to haunt. And so the novel oddly demands that we forget: 'It was not a story to pass on' (1988 [1987], 275). This is not a story to tell again, to share, to keep alive. At the same time, 'This is not a story to pass on' (275). This is not a story we can risk abandoning. It must be passed on, retold, cast and cast again. This story, this memory, this spectre, must be permitted to 'come and go, come and go' (275). Or, if we return again to Malabou's reading of Hegel, *Beloved* encourages us to aim for (and accept) a certain ' "dialectic" . . . action of at once arising and disappearing' (2005, 122). Since the past as plastic never permits – even as it perpetually informs – its final (symbolic) formation, it only emerges (again and momentarily) as a representation of what is coming (again).

CONCLUSION

Morrison's *Beloved*, as an exemplar of aesthetic production since the fall of postmodernism, embraces and even endorses the traumatic undecidability of the past as plastic while implicitly denouncing the perversity such undecidability might authorise. In this sense, the novel certainly seems to engage in what Hutcheon calls 'complicitous critique' (2002 [1995], 2). However, the complicity Hutcheon has in mind does not (strictly speaking) apply here, nor (for that matter) does the critique. For Hutcheon, postmodern historiographic metafiction 'at once inscribes [complicitly] and subverts [critically] the conventions and ideologies of the dominant cultural and social forces of the twentieth-century western world' (11). The critique we see in *Beloved* is ultimately a critique of postmodern critique, a critique of its increasingly dogmatic and irresponsible emphasis on the inescapabilty of an arbitrary and fictitious symbolic universe. At precisely the same time, though, *Beloved* is complicit in accepting and even endorsing this universe. Such complicity ensures the corresponding elements of critique do not simply and naively return us to (a form of) modern ideology. Instead, then, of complicitous critique, *Beloved* engages in a type of affirmative critique – a critique of its own sincere affirmation of the Real. It is precisely this affirmation and this critique that marks *Beloved* as a forerunner to a metamodern era – if, that is, we take 'metamodern' to refer to that which moves us beyond the postmodern while refusing to abandon some of its most challenging lessons. But this is not to suggest that the novel simply 'oscillates between a modern enthusiasm and a postmodern irony' (Vermeulen and van den Akker 2010). What might seem like 'oscillation' is, instead, an effort to negate postmodern irony *while negating its negation*. The novel returns us to the possibility of an ethical account of history by *sublating* its own postmodern skepticism (in a strictly Hegelian sense); it stresses the absoluteness of a plastic Real by presenting its sincere movement towards final apprehension as traumatically infinite. Like any number of texts that have followed it – from novels like Danielewski's *House of Leaves* (2000) and Leyner's *The Sugar-Frosted Nutsack* (2012) to films like Tarantino's *Inglourious Basterds* (2009) and Scorsese's *The Wolf of Wall Street* (2013) – *Beloved* renews the possibility of the objective, the absolute outside limits of the Real while insisting upon the inherent plasticity of those limits. Its various narrative re-formations '[bring] the possible to actuality, [and] manifest a virtuality already inscribed in the essence itself. This virtuality authorizes essence in its free "interpretations" in the same way the "type" legitimates the sculptor's improvisations' (Malabou 2005, 74). The novel's narrative 'improvisations' effect while being effected by (but never wholly inclusive of) that which is un-deconstructable – or rather, if we can return (once again) to Žižek's phrasing, 'the inertia of the [plastic] Real'. In *Beloved*, the elements of historiographic metafiction are thus recast; the focus is no longer on the possibility of rewriting the past but (rather) the *finite* malleability of that past. What we get is a re-formation of historiographic metafiction. What we get is historio*plastic* metafiction.

Chapter 4

Super-Hybridity: Non-Simultaneity, Myth-Making and Multipolar Conflict

Jörg Heiser

The term 'super-hybridity', in its original conception, described a set of artistic practices involving the use of a great number of hugely diverse cultural sources to create work (Heiser 2010a, 2010b, 2012). Initially, the focus was clearly on aesthetic production: the 'super-' prefix was meant to designate a tipping point in quality by way of quantity, under conditions of potentially global digital access, acceleration and accumulation. The discussion responded to works not only being done with more ingredients and faster (thanks to digital tools and the Internet) but also with a shift of focus from the styles or looks cited to the way they are dealt with methodically, such as in the work of artists like Hito Steyerl or Seth Price, or of musicians such as Gonjasufi or Yeasayer.

Like the moniker 'metamodernism' (Vermeulen and van den Akker 2010), 'super-hybridity' sought to describe a new phenomenon. As such, it perhaps overlaps with some of the practices hitherto called 'Post Internet', a term arguably first used by artist Marisa Olson between 2007 and 2010 to describe a relationship of art to the Internet (McHugh 2011; see also Cornell 2013). It is short hand for art production based on a casual use of the Internet as remote communication tool, as well as studio, archive, storage, production machine, stage, circulation engine and auditorium, but not necessarily as a main subject matter. The term has remained slippery but is usually applied to artists born post-1980 who are assumed to be 'digital natives' and whose work often involves surreal collaged materials and imagery, referencing social media tools or online design styles, as well as certain materials associated with high-tech and/or cheap mass production. However, as opposed to 1990s Internet art, these are usually put on display in the 'classic' art gallery context.

Like both 'metamodernism' and 'Post Internet', from the outset, super-hybridity provoked contentious reactions: These kinds of terms always –

still – come with the underlying assumption associated with classical avant-gardes: that they are not only descriptive or even critical-analytical, but *programmatic*. That said, the term super-hybridity initially was indeed implying two 'messages'. The first is that creating by way of using existing sources was not automatically merely unoriginal pastiche, especially if the high number of tropes and sources used de-emphasised 'quoting' as an aesthetic gesture in itself (as opposed to previous postmodernist approaches, lauding themselves for 'challenging' crossovers between, say, two earlier styles/sources, e.g., baroque and brutalism). The second is that ultimately *all* new cultural practices – all ideas – are borne out of the sticky mess of existing practices and ideas, even if in their newness they seek to deny that very fact. What followed from that observation was that concepts of purity – not least those of historical avant-gardes – have a tendency to become obsessive with denying their 'impure' origins. It is in this sense, then, that the aesthetic and cultural forms characterised by super-hybridity should be distinguished from forms typically associated with modernism and postmodernism. That said, they should be situated within today's historical moment and related to the metamodern logic of recycling past styles (see also chapter 1).

Almost two decades after the turn of the millennium, it has become all the more pressing to understand the concept designated by super-hybridity: The conditions of digital, global/local networking have become ever more ubiquitous; social media have become even more unavoidable; and, in the wake of Edward Snowden's revelations, our digital data have been exposed as being subjected to levels of capitalist manipulation and state surveillance unimagined even by the paranoiacs. The hard, dark truth may be that the stickiness and messiness of cultural confluences occurring rapidly in one given place and time are not only corrupted from the outside, co-opted by capitalism and autocratic state tendencies, but may also rot from the inside, as fantasies of purity and purification – intricately linked to ultra-violence and tyranny – seek to find justification in the mythical past while embracing the techno-cultural now. Consequently, super-hybridity needs to be explored as more than just a set of artistic practices, but as a social practice that can be exploited for all sorts of ideological and political ends.

SUPER-HYBRIDITY AND NON-SIMULTANEITY: THE CASE OF IS

Ernst Bloch (1985 [1935]) coined the notion of *Ungleichzeitigkeit*, variously translated as non-simultaneity or asynchronicity. The term describes a clash not of civilisations, but of different stages or periods of progress in social, economic and technological terms *within* what are often the same civilisations. This clashing is the result of a *Schieflage* (imbalance) of factual states of being, of factual imbalances of power, as well as of the various ideological currents abound to agitate, propagandise, distort and twist these factualities.

Crucially, Bloch shifts focus from a largely geographical assumption of difference to a temporal/historic one, thus resulting in the assumption of phenomena originating from very different periods occurring *at the same time* and often in the same place or context. Bloch first developed the idea with a horrified view towards the rise of the Nazis in Germany, explaining their strange, mesmerising power over the minds of large parts of German society with the way they managed, in the wake of a post–World War I identity crisis, to tap into a crypto-romantic longing of the Germans for past, often purely imagined, 'Germanic' glory. It is as if the repressed past and the Tourette-like, blurted-out near future are colliding head-on in the present moment.

In the Cold War era, despite the overwhelming ideology of the East-West confrontation, Bloch reformulated the notion of 'simultaneous non-simultaneity' as a concept involving what he called 'multiverses' (Bloch 1965, 201) of different temporal stages of progress branching out, so to speak, across the globe – a notion he specifically held up against the notion of 'Kulturkreise' ('cultural circle' or 'cultural field') that had trickled down from early twentieth-century German anthropology to mid-brow parlando, assuming geographically defined genealogies of cultural difference across long periods of time.

The practices of the infamous Islamic State group (IS, formerly known as ISIS, or ISIL) can serve as an example of the contemporary resonance of non-simultaneity. In 2014, Islamic State insurgents, known for their ruthless and excessive brutality combined with state-of-the-art military and propagandistic tactics, took control of large parts of Syria and Iraq, of a territory roughly as big as the United Kingdom. On 29 June 2014, the group declared the territory it occupied a caliphate, and its leader Abu Bakr al-Baghdadi was announced as 'Caliph Ibrahim', while dropping the 'Iraq and Levant' part from its name, thus suggesting the aspiration to substantially widen the territorial scope. The claim is, of course, to be in a line of descent from the first caliphs, who were the rulers of the political-religious state created in the two centuries following the death of Prophet Muhammad in 632, an empire that included large parts of North Africa, South Eastern Asia and Spain. However, this claim has largely been refused, seen as ridiculous and even heresy – even among radical Islamist circles who mainly argue that an isolated group cannot declare a caliph without that authority being awarded to the supposed caliph by a consultative council of religious leaders (al-Samad 2014). Furthermore, the invocation of a traditional caliphate order stands in stark contrast not only to what actually was the more recent history of caliphs but also to the way the Islamic State group itself picks and mixes its ideological make-up from wildly different, at times bizarrely contradictive sources – a mix that has proven to be devastatingly efficient in fuelling war atrocities on a grand scale in Iraq and Syria, as well as numerous terrorist attacks around the world.

The last caliph, Abdülmecid II, was expelled from Turkey in 1924. On the night that his residence – the Dolmabahçe Palace in Constantinople (renamed Istanbul in 1930) – was surrounded by Republican troops, Abdülmecid was reading Montaigne (Dalrymple 2014). Prior to his deposal, he had been the chairman of the Ottoman's Artist Society. He was an avid collector of butterflies and painted a picture of a woman reading Goethe's *Faust*, which was exhibited in Vienna in 1918. In exile in Nice, France (where on 14 July 2016, in the name of IS, eighty-six people were killed in a ferocious attack with a cargo truck), one could see him stroll with great dignity along the beach, wearing nothing but swimming trunks and a parasol (Dalrymple 2014). What about his supposed direct successor in office? When Abu Bakr al-Baghdadi declared himself Caliph Ibrahim during midday prayers in a mosque in Mosul, Iraq, on Friday, 4 July 2014, he sported black robes and a black turban, and a heavy bling watch that set the social media ablaze with speculation whether it was a Rolex, a James Bond–type Omega Seamaster or in fact a Swiss-made watch of the Saudi Arabian brand Al-Fajr, which, among other features, has a built-in compass to indicate the direction of Mecca, and a Qur'an bookmark feature which allows you to record the last Sura name and verse number you recited for next time. More important, though, was that al-Baghdadi spoke from the very pulpit previously used by a moderate Sunni imam, executed by Islamic State only a few weeks earlier. While al-Baghdadi's black attire was meant to underline the sober religious authority that many radical Islamists say he claims unjustifiably, the glistening watch seemed a distortion in that image. It is precisely this combination of evocations of the ancient past and an almost futurist technophilia that seems characteristic for Islamic State and that makes them a striking example of super-hybridity and non-simultaneity.

Since its rise to power in Syria and Iraq, Islamic State has issued various shocking propaganda videos, proving itself skilled in using social media such as Twitter, YouTube and Tumblr, and even issuing a smartphone app, to circulate this material. The Berlin-based artist Goscha Steinhauer, in preparation for his video installation *Dreamcatchers* (2015), has voluntarily looked at these videos for too long and too often, in order to get his head around the fact that they are not only shot with often more than one state-of-the-art HDTV camera but that they expose a frightening mixture of excessive, sadist violence and an affinity to Hollywood action movie and video game aesthetics (as shown in figures 4.1, 4.2 and 4.3). Often, the videos include compilations of murdering scenes in the style of 'best kill' online shooting game compilations, put up on YouTube by so-called players to brag about their skills.

Figure 4.1. The video game aesthetic of IS propaganda videos (*First Person Shooters*). Courtesy of Goscha Steinhauer.

Figure 4.2. The video game aesthetic of IS propaganda videos (*Grand Theft Auto*). Courtesy of Goscha Steinhauer.

The opening shot of one particular video is reminiscent of Charles and Ray Eames's famous short film *Powers of Ten* (1968), but instead of gradually moving up into the sky from a couple's comfy picnic, eventually showing us the vista of the entire earth, it's the other way round: a Google Earth zoom leads us closer and closer to and eventually through the clouds, as smooth editing switches to the camera of a small hovering drone that panorama-pans the ruined cityscape of war-ridden Falluja, Iraq. Reaching the ground, the edit switches to troops of fighters on the back of pick-up trucks proudly punching the air with their guns. They often wear white Nike trainers but otherwise are clad in black, with sophisticated fighting gear, including body armour vests. Next, we see them standing in a market place, listening to one of their leaders giving a speech, wielding a Machete-like knife. The next move is that all of the insurgents draw out their passports – whether French or Lebanese or Syrian or another nationality – and tear them apart, as a gesture of joining the new Islamic State land. There is no doubt this kind of video has been successfully used as a recruitment tool attracting young men from around the world who have grown up in often difficult social circumstances, in immigrant communities of Paris, Brussels or elsewhere.

If one needed further proof of the uncanny proliferation of social media tropes within the realm of war and its inflated macho-ism, jihadi insurgents have also flooded Instagram and YouTube with imagery of themselves

Figure 4.3.   Installation view of Goscha Steinhauer's *Dreamcatchers* (2015). Courtesy of Goscha Steinhauer.

posing with kittens. No reason to LOL though: posing with a cat may well be a 'sectarian statement' (Buchen and Delhaes 2014), as the kitten is associated with an early Islamic figure who expressively denounced the Shiites. That figure, in Sunni tradition, is Abu Huraira (which translates as 'Father of the Kitten'), who was not only a lover of cats but also a companion of Prophet Muhammad, and the narrator of hadith (collections of Muhammad's sayings,

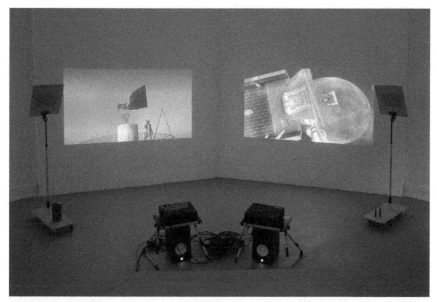

Figure 4.4. Installation view of Goscha Steinhauer's *Dreamcatchers* (2015). Courtesy of Goscha Steinhauer.

supplementary commentaries to the Quran). As such, Shiites have considered Abu Huraira as a liar who supposedly misquoted the prophet as denouncing Ali, who for the Shiites is the rightful successor of Muhammad. Nevertheless, the actual images seem less triumphant gestures of provocation to Shiite onlookers, but more like self-forgotten signifiers of precisely the narcissist longing for intimacy and delicacy and 'immaculate' life that motivates many others to post kitten images on social media.

The perverse amalgam of technophile pop-, meme- and game-culture styles with archaic interpretations of religion, of technicist-narzissist-self-realisational thinking and magical thinking, of versed image propaganda and archaic iconoclasm, is anything but exclusive to Islamist extremists. In fact, the ideological aspect appears to function as a pretext to legitimise the unfettered exertion of brutal power and the acting-out of ultra-violence, while in a state of severely repressed sexuality and mass-psychotic aversion of self-reflection (cf. Améry 1980; Scarry 1987; Theweleit 1987).

SUPER-HYBRIDITY AND NON-SIMULTANEITY: MYTH-MAKING TODAY

We arrive at a hard truth: that even the ones who *explicitly* act towards ethnic cleansing and cultural purity will nevertheless do so with the unfettered self-entitlement to plunder from all sorts of cultural imagery. In his famous 1967 lecture 'Art and the Arts' on the eroding delimitation between artistic disciplines and genres, Adorno asserted that there exists among many people a 'repulsing fear of miscegenation' that 'assumed pathological dimension in the National Socialist cult of pure race and the denigration of hybridity' (Adorno 2003 [1967], 370). What Adorno did not mention in that same treatise was that this very 'repulsing fear' did not keep the Nazis from some of the most absurd hybridisations of cultural sources: in 1920, Friedrich Krohn suggested the swastika as the emblem of the new Nazi party, pronouncedly as a symbol of auspiciousness in Hindu and Buddhist cultures, while some Esoteric proto-Nazis such as Guido von List had simply claimed it to be a Germanic rune; similarly, the cult of a supposed 'Indo-German', Aryan master race came with the absurd claim of purity that never existed, namely that of a 'pure' mix of Indian, Iranian and Northern European descent, while the very term 'Aryan' had been hijacked from linguistics, where it had simply denoted a set of related languages, to now be the name of a supposedly superior Nordic race. Ultimately, the underlying technique is that of a bogus mysticism. That is, the Nazis adopted the technique of willful arbitrariness (a kind of 'I take whatever source suits me, and turn it to fit my objectives' attitude) that worked precisely to conjure mysticism, to create leaders and scapegoats. This technique of pilfering mythical sources for the sake of creating one's own legend is typical for so many war and war crime scenarios: the entire complex of self-legitimising what is ultimately the negation of being a social human being as such is decorated with fantasies of coolness and heroism that are plundered and picked from the pop-cultural and religious smorgasbord as fits. What is so different today is that this technique is used in a bizarrely unstable media environment in which this picking 'n mixing has accelerated up to the point that these myths become not only first available to a small secret cult, before being picked up years or decades later by a strong political movement, but that these bizarre and contradictory ideological constructions become virulent right away, as an almost self-replicating entity.

One of the best documentary films of recent years, Joshua Oppenheimer's *The Act of Killing* (2012) provides a horrific insight into the mentality that goes with the process of self-legitimisation, decades after a crime against humanity. The film's main protagonists all committed mass murders during the 1965–1966 anti-communist purge in Indonesia during which between 500,000 and more than a million people, often of Chinese descent, were killed. Those who committed this genocide have never been held accountable in their country – quite to the contrary: a right-wing regime has been built on these crimes against humanity and, as the film shows, the perpetrators have been hailed as heroes. What is so chilling is the narcissism of the film's protagonists – their sense of entitlement, almost five decades later, as they boast of their horrific crimes. Indeed, one of them, Anwar Congo, readily confesses to have strangled more than a thousand victims with a wire. Strikingly, Oppenheimer persuades his protagonists to re-enact some of their crimes on camera, in order to make them physically feel the tremor, fear and pain of their victims. Initially showing not the slightest sense of remorse, Anwar Congo subsequently weeps, seemingly starting to regret. The perpetrators had started out as the so-called movie theatre gangsters, who had organised black market screenings of Hollywood flicks. They recount how they saw themselves, upon leaving the cinemas in which they saw the latest action movies, as cool Al Capone types, wearing slick clothes and hats, whom no one can stop.

At one point in the film, the protagonists appear on a television chat show and are applauded for their crimes. The scene resonates with fictions such as *The Hunger Games* (Collins 2008–2010; films 2012–2015) or its Japanese predecessor *Battle Royale* (2000), as well as a whole set of 1970s sci-fi movies that tell apocalyptic parables of today's society, such as *Zardoz* (1974), *Logan's Run* (1976) or *The Running Man* (1987). Shockingly, in reality such episodes have already taken place – whether in Indonesia, Iraq and Syria, or in Rwanda, where in 1994 drunken and stoned hosts of RTLMC radio station incited and spurred on fellow Hutus to go out and commit a mass slaughter of Tutsi, to the sound of Reggae reverb sound effects on their voices, and in-between playing fast-paced Zouk numbers, a jump-up music style from the French Antilles that was popular across large parts of French-speaking Africa at the time.

As wars unfold, social media channels are jam-packed with images and accompanying news bits, many of which may be accurate, but a notable number of which are also, simply, faked, using images from previous incidents or even other contexts; for instance, a video from the Syrian Civil War being used to supposedly illustrate how Hamas uses children as human shields or vice versa or how a video of a Syrian father hugging his dead son is relabelled as referring to Gaza (see Mezzofiore 2014a). Comparably, in a flagrantly open attempt to sexualise soldierly brutality, there occurred, during the unfolding of Operation Protective Edge, the 2014 Israeli military campaign launched in Gaza, a Facebook page of 'sexy' IDF support images entitled 'Standing with IDF'. As with the Islamic State kittens, another trope of online meme culture was hijacked, namely that of the write-on-someone's-skin drunk/sexy snapshot: a stream of images of young women with 'I love IDF' statements as well as hearts and/or Stars of David written on their behinds and breasts. The 'sex bomb' logic is reminiscent of 1950s and 1960s tropes that conjoined the awakening 'sexual revolution' with ongoing wars, especially Vietnam. Here, however, all of the images are posted on Facebook with no indication of their respective originators, and almost none showing faces (which plays into sexism of the basest kind, but also simply is a means to render anonymous the individuals in question). Consequently, it is hard not to see these as a very calculated and hampered kind of propaganda that is encouraging as much support for the Israeli troops as it is causing outrage against them. Self-defeating propaganda: yet another phenomenon of a bizarrely unstable media environment in which modes of narcissist presentation and opinion-forming, of scheming and randomisation, converge.

After the Maidan revolution in Kyiv in winter 2013–2014 – and this is already where for many the revolution starts, and for others the 'fascist' regime change is manifested: whether you use the Ukrainian spelling of the capital of the Ukraine, or the Russian which is Kiev – a kind of covert war has unfolded. First, Russia took Crimea, and in Summer 2014, after a Malaysian passenger plane was shot down, speculations abounded over whether the Russian authorities under Putin either had their hand in it, or whether they have, to the contrary, lost control of the separatist rebels (much the same way the Islamic State group has become seemingly uncontrollable by earlier backers) or whether – as especially Russian media were trying to suggest – in fact it was Ukrainian forces who downed the plane. With the Kremlin largely controlling the media and intimidating critical journalists, it is hard to believe the latter insinuation, especially if it turns out that there are facts that even some of the Russian media seem to agree on with sources in other countries: namely, that the two leading figures of the separatists, Alexander Borodai and Igor Strelkov, have been, or possible still are, FSB officers who came straight from Moscow for the 'job'. Strelkov – which is his *nom de guerre*, while his men call him Strelok, meaning 'rifleman' or 'private', and his actual last name is Girkin – is a forty-three-year old Russian who allegedly started his 'career' in the early 1990s as an insurgent supporting Serbian separatists in Bosnia. He was possibly involved in war crimes and the killing of 3,000 Bosnian Muslims (Mezzofiore 2014b). Ever since Strelkov seems to have been associated with the FSB in one way or other.

In regard to our concern over how myth-making converges with technology-induced means of circulation and narcissist self-presentation, how an idiosyncratic mix of historical facts and sources is seemingly magically transformed into a purist cause for separatism, Strelkov is a curious case in point: his big passion is war re-enactments. Having published regularly on *forum antikvariat* – a Russian forum for antique dealers, including those who trade in old uniforms and historic weapons, and so on – he has written under the user name Kotych ('cat'). Strelkov has participated in numerous re-enactments of 1918–1920 battles of the Russian Civil War, taking the role of a White Guard officer (Kashin 2014). There are images of him on the Web in a Roman soldier's attire, as well as in the uniform of Tsarist soldiers from the times of the Napoleonic Wars (Marples 2014). In the Ukraine, Strelkov sported the same moustache and hairstyle – and some claim even military tactics – that he assumed as a historic White Guard officer (Kashin 2014). If Bloch's notion of *Ungleichzeitigkeit* needed to be (re-)enacted as farce, here it is. When Strelkov's soldiers took Slavyansk, they decorated the entrance to the city with a large banner that combined allusions to one of Strelkov's great idols, the White Guard general Mikhail Drozdovsky, using images from the grotesque Hollywood flick *300*, with its computer-animated Spartan super soldiers holding out against the vast Persian superiority, presented as barbaric hordes (Kashin 2014). Again, *Ungleichzeitigkeit* as farce. Farce, though, does not exclude tragic reality; on the contrary, as with many of the Western recruits of Islamic State, video and re-enactment game culture seems to have transmuted directly into real war, actual battles, actual killings and crimes. War has become the adventure holiday for sociopaths, willingly recruited and incorporated by schemers in high places.

Many of the aforementioned events are a mixture of happenstance and manipulation. The job is to develop a sensorium to be able to tell the ingredients apart. In societies enmeshed in the global-local, mass- and social media networks (which is to say, more and more societies), all of us will have to learn anew to tell apart crowd wisdom from mob mentality, proper journalism from fabricated misinformation or fake news and actual spontaneous developments from manipulated ones. To the extent dissident opinion and whistle-blower leaks become more easily available, so do troll comments and fabricated news.

SUPER-HYBRIDITY AND NON-SIMULTANEITY: AESTHETICS AND POLITICS

Against this background it becomes all the more important to distinguish between a hybridity employed to weave a cloak of myth meant to justify and glorify the establishment of tyranny, creating a sharp either/or distinction between the ones partaking in the power thus assumed and those under its thumb; and the kind of hybridity that is geared towards taking apart that very either/or, towards weaving new coalitions between dissidents on both sides of an antagonism. The uncanny marriage between the fantasies of omnipotence as acted out in the virtual realm of social media and the Internet, and the fantasies of omnipotence as acted out in war atrocities, has now and again made glaringly clear that nothing is safe from being hijacked for whatever barbaric purpose imaginable. No technology of decentralised digital circulation and no hybrid cultural technique is safe from being incorporated into political stratagems geared exactly towards diverting them from their inherent emancipatory and liberating potentials. Indeed, we must be alert to these kinds of debased forms of super-hybridity.

Art is a realm in which it is possible to reflect, understand and speculate on socio-political epistemology, on principles of possible progress (as well as regress). But these aesthetic mirror images or doppelgangers of actual socio-political epistemology, including the pathological forms (pathological in that they seek to undermine the very civilisational standards that allow communities to build and flourish in the first place), cannot be the same. To confuse art and political power is itself a form of pathology, à la Gabriele d'Annunzio (who tried to rule Fiume, now Rijeka in Kroatia, in proto-Duce-style), or Yukio Mishima (who tried to carry out a putsch with his own militia): a narcissist self-inflation, from being the ruler of aesthetic cohorts and narrative landscapes to being the ruler of actual armies and countries; from being a great artist to being a great, dangerous idiot. In the current sociotope of globalised, digitally accelerated aesthetic influence (thanks to the Internet and globalised trade, one can almost anywhere in the world be receptive to anything from anywhere else), one could easily imagine todays d'Annunzio as someone who would not be satisfied with a small army in a provincial Italian town.

In the figure of today's super nerd hacker, the claim to aesthetic radicalism and political weight can converge – pathological still, but not as obviously as in aforementioned examples, as both the aesthetic practice and the political ambition take the practical form of code, of technological expertise and of conspiracy. Aesthetic projection, fantasy, aesthetic 'what if . . .' scenarios: they all become code, programming. Fantasies of power and creation that once would have produced a philosophy or a theatre drama now may produce a programme that actually does things to other people's lives in a much more directly manipulative manner. Of course, philosophy and drama could do things to other people's lives as well – agitate, infuriate, stimulate, enlighten them. Now there is also a technicist, functionalist drift involved: we may be hacked, monitored or something may be leaked, or shitstormed, and we may not even fully know or understand, as we become part of the semi-automatic process. Precisely because of this technological delimitation of the distinction between aesthetics and politics in the realm of code, one may have to insist on that very distinction. The fantasies of pure action, of power and triumph, of ultra-violence and ultimate narcissist fulfilment that populate pop culture as well as the (post-)avant-gardes may need to be questioned in terms of their political repercussions already in the realm of aesthetics. Such fantasies certainly should be understood as, in principle, legitimate aesthetic materials that, depending on the aesthetic constellation they are subjected to, can result in great art or debilitating propaganda (and sometimes, disturbingly, a mixture of both). If these fantasies, whether prior or after being subjected to aesthetic constellations, leak back into the political realm – in the sense of confusing the distinction, treating reality like a dream/nightmare, and war like a game – they effectively produce the devastation of that very political realm. Islamic State in Iraq/Syria seems to be the most obvious example of such a process. Here, digital technology doesn't replace that old coupling of magical thinking with political ruthlessness, but accelerates it; they converge.

In the wake of neoliberal capitalist ideology and the devastations it has already effected in the realms of finance, labour and overall ideologies of individualism, we have become accustomed to read cold economic calculation into each and every hot political conflict and war. Even if we find evidence that, say, US companies are directly profiting from war in the Middle East, or that Russia has geo-strategic-cum-economic interests in the Black Sea, that alone does not explain why they would be so stupid to create the mess we're in now. The character of Francis Underwood in US television series *House of Cards* – the ruthless Machiavellian politician aiming to become US president, by all means necessary – formulates it very clearly early on in the series: money is only interesting in as much as it provides power; 'true' political power is superior to money, because it can devaluate, confiscate, annihilate that money and/or its owners. In other words, the neoliberal ideology of financial clout resulting in direct political influence works only as long as there is at least the façade of a reliable civil system, and at least remnants of a civil society that can be exploited and hollowed out from within. If they finally collapse, so does neoliberal ideology – it relates to a democratic, civic society like a parasite to its host; if the latter dies so does it unless it finds another host (which sadly it does quite easily in a globalised financial realm). Of course, Islamic State needs financial support, and they seem to have gotten it from all sorts of sources, most notably from Saudi Arabia and Qatar, who seem to have seen them as a necessarily tool, initially, to fight Syria's Assad regime, and to ward off the Iranian influence in Iraq. But what becomes apparent here, either way, is that ruthless economic and geo-strategic calculation, itself an ideological pathology, can become sucked into political and military processes it ceases to control, leading to devastation that ends all calculation.

CONCLUSION

Super-hybridity is a name for a method of responding to, or exploiting, the technological accelerated possibility of converging sources and influences; it is not an aesthetic programme in and of itself, lest an ethics. Looking at the make-up of the cultural 'surfaces' of our political and social environments, even and especially at times of war, is not a delusionary pastime that keeps us from understanding what is really behind discrimination, brutality, tyranny (i.e. the invisible machinations of economic interest and political intrigue). Rather, looking at these surfaces is the irreplaceable and necessary complement to looking at what is supposedly underneath, unless we want to become trapped again in mono-causal – dare I say purist, dogmatic, totalitarian – concepts of society that are part of what landed us in the current mess in the first place.

The dialectics of enlightenment, one could say, has entered another phase: phase one was about understanding that functionalist, scheming forms of rationalism are anything but immune against tyranny and the excesses of fantasies of omnipotence; and that vice versa merely suppressing these fantasies does not at all equal ethical behaviour. Phase two is about understanding that even the cultural techniques that were borne out of the necessities of warding off these excesses of functionalist rationalism – for example, on the part of the colonised emancipating themselves from colonisers, celebrating, for example, 'impurity' against dominant ideologies of racial purity – are not immune against being sucked into the civilisational breakdowns borne out of the power games of a post 9/11, multipolar world.

Bloch's notion of *Ungleichzeitigkeit* was based both on a Marxist, post-Hegelian philosophy of historic progress and on a more general understanding of enlightenment as a move towards increasing the self-reflexive nature of thought and ethical standards. Even if we were still ironic postmodernists, or whether we have evolved into post-ironic metamodernists, it is evident that simplistic notions of linear progress have long been exposed as illusory and dangerous, and even as we may be tempted by nihilism, it is hard to deny that virtually any idea of reflection and thought – indeed, of philosophy in general – ultimately relies on the assumption that progress is possible, at the very least a progress in understanding what's going on. Otherwise, there would be no point in any kind of reflection. From that assumption it follows that, at least in principle, acting under the guidance of that progress of understanding is possible, as long as it remains accessible as part of the 'heritage' of thoughts that have been thought on this planet. This is not to say that illusion, amnesia, failure and chaos, as well as social and political antagonism, may not prevent that access, lest that progress from happening. The *Weltgeist* has indeed become a ghost, trapped in an old ruin. There is no march towards a bright future, as there is no inevitable slide back towards a dark past. Yet that does not mean that the ideas of how things could be better for all – economically, socially, ethically – are nullified. As soon as we can imagine how things could be better, a principle of progress is implied. This is how I understand *Ungleichzeitigkeit* today.

Chapter 5

The Cosmic Artisan: Mannerist Virtuosity and Contemporary Crafts

Sjoerd van Tuinen

In contemporary culture, handicraft is everywhere. Architects have rediscovered the values of craft in post-iconic times, while artists have developed a renewed interest in the material process of making things. In the past years, the best restaurant in the world was no longer the molecular kitchen of *El Bulli* but the new Nordic cuisine of Red Zepii's *Noma*. As activists have reverted to craft graffiti or craftivism, hipsters are meeting in specialised knitting cafés. Television spills over with cooking shows. Internet theorists celebrate the culture of craft in anything from open source software to web 2.0 to the Fab Lab. In the slipstream of the slow movements, social philosophers implement the ethos of the craftsman in city renovation projects. At a regular pace, a new exhibition about the current state of craft opens its doors to an enthusiastic crowd.

As I argue, the 'artisanal turn' is not just a symptom of postmodern nostalgia, that is, past 'options' or 'instances' allowed to make a second appearance. Rather, it is our very experience of time that has changed. What seemed old can appear authentically new again. Peter Osborne speaks of 'an art of the contemporary' (2011: 115–16) that comes after postmodernism and that involves 'a kind of internal retreat of the modern to the present' (2011: 111). Instead of the modernist new, the avant-gardist tomorrow and the postmodern End of History, contemporary practice inhabits an 'a-synchronous' present (cf. Avanessian 2016a) that we can call metamodern (Vermeulen and van den Akker 2010), where meta- is understood in its etymological sense of 'among' a heterogeneity of (material, technical, social, political, digital, etc.) practices which, in their hybrid togetherness, express and construct the contemporary.

The metamodern interest in crafts and craftsmanship thus has less to do with the idolisation of pre-industrial handicrafts by John Ruskin or the anti-industrial Arts and Crafts movement founded by William Morris than with Bauhaus. For Ruskin and Morris, the basic idea had been that craftsman-ship guarantees workers control over the means and relations of production and thus enables them to retain their traditional form of life. Bauhaus, by contrast, was probably the first major attempt to combine specialised craft workshops with industrial manufacturing and capital investments and, hence, conceptualise modern craft vis-à-vis the historically specific social situation of labour.

Ever since, craft has been emancipating itself from the intimacy of the studio and the corresponding closed guild mind that values only the specifics of its metier and its skills. The recent exhibition curated by Li Edelkoort and Philip Fimmano at Israel's Design Museum Holon, 'For the Gathering: From Domestic Craft to Contemporary Process Exhibition' (2014), establishes direct correlations between material transformation and social congrega-tion. Instead of a concern with labour, the question of craft now seems to be synonymous with our engagement with matter and everyday life. This trans-formation marks less the disappearance of craftsmanship after the end of art than its development into a general media literacy. Given a certain material, what is it capable of?

It was perhaps in this metamodern sense that Deleuze and Guattari, in *A Thousand Plateaus*, proposed the concept of the modern artist as 'cosmic artisan' (1987: 345). For them, modernism is not just the historical moment of the final crystallisation of the canonical fine arts, each with its specific mat-ter and form. Rather, as in Russian constructivism, it is the moment when art becomes exclusively a question of technique, the elaboration and assemblage of any material whatsoever charged with harnessing unformed and unlo-calisable – that is cosmic – forces. Crucially, it has nothing to do with any social-political or other pre-established division of labour. The cosmic artisan does not oppose art in favour of life, but art as a form of life, as an already socio-political project: he is the hero of contemporary DIY culture. He is the Revolutionary Knitter who understands skill and technologies as free actions directly wed to a material movement that exceeds him on all sides: 'The modern figure is not the child or the lunatic, still less the artist, but the cosmic artisan: a homemade atomic bomb. To be an artisan and no longer an artist, creator or founder, is the only way to become cosmic, to leave the milieus and the earth behind' (Deleuze and Guattari 1987: 345).

From the perspective of the cosmic artisan, we can also retroactively reinterpret and reevaluate modern tendencies that were already present in premodern arts and crafts, albeit in a latent and dissociated state. If the con-temporary is a disjunctive synthesis of heterochronic times, it constitutes a drama in which all of the past emerges as our contemporary potential. In what follows, I will argue that the cosmic artisan finds a precursor not in the classical or romantic artists, who belong only to Art's official and exclusive

'History', but in the untimelier becoming of the mannerist craftsman. As Bruno Latour has argued in his 'Compositionist Manifesto', the current geological epoch of the Anthropocene is closer to the sixteenth century than to the self-image of the modern world (2010). A more adequate model of creativity than the artist-genius is the alchemist as cosmic operator. No longer a professional but a transdisciplinary maker and researcher, today's artisan's gentle unruliness and experimentations tend towards a new unity of the arts. Their composition is neither that of God's creation nor that of a romanticised Nature but one of geo-engineering. As a consequence, the relation between past and future becomes fully reversible. Just as metamodernism not merely equals contemporary art but also actualises transhistorical tendencies, I look to the sixteenth century to find in it not a model for the present, but a futuricity that is already included in it and that enables makers to forge new alliances between the oldest and newest of (social) technologies.

In what follows, I offer a mannerist genealogy for metamodern crafts and craftsmanship. Starting from the tensions brought about in matter-form relationships by contemporary digital design practices, I retrospectively problematise the division of labour between design and craft at the very moment it first appeared. In this way I expose an informal or cosmic dimension in both mannerist and metamodern craftsmanship, characterised by an infinite and continuous variation of manners rather than forms. I will then develop some of the ontological, epistemological and political implications of this dimension in the light of recent developments in theory such as New Materialism, Object-Oriented Ontology (OOO) and the care for the plastic relationality of the Self, which themselves are interpreted as expressions of a metamodern sensibility.

HANDS-ON DESIGN: MANNERIST CRAFTSMANSHIP

If there is a relevance of mannerism for contemporary 'art', perhaps even a return of mannerism in contemporary 'design', we must stop looking back to mannerism in terms of the nineteenth-century dialectics between the degradation of the operative into automatised modes of production and the subsequent nostalgia for pre-industrial handicrafts (cf. Cardoso 2010). This division of labour between design and craft already appears in the sixteenth century. Wasn't it Giorgio Vasari who sanctioned the distinction between art and craft or between the major and minor arts in order to save the aristocracy of the three *arti del disegno* and constituted art as a field of intellectual knowledge, thus also providing the self-legitimation of art as a coherent and recognisable order of historical progression? In the mannerist arts of design, everything seems to depend on the strict division of labour between genius and work, conception and execution. Thus Michelangelo famously held that the marble already encloses the idea of the work of art, but that it takes a hand that obeys the intellect to accomplish it. It would be the task of the intellect to actively recognise the form of this content and of the obeying hand merely to free it from the surrounding mass.

Still, this is perhaps only the all too well-known story that culminates in the romantic aesthetics of the artist genius. For whereas in the Kantian aesthetic, the Idea would become irreducible to conceptual rules, mannerism still sought to unite idea and rule, artistic freedom and academic training, in other words, fine art and craftsmanship in a single intuition. This indicates that the mannerists knew that the artist's creativity and self-knowledge cannot be separated from their application in material practice. The hand may be mechanic, but in communication with the spirit it becomes a free machine. Vice versa, there is no art without craft, no *essai-idée* without *métier*. In reality, 'intelligent' design is as obscure a term for artificial objects as creation is for natural objects. The *non-finito* state of works such as Michelangelo's *Captives* (1513–1534) does not refer to some prefabricated idea in general but reflects the artist's virtuosity insofar as the idea, virtually enclosed in matter, does not exist outside the manner of its manual (since *maniera* comes from *la mano*, the hand) actualisation.

Intuitions are not transcendent Ideas but immanent feedback loops. They depend on sensitive and sensible evaluations that pose more problems than they solve, as they demand the very invention of what they are about: making is thinking, and what I cannot create I do not know. This is why contemporary designers and theorists like to compare their work to applied arts such as cooking or gardening, or growing a beard. In art as in nature things come into existence by variation, internal movement and distributed agency. Instead of the realisation of an original, there is only transmission; what replaces method is cultivation (Spuybroek 2012). Design becomes a matter of skill and sentience, of learning to pay attention to, and experiment and collaborate with materials, which present themselves as riddles, as clusters of tendencies one first needs to learn how to read.

At stake today as well as in the sixteenth century, therefore, is not the social division of labour, but the cosmos at large. If mannerism elevated mechanics into the sphere of the formative idea, today different and new machines are capable of acting as formatting forces. With every new medium or technology, there is a reciprocal deterritorialisation between hand and material. Documenting in breathtaking detail the very history of their creation and transformation, Quayola's *Captives #B8–6–0* (2013; see Figure 5.1.) offers a contemporary interpretation of Michelangelo's *non-finito*. They shift the focus from the all too well-known sculptures to how new technologies introduce new tensions and manners in the formal articulation of matter. Ultimately it is not ideas that inhabit matter, but other materials. They always do so, though, in an unpredictable, differentiating manner. This is what makes it

Figure 5.1. Image of Quayola's *Captives #B8–6–0* (2013). Courtesy of the artist and bitforms gallery.

interesting today to speak of new crossovers such as digital handmade, digital gothic or digital grotesque (cf. Johnston 2015).

The operational use of algorithms and computer-controlled robots is not simply a means to an end, that is, a means that allow us to produce forms that were impossible in the past, but a means that generates unpredictable ends and endlessly evolving forms. While canonical distinctions impose the theoretical opposition of form and matter and assign art and craft their own respective media (synthetic materials such as canvas, paper and oil versus natural materials such as wood, clay fibre, and elbow-grease), these oppositions are therefore always already bypassed in practice by an informal and intermediary dimension that is energetic and molecular, something Deleuze and Guattari describe as 'an objective zone of fluctuation that is coextensive with reality itself' (1987: 373). In this zone of indetermination, fine art and applied art, design and craft converge in an abstract and machinic constructivism. They converge with life itself.

ALCHEMY: TRANSFORMING (THE) EARTH

More than with Michelangelo's *non-finito*, the informal dimension of craftsmanship already became clear with mannerist sculptors such as Bernard Palissy or Benvenuto Cellini, the latter generally, from Goethe to Richard

Sennett, being regarded the craftsman par excellence (Sennett 2009: 67–80). Both Palissy and Cellini have been marginalised due to sculpture's lower classification in the *paragone* debate and traditionally count as examples of decorative art. In reality, they were all the more ambitious. Adopting the old idea of Paracelsus or Dürer that alchemy and the arts are the same, they engaged in manipulating and operating nature itself. The task of art, Cellini said, is to animate and 'test the earth' (*per provare la terra*), to isolate, capture and harness its forces by means of liquefaction of its metals (Cole 2002: 16). As a smith, he knew that form is never separable from matter, but that it comes to the fore as a flow, being as much artificially constructed as it is natural. His bronze *Perseus* (1545) is therefore not carved like marble, but cast. In 'Art of the Earth' (an essay included in the *Discours admirables* ([1580] 1996)), Palissy similarly explained how he seeks to channel life itself into clay. Simultaneous with the appearance of the *Wunderkammer*, his casting of teeming pond scenes marks a triumph of assemblage (Falguières 2005: 241–45). The glaze makes everything – stupefying aggregates of fish, serpents, lizards, arabesques, interlacings, angels, volutes and masks – come loose from its context and enter into strange, unnatural machinations, while a multiplication of artificial grottos, gardens and topiary directly confronts the earth's own formation processes.

The exhibition on 'Art and Alchemy' curated by Dedo von Kerssenbrock-Krosigk and Beat Wismer (Kunstpalast Düsseldorf 2014) shows how alchemy has had a lasting influence on modern art, from surrealism to Anselm Kiefer and from Sigmar Polke's art of separation and fusion to Yves Klein's interest in the alchemical roots of oil paint (with pigment and dyes as *materia prima* and the sponge as zone of immaterial pictorial sensibility where matter and spirit interpenetrate). In the late 1960s, the old concept of the artist-alchemist itself resurfaced with Germano Celant's interest in *arte povera*, as the recycling of garbage and its transformation into art opened the work to both social and natural processes. Today it is taken up in Gordon Matta-Clark's *Urban Alchemy* (2009–2010) or Wilhelm Mundt's trashstones (a series of abstract and amorphous lumps (*Klumpen*) beginning in 1989 with *Stone 001* and running well into the 500 stones at the time of writing), shown in Figure 5.2. Composed of the hybrid production waste of the artist's studio but coated in coloured, fibre-glass reinforced plastics, the latter conjures up visions of serial production processes as well as an enigmatic and magical presence. Shiny and reflecting at first, their surfaces quickly reveal their multilayered composition as they are wrapped lithely around an inner core of wood, duct tape, discarded sculptures but also broken electronics and personal items which are all compacted together and preserved like the fossils of our time.

What is new today is that alchemy is not restricted to low tech. In collaboration with art academies, the ceramic industry, several scientific research

Figure 5.2.   Installation view of Wilhelm Mundt's *TrashStones* (aluminium) – Buchmann Box, Berlin. 2012. Courtesy of the artist and Buchmann Galerie Berlin.

centres, museums and galleries, a workplace such as Sundaymorning@ EKWC offers pristine raw materials as well as advanced equipment to artists, designers and architects who want to work with 3D objects. The exhibition 'Ceramix' (Bonnefanten Museum, Maastricht, 2015) curated by Camille Morineau and Lucia Pesapane provides a retrospective, organised according to a blend of old and new categories such as the grotesque, the curiosity, engagement, performance and the installation. It shows how the unexpected reactions in the sober procedures of the baking, kneading and modelling of clay inspires modern and contemporary practitioners – such as Grayson Perry, Filip Jonker, Thomas van Linge, Alexandra Engelfriet, David Zink Yi – to renegotiate the relationship between what the curators refer to as the 'three ponds of creativity' (2015): the natural world, the digital world and their commercial environments. Outside the art world, moreover, this renegotiation coincides with the appearance of what Parikka calls the 'reverse alchemy' (Feigelfeld 2015) of urban mining: just as urban farming finds a new function in building roofs and vacant industrial lots, there is gold to be made from discarded cellphones, which reveals that technical objects, as affordances of metallic arrangements, are never merely technology but first of all elemental parts of the earth.

MODULATING MANNERS: METASTABILITY, METALLURGY, METAMODELLING

For both Cellini and Palissy and for contemporary alchemists applies: if alchemy is a secret knowledge of nature, this is because it seeks to know its material conditions from within; it is to intuit how to pass from one mode of existence to another (Smith 2004: 149, see also 8, 145). Instead of the concatenation of carefully distinguished operations typical of rational organisation of labour, we are dealing with uninterrupted gestures or manners that are contrapuntally related to the complex and variable behaviour of materials themselves. As in metallurgy, there is no division of labour between conceiving and working, because cognition itself is a surveying and following of a material process. Only when the movement is stopped, when the matter-flow is submitted to rigid stratification, does the artisan cease to be a designer and become a mere worker or labourer (Lapoujade 2000).

Writing for the biotechnical individuals of our own age, the alchemist-philosopher Simondon (2012: 12–13) argues that a moving-matter or material is detached from the matter-form model at the same time that the technological operation is detached from the labour model. Life is not only concerned with technology but co-emerges with it. As a consequence, technique is not reducible to automatised work, the imposing of stable form on passive and indeterminate matter to be worked. It is the living milieu of informal manners by which life's materials are integrated in design practices and pass from one metastable manner or state to the next.

This absorption of matter by manner means that we pass from a reductive to generative notion of modelling, or meta-modelling. Carl De Smet, for example, replaces form with formation by working with a foam that retains a memory of its past (e.g. Memories of the Future 2012). Aranda\Lasch work with crystallographic structure as organising force (e.g. Grotto 2005). And with the Mycelium Chair (2013) Eric Klarenbeek combined growing material derived from protocells with an emerging technology such as 3D printing. After metallurgy, then, contemporary designers use new materials to blur the gap between the non-living and the living. Besides engaging the right materials, however, they also need syntactical or plastic methods, tools, technologies and concepts to accelerate matter or slow it down. These tools of configurability can be of varying levels of abstraction, from an algebraic alphabet (cf. alchemy's *mathesis* in which material articulation and mathematical calculation are mutually implicative) for probabilities and possibilities to CNC systems and simulation software. But what is crucial is that, being both instrumental and constitutive, they are not representational, but constructive; they mediate and effectuate what they are about. As Luciana

Parisi says, there is a continual adaptation or 'contagion' between algorithms, mechanical arts and real-time physical movement (2013: ix).

RENEWED MATERIALISM: PRACTICE-BASED AND OBJECT-ORIENTED

The metaphysical core of metamodern design can be summed up as follows: there is creation and design everywhere, but not everything is created or designed. Is this betting on the alchemy or metabolism of informal creative processes the ideology of today's hackerspaces?

There are many signs that today, after decades of postmodern idealism or culturalism, we are witnessing a renewed materialism. According to Sennett, to be a 'cultural materialist' means to refrain from explaining things by, and thus reducing them to, what they are not (2009: 7–8). Instead of explaining works of art by reducing them to a mirror of socio-cultural norms, economic interests, linguistic conventions or religious convictions, we must turn to the works themselves in their tangible, sensual, non-conceptual and non-anthropocentric reality. Ideally, this is what fieldwork (as opposed to laboratory experimentation) in science or practice-based research (as opposed to 'doing theory') in art means. The new importance attached to tinkering in design is matched by the renewed interest in metallurgy and the science of materials in science and technology studies.

Of course, if cultural materialism is to be a real movement and not just remain an idea, it has to go beyond the politeness and good will of some pre-established subjective attitude. As Manuel De Landa has repeatedly argued, whereas hylomorphism is always mind-dependent, material entities are mind-independent (De Landa 1997: 39). Only what is mind-independent must be produced in the slowness and unpredictability of historical, evolutionary, embryological and physico-chemical processes. Besides practice-based, we must therefore also become object-oriented. What Graham Harman has recently called 'tool-being' (2005: 135) is the epiphany of the craftsman: the disconcerting experience that his tools and materials exert their own reality and possess a vitality far beyond the subject-object correlation. When things come in the mode of being of ready-to-hand (*zuhanden*, as Heidegger says) as opposed to present-to-hand (*vorhanden*), we can use them only by allying ourselves with their autonomous propensity. And while they generally vanish and lose their singularity in the general equipmental effect, they regain an excessive presence at the moment they break. This is why the proponents of OOO see object-orientedness as a relation that is neither theoretical nor practical but aesthetic – with Harman and Steven Shaviro approaching this presence from the side of beauty and Timothy Morton approaching it from the side of the sublime. Either way, aesthetics is the sensibility or feeling of an object for its 'sheer sincerity of existence' (Harman 2005: 135).

FROM MAGIC TO TECHNICS: THE BEAUTIFUL AND THE SUBLIME

Perhaps the necessity of breakdown of the traditional theory-practice schema is also where the contemporary rupture with alchemy and metallurgy takes place, and a breakthrough becomes possible that is not just aesthetical but also technical. Alchemists put their trust in a vital, perhaps we can call it romantic, liaison between humans and their world, which has become completely inaccessible to modern technoscience. Today more than in the past, the hylomorphic division of labour implies a scission of action and a kind of alienation, such as becomes clear from the fear of robots taking over work. As Simondon has argued, the domination of humans over humans even derives from this more fundamental domination of humans over nature rather than vice versa. Instead of returning to a magical unity, then, it is only through contemporary technics that we may come to construct a new modality of the transductive relation of humans to things, and in this way also of new transindividual relations among humans. For labour to become a collective activity again it must take on a position in the technical work-net that binds human and non-human actors alike: 'We should be able to discover a social and economic mode in which the user of the technical object would be not only the owner of the machine but also the one who chooses and maintains it' (2012: 341). In other words, responsibility and care must be based on a technical and no longer magical commonality.

This means, firstly, that today's fascination with handwork should not be confused with the nostalgia for the transparency of the crafted product with respect to its production. After all, Marx had already pointed out that production cannot be rendered visible or absorbed in the product. Representation always comes too late, since the product of production is the plane of representation as such. As Egenhofer (2010: 7–8, 198–99) argues, a contemporary production aesthetics therefore does not imply a preference for handwork or the unicity of a work in the age of serial reproduction. Rather, it starts from the fissure between representation and becoming, having to deal with the having become of the real as well as its means of reproduction and representation. The notion of the vibrancy of matter is perhaps only the sublime cipher of this disparity, whereas metamodern craftsmanship expresses an impatience with the paralysis (e.g. climate skepticism) caused by our inability to oversee the becoming of integrated world capitalism since the economic, ecological and geopolitical crisis of the 2000s.

A second lesson is that artisanal intuition does not develop at free will and that its efficacy depends on the resistance and ambiguity it meets. The craftsman, Sennett (2009) tells us, is always engaged in a bodily combat with reality, deciding in split-seconds, not by measuring and talking but by learning from contingency and constraint. This is why the mannerists valued virtuosity (*virtuosità*) and the speed of execution (*prestezza*) above all else. This love for speed must be understood in conjunction with the equally mannerist will to difficulty (*difficoltà*) – the intense exploration of the liminal zone between raw material and pure form. We need to get rid of the classical conflict between necessity and freedom. Life, for Palissy, is not just much swift, elegant movement, but also the slow fermenting process of a swamp. In a culture of rapid change, likewise, slow movement does not equal a lack of speed. Rather, slowing down is a particular assemblage of speed, an a-synchronisation of the present and thus a reclaiming of time from rational homogenisation. Speed exists in direct connection with the contingency and roughness of material flux, such that there can be no authority of skill without an intrusion of indeterminacy and otherness that slows down the question of failure and success.

Hence there is the oscillation between the two irreducible moments of aesthetics, the sublime and the beautiful, or between the sense of intrusion and the feeling of sympathy. Only when our relation to the world is problematised by the disparity of materials can we profit from their affordances and befriend resistance with only minimal force. Vice versa, we cannot immediately relate to the infinite and must attune with vital processes through finite composition. This was already Ruskin's aesthetic and non-ideological critique of capitalism. Perhaps this demand for proportionality also implies that we finally have to rid ourselves of the concept of design if we want to understand what is revolutionary about craftsmanship. If design is about problem solving and operativity, craftsmanship is about problem finding and inoperativity (e.g. the self-destructing DRM chair, 2013). The craftsman thus articulates something that lies beyond the good intentions and optimism of design and the postmodern fascination with the technical sublime. Whereas Rem Koolhaas' affirmation of the infinite, for example, is still a cynical expansion of scientificism, crafters know that there comes a point when you can't improve by doing better and finitude, perhaps even beauty becomes more important than the sublime. Learning is not only about how to do things, but also about why you are doing this and with whom. There is no general response, only the informal processes in which we become a machine among other machines, or one manner of producing coherence in matter among others. The artisan is cosmic precisely to the extent that he inhabits this interstitial, self-reflective space.

RELATIONAL SUBJECTIVITY: VIRTUOSITY, VIRTUE, VIRTUALITY

In mannerism the artisan is traditionally said to part way with the anonymous swamp of his colleagues and emerge into the solitary figure of the artist under the sole authority of originality. Of course, it was lucrative to have this authority. Outside the guild orbid of assay and raw material, goldsmiths made more money as artists than their peers in crafts. However, as Sennett has shown, originality does not equal autonomy. The newly gained inner life came at the price of social estrangement. Vasari's *Lives* reads like an early modern taxonomy of the pathologies of the artist's psyche. Worse still, individual autonomy comes at the price of a loss of speed and agency, or indeed of a fundamental crisis of belief in the world: 'The master's own mastery changed in content; claims for his distinctiveness and originality now posed a motivational problem for him' (Sennett 2009: 74). This becomes abundantly clear from post-fordist conditions of labour, where managers have seized the image of the creative artist for themselves and demand from the people on the ground to mirror themselves on it. The illusion that everybody can be a designer without appropriate training in fact reveals that, whereas the workshop was a recipe for binding people together in a way that enabled them to deal face to face with issues of authority and mastery, originality is bad for coherence in basically any level of our relations: those to ourselves, those to others and those to our physical environments.

Here, another aspect of craft becomes important: discipline, or the convergence of design and use, production and exercise. There can be no mastery of design without constant rehearsal. Craftsmanship is not just about making things, but it is also about making ourselves in relation to the world. In the words of Anish Kapoor, 'In the end, what one's working with is oneself. Every piece of sculpture, every drawing, every painting is a kind of chemistry. It's like an alchemy' (Dupré, von Kerssenbrock-Krosigk and Wismer 2014: 17). The contemporary artisanal turn points, then, to the compelling question, provoked by metamodern conditions, of how we must shape our lives together with others in a network and media society.

Instead of rejecting the allegation that their craft was one of mere work, the mannerists related sculpture's exercises to a spiritual presence. The repetitive training of skill in mannerism was part of a more general revival of interest in exercises of man on himself through one medium or another. The autobiography of Cellini, that great anti-Vasari, reads as a sort of care of the self based on *esercizi* or *lavori* by which he elevates himself from the profane to the sacred. *Disegno*, for him, was not the end of knowledge, but the means to grace; it made his art significant not just as a form or idea, but as a work, an *opera* (Cole 2002: 111). As such, it stands at the very intersection of sculpture and morality: virtuosity is directly related to virtue. If the intuition transports us into the interior becoming of things themselves, then mastery is inseparable from the responsibility for what is being brought forth. It demands a delicate and tender care for an existential urge which is not ours, but of which we nonetheless form an inextricable part and on the continuation of which we depend.

For this reason, contemporary political philosophers from Sennett to Peter Sloterdijk and from Bernard Stiegler to Paulo Virno and Giorgio Agamben are rediscovering craftsmanship as a model for an engaged life. Under the real subsumption of labour by capital, public life no longer transcends manual labour. Instead, it is in integral skilling that they find the conditions for literacy and civic maturity. For more than the mere acquirement of competence, a skill makes us experience the effect of *how* we connect and cohere. Like virtue, virtuosity is irreducibly public or virtual. Being neither the property of a subject nor the quality of his actions, a virtue's only mode of reality is that of virtuous use. Even when our habits are enacted mainly in the disciplined and controlled manner of private subjectivity, we are only the individuations of the relations of which we are composed and through which we inhabit the world. Thus whereas conscious intentionality is always temporally dephased from the agency of its media, the mastery of skilled labour triggers an agency that makes us interested and could even provide a sense of dignity in our collective modalities and assemblages of subjectivation.

From the earth to the brain, we inhabit a plastic continuum of interdependencies. On each of its levels, networks or planes, consistency isn't just a matter of subjective attitude or objective structures. Rather, it is produced in and through gestures and acts, the performative coherence of which is aesthetic as much as it is technical. As Stengers (Stengers and Despret 2014) says, the cosmos is not created *ex nihilo* but comes about by being articulated as a body of virtual reciprocity. It doesn't exist apart from a politics and a *politesse*, a cosmopolitics. In a similar vein, my proposition is that nature or the earth itself should be regarded as mannered. Just as artfulness does not, by itself, make works vain, our ecological crisis is not simply a consequence of the total artificial mediation of nature through technology. It is true that ubiquitous computing leads to a loss of *savoir-faire* of the worker and the loss of *savoir-vivre* of the consumer. As Bernard Stiegler has pointed out, both are cases of proletarianisation and immiseration (2010: 33). But every technology is a *pharmakon*. We need new technologies of subjectivation, and hence new skills and designs, that are equally artificial. As in the practice of diplomacy, craftmanship here could assume a self-referentiality with a ritual significance; making an object in the right way could be a question of devotion and proper form (Cole 2002: 13–14).

CONCLUSION

The return of craftsmanship offers a key to understanding the present, provided that we associate this return with the sixteenth century and not with the nineteenth century. In the sixteenth century begins the history of the gradual reversal of the opposition between individual genius and collective industry into that between unskilled mass production design and small-scale neo-crafters. In contrast, the nineteenth century is based on desingularisation, such that the craftsman is less a mediator between conception and execution than simply the enemy of the machine that produces non-biodegradable trash. The contemporary convergence of art, craft and design, by contrast, is about resingularisation. Instead of standardisation, design processes happen among or within machinic modes of production in the form of a testing of new materials, customisation of technologies and an active care for their waste, just as contemporary technology turns design into a kind of generalised craftsmanship.

Of course, many of today's so-called workshops, labs and breeding grounds are not productive spaces but places for the incapacitating consumption of originality, or what I would call the *tabula rasa* experience. The use of handmade sketches which characterise the design process of architects such as Renzo Piano or Frank Gehry merely leads to an affected illusion of a proper engagement with matter. Ultimately, this is also the problem of Sennett's approach to craftsmanship, which never arrives at the question of technology. In both cases, craft is no more than a false concretion of the real abstraction of money and technoscience, which is itself based on the ever-increasing split between *Kopfarbeit* and *Handarbeit*. If craftsmanship is anything meaningful today, it must therefore be based on the reversal of the old idea that it is possible to design without making. What matters is media literacy, or rather, eco-literacy or cosmo-literacy.

Artistically speaking, the return of craftsmanship and mannerist virtuosity marks a rematerialisation of the art object. Socio-economically speaking, it undoes the traditional division of labour between the conceptual and executional moments, now that work has become increasingly networked and immaterial. Ecologically speaking, craftsmanship puts us back in touch with shared social and material conditions of production. Do these three tendencies taken together constitute defining traits of 'a new sobriety' in metamodern times? I prefer to speak somewhat less self-confidently but more alchemically of a new minimalism, in the sense that Deleuze and Guattari describe the modus operandi of the cosmic artisan, for whom sobriety is 'the common prerequisite for the deterritorialization of matters, the molecularization of material, and the cosmicization of forces' (1987: 344).

AFFECT

ii. Metamodern Affect

Alison Gibbons

In Jameson's account of the postmodern, the loss of historicity, affect and depth are interrelated. Indeed, we might interpret what Jameson calls 'the waning of affect' as a human response to the disintegration of history, the superficiality of postmodern representation, and the free-floating signs or intensities of a mediatised consumer bubble. Jameson, after all, speaks of 'a fundamental mutation both in the object world itself – now a set of texts or simulacra – and in the disposition of the subject' (1991 [1984], 9).

To explain his conception of the waning of affect, Jameson compares two works of art – Vincent Van Gogh's 'A Pair of Boots' (1887) and Andy Warhol's 'Diamond Dust Shoes' (1980). Van Gogh's painting is a still life that calls up the reality on which it is based, that is, the life of an agricultural labourer such as who would wear the depicted boots. Jameson offers two hermeneutic readings of Van Gogh's work. Firstly, the image is a 'transformation of a drab peasant object world into the most glorious materialization of pure color in oil paint' (1991 [1984], 7). This, in itself, is 'to be seen as a Utopian gesture' (7). Secondly, 'the peasant shoes slowly re-create about themselves the whole missing object world which was once their lived context' (1991 [1984], 8). Thus in the modernist image, Jameson argues, a hermeneutic interpretive operation is possible; as such, it intimates an 'ultimate truth' (8).

The hermeuneutics of Van Gogh's painting contrasts with Warhol's silk-screen canvas; Warhol's shoes are shown in black and grey, like a photographic negative – an image of an image rather than a depiction of a world with depth. The different depths of representation both embody and offer different affective sensibilities. While Van Gogh's work demands empathy for the owner of the boots and the associated poverty-stricken rural life (thus, also instigating in the viewer an impulse towards social transformation),

Warhol's image disbands any form of meaningful response. In turn, meaning-ful emotion becomes a postmodern fallacy since the unified modernist self, experiencing internal emotions in response to the external world, is dissolved. As Jameson puts it, 'The liberation, in contemporary society, from the older anomie of the centred subject may also mean . . . a liberation from every other kind of feeling as well, since there is no longer a self present to do the feel-ing' (1991 [1984], 15). With the very notion of a feeling subject displaced, feelings themselves become 'free-floating' and 'impersonal' (18).

In recent times, there has been what has widely been called an 'affective turn', whereby either the rise of affect is seen to have occurred in parallel with the demise of postmodernism (cf. Woodward 1996; Nicholson 1999; Clough 2007; Pellegrini and Puar 2009) or else Jameson is judged to have done away with affect too readily. Massumi's (2002, 27) provocative dismissal of Jame-son is perhaps the most well known:

> There seems to be a growing feeling within media, literary, and art theory that affect is central to an understanding of our information- and image-based late capitalist culture, in which so-called master narratives are perceived to have foundered. Fredric Jameson notwithstanding, belief has waned for many, but not affect. If anything, our condition is characterized by a surfeit of it.

Massumi is not alone in questioning the waning of affect; Grossberg (1992, 222) and Berlant (2008, 7) uncouple it from the postmodern condition altogether. The relation between postmodernism and affect is, however, somewhat more complicated. Affect, as it is conceived in contemporary Affect Theory and much influenced by Deleuze (2002 [1981]), is ontological rather than situational (as in Jameson's view) and thus already disconnected from subjective experience. Pieter Vermeulen expounds, 'While affects are non-cognitive and non-representational intensities that take place outside of consciousness, emotions emerge when such intensities are narrativised, named and represented as part of individual experience' (2015, 8). The latter reference to individual experience begins to make things clearer: Jameson's renowned expression 'the waning of affect' uses the term 'affect' somewhat distinctively, since in equating it with a thinking, feeling human subject – a 'bourgeois ego or monad' (1991 [1984], 15) – Jameson is in fact speaking of emotion (cf. Buchanan 2006, 92–93; Duncan 2016, 39–42). In the postmod-ern moment, such emotion is unavailable (for instance, due to the subject's bombardment with stimuli in a situation in which lifestyles, consumerism and mediatisation engulf social space).

In interview with Stephanson, Jameson refines his use of the term 'affect'. He asserts that postmodern depthlessness results in a 'transformation of the depth of psychological *affect*, in that a particular kind of phenomenological or emotional reaction to the world disappears' (1988, 4; original italics). This entails a 'changeover' from 'hermeneutic emotion' to '*intensities* of high and lows' (1988, 4; original italics). Moreover, 'highs and lows really don't imply anything about the world, because you can feel them on whatever occasion. They are no longer *cognitive*' (4–5; original italics). Thus, when Jameson outlines the 'waning of affect' in 'The Cultural Logic of Late Capitalism', the 'free-floating', 'impersonal' state of 'euphoria' (1991 [1984], 16) that he equates with the postmodern condition is somewhat comparable to the pre-personal, a-signifying, non-subjective intensity of affect in Affect Theory, but only insofar as these intensities are (in Affect Theory) not yet – cognitively, psychologically – processed into meaningful emotional response. Whereas the postmodern moment is characterised by a waning of affect and the vanishing of hermeneutic options, the affective turn in Theory might be seen to parallel a growing body of work that shows that contemporary art works display something akin to a return of affect. In the contemporary, then, we can perhaps speak once more of a hermeneutics of the self, a will and ability to process intensities so that we can articulate meaningful emotional reactions or cognitive responses to today's social situation in which another affective modality has substituted yesterday's fragmented and fragmenting euphoria.

The chapters in this section of *Metamodernism: Historicity, Affect, and Depth after Postmodernism* all, in their own ways, explicate the return of affect. Lee Konstantinou, Nicoline Timmer and I all consider how affect is manifest in contemporary fiction. Konstantinou starts from the premise that as a defining feature of the postmodern, irony is an ethos that is damaging in its sceptical passivity and dismissiveness. David Foster Wallace's call to arms in 'E Unibus Pluram' is, for Konstantinou, a jumping-off point for an entire contemporary project – what he calls postirony – in literature as well as in film and TV. Outlining four forms of postironic literature, Konstantinou shows that postirony does not dismiss irony altogether. Indeed, it preserves some aspects of it but uses it for different purposes. Nevertheless, implicit in Konstantinou's argument is that postirony can be seen as a new emotional ground tone that succeeds that of postmodernism.

Nicoline Timmer's chapter also sketches a new tone, similarly departing from David Foster Wallace's work. Wallace, Timmer argues, reacts against postmodern strategies of self-representation that deconstruct subjectivity, in part because if postmodern subjectivity is fragmented, it also appears to be excused of moral responsibility. Timmer demonstrates that Wallace's writings show this dissolution of ethical commitments to be problematic. Mapping out a new sense of self, Timmer instead advocates defenselessness. For Timmer, defenselessness entails sincere self-discovery even amid ironic commentary. Such a sincere uncovering of selfhood occurs through relationality – both the self's relation to its own feelings and the self's relation to others. In this way, Timmer's discussion can be aligned with other writings on the contemporary that conceive of contemporary identity as having moved beyond a postmodern, poststructuralist model towards relationality (cf. Moraru 2011; Gibbons 2016).

My own contribution to this volume also engages with relationality as an important dimension in contemporary subjectivity and affect. I integrate a post-positivist understanding of identity into the metamodern paradigm. The post-positivist model of identity sees both essentialism and postmodernism as unhelpful, but rather than abandon them it argues that the two exist in tension. Contemporary identity is therefore both driven by a desire for meaningful personal emotional experience while being aware of the constructed nature of experiences, particularly in relation to social categories of identity. By analysing two works of contemporary autofiction, my chapter argues that it is possible to speak of a distinctly metamodern subjectivity, to which affect is central.

Finally, in their chapter, Gry C. Rustad and Kai Hanno Schwind reflect on the contemporary sitcom. They contend that a metamodern sensibility has emerged and while some of the stylistic features of the postmodern might linger on, they are used to different ends. Unlike in postmodern equivalents, metamodern sitcoms use devices such as irony, pastiche, and parody to articulate emotive affect. Irony clashes with authenticity to render characters as flawed and complex subjects; a hyperreal style such as animation is used not to flatten the characters (and confine them in viewers' eyes to performers) but to render emotional depth. Unlike the cool, flat, unemotive postmodern sitcom, metamodern sitcoms have what Rustad and Schwind call a 'warm' tone, urging viewers to vicariously connect with the social, human situation they depict and empathise with the characters therein.

Throughout the four chapters, common themes emerge, such as the importance of collectivity or with-ness, the persistence of irony even if it is now kept in check by sincere undertones and overtones, and the continued prevalence of self-consciousness and metafictive practice. The chapters are also not exclusively interested in affect. Each also feeds into the arguments about the return of historicity and depth that frame the other sections of this volume.

Chapter 6

Four Faces of Postirony

Lee Konstantinou

> The virus of irony is as widespread in California as herpes, and once
> you're infected with it, it lives in your brain forever.
>
> — Neal Stephenson, *Cryptonomicon*

Over the past thirty years, we have repeatedly been warned that we live in an
age of irony. From the liberal satire of *MAD* comics and the improvisational
comedy troupe Second City to recent television programmes such as *The
Daily Show with Jon Stewart* and *The Colbert Report*, irony has moved from
the margins to the centre of media culture in the United States and Western
Europe. As David Foster Wallace put it, in a 1993 interview with McCaffery,
'Postmodern irony's become our environment' (2012, 49). Such observations, which treat irony as a major feature of postmodern media culture, usually precede declarations that irony either has died or ought to be killed. As
early as 1989, *Spy* magazine lamented what it called the 'Irony Epidemic' in
American culture, fearing 'it's almost enough to make a person turn earnest'
(Rudnick and Andersen 1989, 98). In response to this epidemic, Wallace's
essay, 'E Unibus Pluram: Television and U.S. Fiction', called for the rise of
a 'weird bunch of anti-rebels, born oglers who dare somehow to back away
from ironic watching' (1997, 81). Purdy likewise condemned the 'crude
dismissiveness that is our contemporary irony', as represented by television
programmes such as *Seinfeld* and *Beavis and Butt-head*, calling for a return to
belief, public-mindedness and emotion (1999, 214). After the terrorist attacks
on 11 September 2001, irony again 'died' or 'ended', which was the 'one
good thing' that might 'come from this horror', in the words of Rosenblatt
(2001). But irony didn't remain dead for long. In a 2012 *New York Times*
column, Wampole expressed her fear that contemporary irony promulgates
'a vacuity and vapidity of the individual and collective psyche', and she

searched for examples of 'nonironic living'. For many writers 'who came of age under postmodernity', as Zadie Smith puts it (2007), the dominance of irony has come to seem like a crisis.

Many contemporary novelists – such as Wallace, Smith, Chris Bachelder, Rivka Galchen, Jennifer Egan, Dave Eggers, Jeffrey Eugenides, Jonathan Franzen, Sheila Heti, Jonathan Lethem, Tao Lin, Salvador Plascencia, Richard Powers, Neal Stephenson, Colson Whitehead and Karen Tei Yamashita – regard irony as an essential component of postmodern culture and fear that it has caused various social, political and philosophical maladies. Such writers define irony as an ethos, a stance that interprets the world and language via a corrosive practice of symptomatic, sceptical or paranoid reading. In the face of postmodern culture, transcending irony's limitations becomes an urgent artistic, philosophical and political project. I call this project *postirony* (Konstantinou 2016a). Postironists don't advocate a simple return to sincerity – they're not anti-ironists – but rather wish to preserve postmodernism's critical insights (in various domains) while overcoming its disturbing dimensions.

In analysing this postironic project, this chapter participates in a broader effort to map the cultural dominant that succeeds postmodernism. Alongside metamodernism, many terms have been suggested – globalisation, dialogism, cosmodernism, altermodernism, remodernism, digimodernism, performatism, post-postmodernism – to name this new period. Whatever term we prefer, no theory of the new cultural dominant can proceed without first addressing the difficult problem of irony. I use postirony herein not to name a period concept or new cultural dominant; instead, postirony designates the effort to move beyond the problems that irony has created for contemporary life and culture. Though I myself avoid the prefix 'meta-' (I don't write of metairony because the term is too easily associated with metafiction), postirony names an especially popular response to the 'metamodern structure of feeling' that van den Akker and Vermeulen outline in the introduction to this book and elsewhere (2010). The ambivalence registered by their concept eloquently describes the cultural conundrums that characterise everyday life, and especially work life, under neoliberalism in the Global North, beginning with the market triumphalism that greeted the fall of the Berlin Wall in 1989. Metamodernism names a confused sense of oscillating between different artistic, philosophical and political possibilities, an oscillation that has generated affects we might, following the terms van den Akker and Vermeulen use, call amongness, betweenness and afterness. Van den Akker and Vermeulen's analysis makes perspicuous the hesitancy, uncertainty and confusion with which postironists have undertaken more and less ambitious efforts to move beyond postmodern irony in search of firmer emotional, artistic and political ground.

Postirony therefore goes well beyond the literary world, encompassing various reassessments of artistic postmodernism, poststructuralist theory, sceptical philosophy and the hermeneutics of suspicion. Nevertheless, this chapter focuses on postironic literature (mostly fiction), offering a typology that lays the foundation for more far-ranging analyses. Postirony is not a synonym for New Sincerity, although critics have applied both categories to many of the same texts. A. D. Jameson has described New Sincerity as a set of 'shared [literary] devices and patterns of device' (including '[l]ots of autobiography', '[m]inimal punctuation' and '[s]elf-revision') that is 'so transparent and unmediated and unaffected that many have failed to see the devices at work' (2012). Kelly defines New Sincerity as a method for deal-ing with a situation in which 'the anticipation of others' reception of one's outward behavior begins to take priority for the acting self, so that inner states lose their originating causal status and instead become effects of that anticipatory logic' (2010, 136). Though convincing in their own terms, these investigations either ignore the problem of irony or alleviate its tortures pre-maturely by presuming that sincerity is what stands in opposition to irony. In contrast to New Sincerity, the term postirony doesn't decide in advance what follows the age of irony. The term postirony also reminds us that there are as many solutions to the problem of irony as there are analyses of the problem to begin with and predicts that contemporary postironic art will be heterogeneous.

To organise this heterogeneity, I will distinguish between how artists react to postmodern irony as form and postmodern irony as content. When discuss-ing postmodern irony as content, I refer to characteristically ironic social phe-nomena, institutions, doctrines, theories and attitudes that might become the subject matter of literary art. Postmodern irony as form, meanwhile, desig-nates characteristically ironic styles, genres and modes of presentation. Form and content are, of course, never fully separable. One can imagine a genre, say metafiction, manifesting either as content or as form, as a story *about* metafiction or as an example *of* metafiction. Moreover, from a dialectical perspective, we should also account for how the form of social reality itself (e.g. neoliberal economic policy) is amenable to or resists representation and ironic critique, and how literary art reshapes social reality. Nonetheless, dif-ferent postironic artists evince different attitudes towards each artistic level, and further socio-political research will benefit from a clear initial descrip-tion of postirony's aesthetic field. From the division of postmodern form and postmodern content, four structurally distinct literary responses become visible. These four responses correspond to four distinct contemporary artis-tic modes: motivated postmodernism, credulous metafiction, the postironic Bildungsroman and relational art. Although these types do not exhaust the

Anglo-American literary field, they describe aesthetic-conceptual attractors towards which contemporary writers are drawn.

MOTIVATED POSTMODERNISM

We might first observe that postmodern irony has never disappeared. Its imperium – as both form and content – is arguably stronger than ever. In fact, calls for postirony depend for their force on irony's prevailing power. Much contemporary fiction indeed continues to pursue postmodern styles and subject matter. Describing recent fiction, Green labels the present 'late postmodernism', arguing for continuity with an earlier generation, though he qualifies his argument by saying 'we are no longer postmodern in quite the same way as when the concept was first set loose' (2005, 1). Under the reign of late postmodernism, 'generalized irony, self-reflexivity, intertextuality, formal play, pastiche' have 'become standard features of many movies and television shows' (41).

Some authors don't mind that characteristically postmodernist techniques have migrated from elite to popular culture. One thinks immediately of Mark Leyner – author of *My Cousin, My Gastroenterologist* and *Et Tu, Babe* – whom Wallace condemned for being a purveyor of shallow 'Image-Fiction' (1998, 50). In Wallace's view, Image-Fiction responds to a world in which 'we can eat Tex-Mex with chopsticks while listening to reggae and watching a Soviet-satellite newscast of the Berlin Wall's fall' (1997, 52). Observing a postmodern world on television, these artists make art that redeploys postmodernism not as critique but as a representation of the world as it is. For example, Tom Carson's (2004) novel, *Gilligan's Wake*, marries Joycean stylistic experiments to a reimagining of the television programme *Gilligan's Island*. Carson not only regurgitates US pop culture, but he turns *Gilligan's Island* into a Rosetta Stone for deciphering the ultimate truth of the American Century. It is hard to see a novel such as this as anything other than an intensification of postmodern pastiche. This same sitcom is also a subject of nostalgic satire in Wallace's first novel, *The Broom of the System* (1987), which features a bar called Gilligan's Isle. Here, neither postmodern form nor postmodern content is rejected, but intensified, often in the interest of a higher verisimilitude. This is part of what Nealon means when he describes post-postmodernism as 'an intensification and mutation within postmodernism' (2012, ix).

When postmodernism intensifies or becomes late, however, postmodernism's irrealism, antirealism, pastiche and reflexivity cease to stand as examples of critique. They no longer undermine, subvert or short-circuit older representational codes, becoming instead the ground for new, fully functional representational codes. Putting to one side the question of mimesis, I prefer the term motivated postmodernism to describe the practice of justifying postmodern literary techniques as verisimilitude. Examples of motivated postmodernism include novels by Richard Powers, Jonathan Lethem, Rivka Galchen, Ian McEwan, Mark Haddon, John Wray. Roth (2009) discusses their fiction as examples of the 'neuronovel', which medicalises the 'experimental impulse', turning modernist (and I would add postmodernist) style into 'the language of crazy'.

Postmodern techniques have likewise been repurposed as adjuncts to the digital age. Kenneth Goldsmith's vision of Conceptual poetry – as seen in *The Weather* (2005), *Traffic* (2007) and *Sports* (2008) – is one prominent example of how digital technologies motivate well-established neo-avant-garde and postmodern formal experiments. Goldsmith repackages a tradition of Conceptual art, appropriating Sol LeWitt's 'Sentences on Conceptual Art' (1969), but makes his formulations seem (paradoxically) original by associating it with 'today's digital world', 'the manipulative properties of digital media', properties that are 'inherent to the digital' and so on (2011, 218, 81, 32). Goldsmith proposes that new technologies necessitate not only new poetic practices but also his preferred appropriative practices. To complain that Goldsmith's art has many pre-digital precursors misses the dimension of his project that is genuinely new. What is new is the evacuation from Goldsmith's art of any social, political or cultural agitation. Contemporary Conceptual poets, he writes, discussing Vanessa Place's work, 'leave it to the reader to pass moral judgment', refusing to 'dictate the moral or political meanings of words that aren't theirs' (2011, 101). Conceptual poetry thereby proffers 'realism beyond realism', a 'hyperrealist' form of art, 'a literary photorealism' (101). This is the poetry of a literary world where postmodernism is academic, where the cut-up routines that seemed to have so much subversive potential for writers such as Burroughs and Acker have become merely routine. Goldsmith produces proudly 'unreadable' Conceptual poetry, which he then provides the interpretive master key for in his essays (2011, 144). Goldsmith's inclusion of a lesson plan is the key feature of his book of essays, *Uncreative Writing*. If we live in what McGurl, speaking of such 'autopoetic' artistic practices (2009, 34), calls the programme era, if both literary art and critical analysis often arise from the same social or institutional location, sometimes from the same person, our capacity for critical irony (sceptical, suspicious or paranoid hermeneutics) has, in some important sense, diminished. How, after all, does one conduct a symptomatic reading of one's own artistic productions?

Those who continue using postmodernist techniques also invoke new forms of global interconnection to motivate their practice. As Heise notes, globalisation has been 'gradually replacing earlier key concepts in theories of the contemporary such as 'postmodernism' and 'postcolonialism' (2008, 4). Writers such as Leslie Marmon Silko, Karen Tei Yamashita, J. M. Coetzee and Juliana Spahr have, to different degrees, globalised and redescribed (using ecological terminology) postmodern themes. In pursuit of a form that might represent global interconnection, motivated postmodernist writers make use of what Ngai (2012) and Jagoda (2016) independently call 'network aesthetics', literary techniques designed to represent networked societies, economies and political systems. Spahr's (2005) poetry volume, *This Connection of Everyone with Lungs*, highlights the difficulty of achieving ironic distance in a globalised world. Writing from Hawaii, Spahr investigates '*what I was connected with, and what I was complicit with, as I lived off the fat of the military-industrial complex on a small island*' (2005, 13; original italics). Spahr's interest in connection and complicity – classic postmodern tropes – leads her to deploy a first-person singular and plural subject that treats seriously the co-implication of every person in the War on Terror, and speaks for and with others at various locations around the world. She speaks eloquently of 'boundaries and connections, locals and globals, butterfly wings and hurricanes' (2005, 20). Her attempt 'to speak with the calmness of the world seen from space' fails, leaving her confused, because 'the world is spinning in some way that I can't understand' (36). Ironic exile from the imperial homeland, a concept her collective lyric speaker briefly contemplates, is rejected as impossible. After all, where on earth could you go to escape the Empire? If, as Hardt and Negri argue, Empire 'actually thrives' on 'difference, fluidity, and hybridity' (2001, 138), what good will critical irony do? Even the 'blank irony' Fredric Jameson describes (1991 [1984], 17) no longer seems an apt way of describing the artworks of Goldsmith or Spahr.

Motivated postmodernism recasts the postmodern aesthetic project, evacuating from it any lingering challenge to existing reality or dominant modes of perception. Postmodernism becomes, in this view, merely a way of registering the features of that reality. Thus, these authors either show no interest in criticising that reality or fear that the critical function has itself been absorbed into power. From this vantage point, there is little for the artist to do other than re-describe the contemporary world of intensified postmodernity, to repeat the characteristic gestures postmodernists already pioneered, sometimes even from within an academic sinecure, justifying one's practice as a kind of realism.

CREDULOUS METAFICTION

Other writers use characteristically postmodern forms, especially metafiction, to narrate traditional (or at least non-postmodern) themes, plots and social worlds. More specifically, postmodern form is used to reject postmodern content, either denying the validity of theories of postmodern reality, or more commonly trying to move beyond its failings. Accepting that they live under a global regime of postmodernity, writers of credulous metafiction nonetheless want to find a way to revive or reinvent the values, commitments and practices thought to be characteristic of life before its debilitating onset. Wallace is the most prominent figure to embrace this project (see also Timmer, this volume). He describes himself as 'using postmodern techniques', a 'postmodern aesthetic', 'but using that to discuss or represent very old traditional human verities that have to do with spirituality and emotion and community and ideas that the avant-garde would find very old-fashioned' (quoted in Roiland 2012, 36–37). Holland has used the term 'postmodern realism' to describe this project, discussing 'fiction written within the postmodern period that subscribes to conventions and ethics of realism' (2012, 230). Such writers rarely think they can turn back the clock (postmodernism cannot be ignored or wished away), but they long to restore what postmodernism destroyed or deconstructed, without resorting to reaction. As McLaughlin argues, such literature explores 'how to live in the world with incomplete systems of knowledge, how various systems of knowledge can be linked together or embedded within one another to create a contingent but useful structure' (2012, 221).

In addition to Wallace, writers who have followed this path include Dave Eggers, Salvador Plascencia, Helen DeWitt, Jonathan Safran Foer and Zadie Smith in *The Autograph Man* and *NW*. I have described this postironic tendency as credulous metafiction (Konstantinou 2016a, 176–84). As Elias rehearses it, standard-issue postmodern metafiction 'relinquish[ed] representations of the real . . . and turn[ed] to the philosophical and ethical questions of what representation essentially *is*' (2012, 16; original emphasis). By contrast, while credulous metafiction embraces the irrealist or anti-realist tendencies of postmodernism, it rejects postmodern metafiction's historic project of debunking convention, belief and investment in fictional worlds. In short, credulous metafiction uses metafiction not to cultivate incredulity or irony but rather to foster faith, conviction, immersion and emotional connection. Dissociated from irony, metafiction becomes a means of returning to 'old-fashioned' content (Wallace quoted in Roiland 2012, 37).

Short stories like Wallace's 'Octet' (1999) and 'Good Old Neon' (2004) try to convince us that what we initially thought were gimmicky experiments are in fact elaborate attempts by the actual author, rather than the implied author, to communicate directly with us – with '100% candor' (Wallace 1999, 148). Similar examples abound in the contemporary literary field. Dave Eggers uses a range of self-conscious techniques to narrate his memoir, *A Heartbreaking Work of Staggering Genius*, with a greater degree of honesty, going so far as to use an addendum in the 2001 paperback edition of the book called 'Mistakes We Knew We Were Making' to make clear 'what was clear to, by my estimations, about 99.9% of original hardcover readers of this book: that there is almost no irony, whatsoever, within its covers' (2001, 33). Though it might be tempting to view this disavowal of irony as itself a form of irony, I would argue that Eggers very much means what he writes, that he obsesses over the hypothetical 0.1 per cent of readers (coded as snarky critics) who might misunderstand or misinterpret him.

Similarly, Charlie Kaufman's screenplays are exquisite metafictional machines meant to inspire rapture and love. Kaufman's *Adaptation* (2002), for example, dramatises the quasi-autobiographical character Charlie's struggle to complete the screenplay to *Adaptation*, based on Susan Orlean's *The Orchid Thief* (1998). Kaufman invents a fictional identical twin brother for Charlie, named Donald, who ends up writing the second half of the screenplay, and who receives an official screen credit beside Kaufman. Indeed, the style of the actual film dramatically changes tone when Donald takes over writing the screenplay within the film. Kaufman constructs this metafiction not to expose the conventionality of cinematic art but, as Landy has persuasively argued, to 'rescue nonnarrative phenomena from the tsunami of diachronic thinking' (2011, 498) – in particular, to help us appreciate the beauty of flowers in a state of stillness. Helen DeWitt and Ilya Gridneff's odd self-published novel *Your Name Here* (2006) uses archly metafictional forms – the authors explicitly invoke Italo Calvino's *If on a Winter's Night a Traveller* (1979) and reflect openly on their desire that *Your Name Here* become a best seller – in a strange, but ultimately earnest effort to do for the languages of the Middle East – 'Arabic, Hebrew, Farsi, Pashtu and other so-called "exotic" languages' (2006, 23) – what Tolkien did for invented languages like Elvish.

Writers working in this mode presume that postmodernity has inured readers to experience, affect, belief or conviction. Though not identical, credulous metafiction resembles what Eshelman has called performatism, a post-postmodern cultural mode that challenges 'the split concept of the sign and the strategies of boundary transgression of postmodernism' (2008, 1; see also Eshelman, this volume). Performatist artworks often deploy a 'double framing' technique that puts an 'ostensive scene' in conflict with endless contextualisation of that scene (2008, 91). The artist's goal is to get readers to believe in the truth of the ostensive scene – such stories do not merely communicate meaning but try to change the reader's actual beliefs. Credulous metafictionists treat postmodern forms as tools for reconstructing readers' lost capabilities. Artistic form is not, as for motivated postmodernists, representational. In credulous metafiction, form is tactical or instrumental. It's designed to do something to us.

Plascencia's (2005) *The People of Paper* exemplifies this mode. Making use of innovative book design, featuring separate columns of text for each character, die-cutting words from the pages of the hardback edition, the novel tells the story of Federico de le Fe, who organises a war against 'Saturn, against the invasion that infiltrated their thoughts and overheard even their softest whispers' (2005, 46). At times, Federico's effort is described as 'the war on omniscient narration (a.k.a. the war against the commodification of sadness)' (2005, 218). The novel is initially dedicated 'to Liz, who taught me that we are all paper' (7). Halfway through the book, Liz intervenes in the novel, explaining in a first-person chapter how she 'replaced' the character Sal 'with a white boy' (138). She complains about how she is rendered in the novel, and implores, 'You need to remember that I exist beyond the pages of this book', and writes, 'Sal, if you love me, please leave me out of this story. Start this book over, without me' (138). And Sal does, beginning the novel anew, but with a different dedication page, and repeating the title page. Plascencia's fascinating novel is too complex to analyse fully in these pages, but what should be clear is that Plascencia uses metafiction precisely because sadness has been commodified, and because his practices as a writer (identified with the figure of Saturn) are the vehicle through which sadness is commodified.

Participating in a literary field that asks writers – especially writers of colour – to repackage and serve up authentic ethnic experience, Plascencia worries that he is himself a commodifier of sadness. The same worry preoccupies Henry Park in Chang-rae Lee's *Native Speaker* (1995), another novel that, as Rhee suggests, borders on metafiction when it links 'the multi-ethnic intelligence-gathering operation led by Dennis Hoagland to the market and cultural conditions of Asian American writing' (2011, 157). How, Plascencia asks, can one communicate sadness, both individual and collective, under such conditions? Whether or not Plascencia is being literally autobiographical, his book introduces autobiographical elements into metafiction in order to bypass barriers, identified with 'commodification', that ostensibly neutralise the reader's ability to experience sadness. As Saldívar argues, Plascencia's novel seeks 'to claim sincerely the utopian vision of achieved freedom and justice all the while not believing in their attainability' (2011, 582). In staging a rebellion of characters against the author (Saturn) within the novel, an attempted murder of the author, Plascencia hopes to remind us of what exists 'beyond the pages of this book' and thereby to liberate sadness from the circuits of literary commodification.

POSTIRONIC BILDUNGSROMAN

Perhaps the most popular postironic mode is the postironic Bildungsroman. These novels reject postmodern form and postmodern content at one stroke. They ostentatiously revive historical forms of realism (and other outmoded genres) to show that these conventions retain their emotional, intellectual and representational power. Such novels are a type of Bildungsroman because they often dramatise the development of central characters from a naïve origin through a phase of irony en route to a final postironic condition. Like the historical Bildungsroman, these texts evince a *'predisposition to compromise,'* in Moretti's terms (2000 [1987], 10; original italics). Unlike novelists who merely write in a realist mode, purveyors of the postironic Bildungsroman put realism into conflict with postmodernism. These writers don't so much reject irony *tout court* as imagine it to be a necessary, but temporary, stepping stone toward a full appreciation of the power of tradition. This is the compromise that allows the postironic Bildungsroman to evade charges of naiveté.

The great emblem of this mode is Jonathan Franzen. In his widely cited essay, 'Mr. Difficult', Franzen casts off his former devotion to postmodernism, rejecting this literature (which he calls 'Status' fiction) in favour of art more concerned with the needs of the reader (what he calls 'Contract' fiction). After ceasing his pursuit of Status, Franzen embraces the need to write according to the Contract of conventional forms, offering the reader 'pleasure and connection' (2003, 240). Whether they're neo-Victorians or middlebrow realists, writers such as Franzen make traditional fictional forms into anti-postmodern statements. To be recognised as anti-postmodern statements, such novels dramatise the rejection of postmodernism and postmodern irony within their fictive worlds. In the case of *The Corrections* (2001), Franzen ritually humiliates one of his characters, Chip Lambert, who is confronted by a skeptical undergraduate student with whom he ultimately has a disastrous affair. Despite the fact that he has 'a hundred percent voting record with the Queer Bloc', Chip comes to find his favourite 'theories sounded somewhat lame when he wasn't lecturing to impressionable adolescents' (2001, 83–84). Once cured of his poststructuralist delusions – and after engaging in a zany postmodern plot involving a Lithuanian financial scam that notably happens outside the novel's diegesis – Franzen rewards Chip with an age-appropriate relationship with a 'successful young doctor' (2001, 565).

Among postironic Bildungsromans, I would include Jeffrey Eugenides's *The Marriage Plot* (2011), Zadie Smith's *On Beauty* (2005), Rachel Kushner's *The Flamethrowers* (2013), Jonathan Lethem's *Fortress of Solitude* (2003) and *Dissident Gardens* (2013), Jennifer Egan's *A Visit from the Goon Squad* (2010), Neal Stephenson's *The Diamond Age* (1995) and perhaps most surprisingly Barack Obama's 1995 memoir, *Dreams of My Father* (see Konstantinou 2016b). Many of these books evince the realist response to postmodern irony, although not all of them are strictly realist. Elsewhere I have discussed what I call the 'storytelling neorealist' strain of this mode (Konstantinou forthcoming). All of these books, in one form or another, represent moves from naiveté through irony to cynicism to postirony. Sometimes, the author herself undergoes this journey. At other times, one or more characters do so. At still other times, the reader is asked to become a postironist. Smith's

On Beauty, for example, dramatises the conflict between two Rembrandt scholars, the poststructuralist Howard Beasley and the neoconservative Monty Kipps. Howard's son grows disillusioned with his father, is tempted by Monty's neoconservatism, but ultimately rejects both orientations; both are, in different ways, too ironic. *On Beauty* distributes its story of development across a range of characters. Though none is a proper protagonist, it's still reasonable to describe the novel as a Bildungsroman to the degree that the reader is positioned to consider and then reject postmodern irony.

Eugenides's *The Marriage Plot* perfectly exemplifies this trajectory, consciously invoking the Victorian Bildungsroman, though the book divides its narrative of development between two characters. When we meet the novel-loving Brown senior Madeleine Hanna, we are invited to 'look at all the books', her collection of mostly Victorian, late Victorian and middle-brow novels (2011, 3). Set in 1982, we follow Madeleine as she takes a class in semiotics and is awakened to the conventionality of realist fiction. Discovering Roland Barthes's 1977 *A Lover's Discourse*, she considers the proposition that 'if you became aware of how love was culturally constructed and begin to see your symptoms as purely mental . . . then you could liberate yourself from its tyranny' (2011, 79). We might be tempted to read the book's realist style – and its central love-triangle – ironically, to treat the book as metafiction. Madeleine, however, rejects the view that deconstructing love liberates one from its grip, concluding that 'the problem was, it didn't work. She could read Barthes' deconstructions of love all day without feeling her love for Leonard diminish the teeniest little bit' (2011, 79). By the end of the novel, as Madeleine and other characters come to understand the inadequacy of theory as a guide to life, we find ourselves being asked to affirm Eugenides's straightforward style, to become neo-Victorianists alongside Madeleine. The novel ends on a note of disillusioned realism, with the character Mitchell (who undergoes his own Bildung and who has been identified with Eugenides himself) realising that Madeleine was indeed 'his [romantic] ideal, but an early conception of it, and he would get over it in time' (406). The novel's titular marriage plot ultimately fails, but in the name of a higher sense of realism and historicism. The book thus simultaneously dramatises the journey of its characters, its author and its implied readers; all emerge from the gauntlet of postmodernism on firmer foundations, having rolled back both postmodern form and postmodern content, weary but non-cynical realists.

RELATIONAL ART

The final postironic mode I will discuss uses realist, minimalist or middle-brow forms to depict postmodern reality. This literature, which participates

in a broader artistic interest in relationality, and which speaks most directly
about the metamodern structure of feeling, turns away from ironic forms typically associated with aesthetic postmodernism in the hope of more directly
apprehending an underlying reality that postmodern theories of mediation
took to be inaccessible. The resulting artworks often employ a powerful aesthetic of awkwardness and can be incredibly uncomfortable to read or view.
Kotsko suggests that awkwardness might serve as the dominant aesthetic category of the era that succeeds the age of irony (2010, 24). In Kotsko's view,
irony, as a defence against the awkward reality of capitalism, eventually
'exhausted itself', leaving the rawness of awkward relationality exposed (24).
Though a range of other artists work in this mode (see Bourriaud 2002 [1998]
for a discussion or relational art), I identify the dominant literary strand of
relational or affective art with the novelist and poet Tao Lin, as well as with
writers published by his small press Muumuu House (such as Sam Pink and
Marie Calloway), with the short stories and films of Miranda July, with books
such as Sheila Heti's *How Should a Person Be?*, and with the cinematic genre
of mumblecore (directors such as Andrew Bujalski, Joe Swanberg, Jay and
Mark Duplass), as well as popular television programmes (some of which
Kotsko discusses) such as Ricky Gervais's *The Office* and *Extras*, Larry
David's *Curb Your Enthusiasm*, Mitch Hurwitz's *Arrested Development*,
Louie CK's *Louie*, Lena Dunham's *Girls* and Maria Bamford's *Lady Dyna-
mite*. Relational art gives us postmodern reality by means of non-postmodern
form. Critics have had a polarised reaction to this art. Some celebrate its
genuineness or representativeness or true-to-lifeness; others condemn it as
precious, mannered or lacking in evidence of craft. Relational art is the sort
of writing A. D. Jameson (2012) has in mind in his description of New Sincerity. With its flatness of tone, rambling plots, autobiographical content and
notable lack of interiority, this art draws attention to the gap between reader
and writer, showing the difficultly of deciding whether an utterance is ironic
or sincere in the absence of tonal or affective cues, staging the author's failure
to communicate.

    In the popular genre of mockumentary (see Rustad and Schwind, this vol-
ume), such as *The Office* or *Parks & Recreation*, directors and screenwriters
use reaction shots – especially moments when straight-man characters look
directly at the diegetic camera – to perform the function the laugh track once
served. These reaction shots simultaneously enhance the mockumentary's
reality effect and create an almost unbearable feeling of awkwardness for
some viewers. Rather than create a sense of communion between viewer and
character, I would argue, the character's gaze at the diegetic camera reminds
the viewer of the broken intersubjective space between people. The character's gaze is designed to fail to substitute for the normative force of the laugh
track. Whereas the laugh track is literally meant to signal that it's time to join

the community's laughter, these mockumentaries to different degrees leave the burden of navigating the depicted scenarios to the viewer. Like other relational art, the mockumentary draws attention to the difficulty of navigating ambiguous social norms.

Lin is the most accomplished literary example of this mode. One critic has described the author's 'biplanar ability to convince a generation of sincerity-starved young men and women to embrace his realist, single-entendre fiction while convincingly presenting himself as the inveterately hip jester of the online-spawned lit scene' (Tyrone X 2012). Lin's *Shoplifting from American Apparel* is characteristic of his style. The novella features frequent Gmail chat transcripts and text messages, proffers flat or low-affect dialogue and follows a central character, named Sam, who in all biographical particulars resembles Lin and whose titular act of shoplifting is committed without commentary or warning or, for that matter, motivation. This is the novella's opening paragraph (Lin 2009, 5):

> Sam woke around 3:30 p.m. and saw no emails from Sheila. He made a smoothie. He lay on his bed and stared at his computer screen. He showered and put on clothes and opened the Microsoft Word file of his poetry. He looked at his email. About an hour later it was dark outside. Sam ate cereal with soymilk. He put things on eBay then tried to guess the password to Sheila's email account, not thinking he would be successful, and not being successful. He did fifty jumping jacks. 'God, I felt fucked lying on the bed', he said to Luis a few hours later on Gmail chat. 'I wanted to fall asleep immediately but that is impossible. I need to fall asleep. Any second now. Just fall down asleep'.

This passage deploys realist conventions – designating characters, settings, times and situations – towards unconventional ends. Each sentence lacks adjectival or adverbial modification, and the actions described include few contextual affective cues. Sam's self-reported 'fucked' feeling is not motivated, and Lin's sentences do not, when taken together, cohere into a unified action. The sentence 'He put things on eBay' may appear in proximity to 'He did fifty jumping jacks' but no clear narrative relationship exists between putting things on eBay and doing jumping jacks (or, for that matter, eating cereal with soymilk, looking at email, etc.). Lin's novella is composed almost entirely of such disarticulated, perfunctory sentences. He rigorously fails to distinguish or distinguishes only weakly between description and narration, possibly creating a stylistic analog for Sam's desultory progression through life. But even to say that Lin rigorously creates a specific style to achieve certain aesthetic effects begs the question Lin's writing raises. After all, to what degree does Lin rely on any conventional notion of craft to achieve his (for some readers powerful, for others irritating) aesthetic effects? I would argue that relational art turns the reader or viewer's uncertainty about how to answer this question, the oscillation between mutually exclusive but seemingly valid interpretations, into its primary aesthetic effect.

Awkwardness is, of course, not the only affect one finds in popular examples of relational art, but it is quite common, perhaps because it is an especially palpable affect for those interested in artistically exploring failures of intersubjectivity. One might also look to the ascendance of autofiction (see Gibbons, this volume), particularly the example of Chris Kraus. The postironic mission of relational art has an affinity with object-oriented ontology, speculative realism and other new materialisms that, inspired by Deleuze and Latour, similarly recode poststructuralist notions formulated in terms of discourse analysis into an ontological register. The emphasis of such new materialism, in texts such as Bennett's *Vibrant Matter*, is on the strange, agent-like, networked relations between objects. Good candidates for literary analogues of the new materialism might include books such as Nicholson Baker's *The Mezzanine* (1988), with its intensive focus on the history of consumer objects; Ben Marcus's *The Age of Wire and String* (1995), which invents strange new kinds of object and renders familiar objects newly strange; or novels that use essayistic form and uncaptioned photography to dramatise the observations of wandering protagonists, such as W. G. Sebald's *The Rings of Saturn* (1995), Teju Cole's *Open City* (2012) and Ben Lerner's *Leaving the Atocha Station* (2011). Obsessed with relationality, the reader-writer relationship, and intersubjective problems, this strain of postironic literature is, along a variety of lines, overwhelmingly affective in its dominant ambitions.

CONCLUSION

The typology outlined in this chapter represents four significant tendencies in contemporary fiction. Each of my four categories – motivated postmodernism, credulous metafiction, the postironic Bildungsroman and relational art – describes a range of texts, and many texts exhibit multiple tendencies and ambitions. Though I described it as an example of relational art, a 'novel from life' such as Sheila Heti's *How Should a Person Be?* can also be read as a postironic Bildungsroman or as credulous metafiction. Likewise, a novel such as Jennifer Egan's *A Visit from the Goon Squad* distributes its story of development beyond irony across numerous characters at the same time that it motivates its mildly postmodern form with references to digital technology. Nor do the strategies represented by these four modes exhaust the formal or intellectual possibilities of the postironic project. The four described here have proven to be popular, but they may develop along unpredictable lines. Whether one or another version of postirony will grow beyond these bounds, whether postirony itself will become hegemonic, is still an open question, although the aesthetic project seems increasingly dominant with every passing year.

Finally, we must address the important question of why these versions of postirony have become prominent – and how their ascent relates to the broader literary field and neoliberal society. For recent studies that suggest answers to these questions, see Smith (2015) and Huehls (2016). Jameson (1991 [1984]) has suggested that developments in the arts need to be analysed in relation to concomitant developments in the history of capitalism. Nealon (2012) has attempted to correlate post-postmodernism in the arts with globalisation and neoliberalism, but he does not develop a detailed account of how the structures characteristically associated with neoliberalism – privatisation, deregulation, financialisation and capital mobility – correspond to the cultural logic of the present. Why might postirony (as opposed to irony or non-irony) become an appealing aesthetic project for the neoliberal entrepreneur charged with managing her own stock of human capital? Why isn't irony compatible with the stance of the well-heeled neoliberal? This chapter ends by suggesting that the dominant neoliberal cultural unit is not the individual entrepreneur, as is commonly assumed, but the temporary group or project-based team. The feeling of oscillation that van den Akker and Vermeulen discuss in the introduction of this volume can ultimately be traced back to the emergence of new norms governing the individual's relationship to the globalised labour market. Boltanski and Chiapello's (2007) magisterial analysis of neoliberal management rhetoric, *The New Spirit of Capitalism*, supports this conclusion.

Under the regime of what Boltanski and Chiapello call the 'projective city,' the 'modern firm' is imagined to be 'a slim core surrounded by a conglomeration of suppliers, subcontractors, service providers, temporary personnel making it possible to vary the workforce according to the level of business, and allied firms' (2007, 74). Within this networked vision of flexible capitalism, individual workers 'must be organised in small, multitasked teams' who work together project by project (74). Such 'projects are a fetter on absolute circulation, for they demand a certain engagement, albeit temporary and partial, and presuppose monitoring by the other participants of the qualities that everyone brings into play' (107). The team's emphasis on 'a certain engagement, albeit temporary and partial,' hints at a plausible explanation for the rhetorical and cultural power of postirony for community-oriented, philanthropic enterprises such as Dave Eggers's McSweeney's. In short, postirony might well be viewed as a useful affect or attitude for project-oriented or neoliberal enterprises.

In the prior era of embedded liberalism – the alliance between labour, capital and the state that characterised midcentury capitalism – one's performance in a capitalist firm (and one's public avowal of commitment to the firm) mattered more than one's authentic beliefs or reputation for 'engagement'. Under such circumstances, irony could be viewed as a valid or effective means of surviving corporate life, the 'protective coloration' the organisation man adopted in order to 'disarm society', to remain hip in a square world, as William H. Whyte put it in *The Organization Man* (2002, 11). By contrast, under project-oriented speculation-obsessed neoliberalism, the worker finds her situation to be more vexed. In a global sense, the dissolving acid of the market has not ceased to melt down all values and beliefs; the individual worker or artist has little foundation to stand on. Nevertheless, she must increasingly commit locally and temporarily to the specific speculative endeavour, to the task at hand, which requires a self-subordinating stance we might fairly describe as contingent belief. Whether you're a worker in the start-up or the member of a band or an individual novelist (in a networked alliance with an agent, publicity director, imprint editor), you must cultivate sincere commitment, intrinsic motivation and earnest engagement – for at least as long as the alliance remains intact. It seems reasonable to infer that the new normative horizons of work, which not only affects artists but often holds up the artist as an idealised kind of worker (Brouillette 2014), can have multifarious effects on the form and content of contemporary literature. After your precarious alliance dissolves, whether in success or failure, you must exhibit the flexibility, openness to contingency and self-ironising capacities to move on to the next endeavour. Such is the condition of postirony.

Chapter 7

Radical Defenselessness: A New Sense of Self in the Work of David Foster Wallace

Nicoline Timmer

One day as I was walking home, immersed in my own thoughts, suddenly a man in a long overcoat approached me from across the bridge, and in passing he asked me a question. Since I had never seen this person before, and although I was the only other person around, I was not sure the question was addressed to me: 'Are you alright?' His words somehow had an enormous effect. Was I alright? I was so much struck by this direct approach that I failed to answer, and felt, immediately, that I had missed an opportunity of grand proportions. I start with this personal encounter, the true significance of which is hard to convey in a verbal account, because I believe it will help me introduce certain aspects of David Foster Wallace's writing that are difficult to approach purely from a theoretical or critical distance.

At the heart of David Foster Wallace's work, there is something which seems to elude conceptualisation altogether; it is circumscribed in 'Octet', one of his most interesting stories, as 'a sense of something', 'something urgent and human', a 'nameless ambient urgent interhuman sameness' which is 'maddeningly hard to pin down' as the narrator willingly admits (Wallace 2001 [1999], 123, 130, 133, 123). When trying to bring to light these hard-to-pin-down urgencies in a critical analysis of his work, it is difficult not to feel that failure is unavoidable. But this sense of failure parallels that of many of the characters and narrators in Wallace's writing – so that at least you will have the odd sensation of being close to something very relevant while failing, and perhaps even because of it. This chapter builds upon a book-length study in which I analysed Wallace's works, alongside work by Dave Eggers and Mark Z. Danielewski, as exemplary of a new direction in fiction writing that I labelled post-postmodern (Timmer 2010; see also McLaughlin 2004, 2012), and which resonates with what Vermeulen and van den Akker have called metamodern (2010). Since writing that book my concerns have shifted, from articulating what is new and different in contemporary theory, fiction and culture to getting closer to what has been there all along, just not in plain sight ('something urgent' indeed): a dimension of being human that – especially for those who were brought up on a steady diet of post-structural theory – for a long time seemed secluded, off-limits, almost unimaginable and certainly intangible.

ETHICAL EXPERIENCE

This dimension of being human is perhaps exactly that which Ludwig Wittgenstein ordered we should be silent about ('must pass over in silence') (Wittgenstein 2001 [1922], 89). Not that he felt it was in any way unimportant, quite to the contrary, but it involves an array of experiences that when put into words easily amount to non-sense. In his moving 'Lecture on Ethics', from 1929, Wittgenstein singles out three experiences ('this is an entirely personal matter', he inserts) to illuminate what he means (1929, 6; all quotations for this source are from Ts-207, the normalized transcription.). The 'experience par excellence' for him is when '*I wonder at the existence of the world*'; secondly, there is 'the experience of feeling *absolutely* safe' (6; all emphasis original); and thirdly – a bit less prominently put forward – the experience of 'feeling guilty' (8). These are what Wittgenstein refers to as ethical experiences.

For Wittgenstein, even stating these experiences feels as a misuse of language. Why? Because language should only be used to state facts, which can be judged true (or not) relative to a certain situation or goal. In contrast, the ethical experiences he tries to convey have an intrinsic or absolute value, not a relative value. This is why Wittgenstein calls them 'supernatural' (1929, 5) or 'mystical' on other occasions (2001 [1922], 88); they escape the world of facts, and thus escape language.

But why, we can wonder, would such an ethical experience not also be a fact? After all, as Wittgenstein himself acknowledges, experiences 'have taken place then and there, lasted a certain definite time and consequently are describable' (1929, 8–9). Yet the experience of feeling absolutely safe is of a very different kind to the experience 'I am safe in my room, when I cannot be run over by an omnibus' (7; Wittgenstein's example). Ethical experiences are true 'whatever happens' (6), Wittgenstein insists. However, if this is the case, why could this not also be a fact, then, that some experiences just happen to have an absolute value? To this not so unreasonable counterargument (which he incorporates into his lecture), Wittgenstein reacts not with a logical-philosophical demonstration of his way of reasoning, but with a certainty which comes to him 'in a flash of light', namely: 'not only that no description that I can think of would do to describe what I mean by absolute value, but that I would reject every significant description that anybody could possibly suggest, *ab initio*, on the ground of its significance' (10; original emphasis). The expressions he had to use for conveying these absolute experiences are necessarily nonsensical: 'For all I wanted to do with them was just to go beyond the world and that is to say beyond significant language' (10).

It is this gesture of reaching beyond language that I want to explore in the work of David Foster Wallace, to locate instances in Wallace's writing when the outline of a new ethics is (almost) within reach. It is in this gesture – of reaching beyond language, with language – that something approximating 'something urgent' comes to the fore or that 'something urgent' is approximated. That something might be proximity itself, a proximity to the other, present all along in the solipsistic experience worlds that Wallace depicts with such vigour and stylistic lenience.

SOLIPSISM

Wallace had truly absorbed the work of Wittgenstein. In an interview with Larry McCaffery in 1993, he discussed why he considered Wittgenstein to be 'a real artist', namely because 'he [Wittgenstein] realized that no conclusion could be more horrible than solipsism' (McCaffery 2012, 44). The problem of solipsism is key to Wallace's whole oeuvre. Already in one of his earliest stories, the ambitious novella 'Westward the Course of Empire Takes Its Way' [henceforth 'Westward'], 'solipsistic solipsism' is the horrid vacuous core around which this multi-layered narrative swirls (1989, 337). It is diagnosed (by the narrator) as a very '*contemporary* flaw' to which most of his characters have fallen prey (304; my emphasis). This is especially true of the character Mark, an aspiring young writer, who thinks 'he is the only person in the world who feels like he is the only person in the world. It's a solipsistic delusion' (305). What is interesting is that this flaw is diagnosed to be a delusion, suggesting that there is a way out, perhaps a reality check possible that would reveal solipsism to be untrue or illogical somehow.

Bearing Wittgenstein's remarks in mind, the question, then, is whether this antipode of solipsism is a truth (or sense) that can be put into words. 'Westward' offers flight lines in fiction, and at least reaches for this other truth, but in a contorted way. Its contortion has to do with the complex narrative trajectory of the story, which continually threatens to take itself as its sole object. That would turn it into metafiction, a form of writing that is much distrusted – by both the narrator and by Mark, who is put forward as the heir-apparent of postmodern literature, and destined to 'sing to the *next* generation' (1989, 348; original italics).

'Westward' is one of three almost manifesto-like stories Wallace wrote in which the problem of solipsism is very explicitly linked to postmodern meta-fictional writing and the style of hyper self-conscious thinking associated with it. Apart from 'Westward', 'Octet' (2001 [1999]) is a clear example; 'Good Old Neon' (2004) too can be read as an attempt to tackle the great horror of solipsism by testing out new narrative strategies that might surpass or overcome the dead end to which postmodern writing and thinking has led. It is therefore useful to spell out how exactly postmodern writing and thinking is – in Wallace's work – associated with solipsism, even if it results in a bit of a digression, albeit a digression that marks much of Wallace's writing. Meta-fiction – and reflecting on its workings – leads to 'the sort of inbent spiral that keeps you from ever getting anywhere', as one 'David Wallace' at the end of 'Good Old Neon' acknowledges, half in despair (2004, 181).

We should keep in mind that it is a conventionalised form of postmodern-ism that stands accused, and metafiction as a standard operating procedure. It is what has become of postmodernism that causes alarm; the arrow is not nec-essarily pointed at the treasured classics of postmodernist fiction themselves (although, they too may already harbour something very wrong). 'Westward', for example, is an ignited critique of, but also a covert homage to, 'Ameri-can metafiction's . . . most famous story' (1989, 237), which is 'Lost in the Funhouse' – written (of course) by John Barth. In the 'Westward' storyworld, however, the author is named as Professor C. Ambrose, a teacher of Mark. This teacher, master of metafiction, has, a few years after the publication of his much-acclaimed story, fallen into disgrace by selling out to an advertis-ing guru who is going to commercially exploit the concept of Funhouses. Mark finds it 'ironic' that what initially had been a sincere attempt at 'critical integrity' (being upfront, within the text, about the artificiality of textual con-struction) ends up being easily appropriated 'by the very pretend-industry' that the first generation of postmodern authors wanted to critically address (1989, 269).

What is suggested is that there may be something inherent in metafiction that lends itself very well to such exploitation. Metafiction itself is regarded as being exploitive: the overt self-reflectivity of metafiction is exposed to be a manipulative tactic. In the story 'Octet' this is, a bit more aggressively than in 'Westward', summed up as the ' "Hey-look-at-me-looking-at-you-looking-at-me" agenda of tired old S.O.P. metafiction' (2001 [1999], 130). The textual gesture of 'Hey Look' – look, this is a story that has been constructed (and I involve 'you', my addressee, in the process of its construction) – is a ges-ture that seems sincere enough and is directly addressed to the reader. Yet, in 'Octet', it is experienced by the narrator as pointing only to the self-conscious writer, to 'the dramatist himself coming onstage from the wings' (2001 [1999], 125). This makes it into a 'highly rhetorical sham-honesty' (125), a strategy that screams 'Please like me' (131).

In 'Good Old Neon', too, this fraudulence is dissected in detail, personified by a young man reflecting endlessly on his strategies to 'impress people and manipulate their view of me' (2004, 154). He is very aware of his manipulative ways, but self-awareness of too much self-awareness only aggravates the problem, leading to a 'vicious infinite regress' (147). Likewise with metafiction. Reflecting on metafiction's operational practices, critically reflecting *on* metafiction *in* fiction, will only come off as just another layer of metafiction. It thus appears almost impossible to somehow directly point at the real problem. But what is the real problem?

In 'Westward' metafiction is judged by Mark to be 'the act of a lonely solipsist's self-love' (1989, 332). Why metafiction still 'exerts a kind of gravitylike force on Mark' (293), making it so difficult for him to break free from it, has to do with the parallel that is constantly being drawn between the self-reflectivity characteristic of metafiction, and the strategies the human figures populating Wallace's fiction employ to construct a 'self'. Both metafiction and these tactics of self-presentation are performative in nature, or, as the young man in 'Good Old Neon' realises: 'My own basic problem was that at an early age I'd somehow chosen to cast my lot with my life's drama supposed audience instead of with the drama itself' (2004, 176). Metafiction is accused of doing the same thing: the dramatist coming on stage from the wings to present himself to the audience: look at me (looking at you [looking at me]).

Metafiction apparently caters very well to the insecure self, a self that constantly needs to assert its presence by being neurotically upfront about its own insecurity (is this real, am I real?). 'Octet' offers entertaining examples of this type of behaviour to hammer the point home. Such an insecure self needs constant confirmation. Metafiction's intra-textual acknowledgements of artificiality gratify and validate the hyper self-conscious writer, narrator, character (and reader?), who are all too aware of the constructed nature of their own identity. They can thus find in metafiction a confirmative clever analogue to the form of self-construction they have to perform on a daily basis. (It has, in that sense, become a very realistic literary device.) Nevertheless, this is the kind of validation and gratification that the characters and narrators in Wallace's fiction have grown tired of. They have discovered that all this overt cleverness only makes them feel more lonely. However simple it may sound, much of Wallace's work is directed at combating this loneliness – a loneliness that seems, from an intellectual standpoint (of the lonely solipsist), to be the only logical outcome since it is caused by the inbent spiral of self-reflectivity. It is perceived as horrible, and must, with clichés if necessary, be combated, corrected, overcome.

The road taken in 'Westward' is still very much dependent on the cleverness that seems to block what is actually wanted, which is to really value something (sidestepping desire, which is so easily commercialised). Wallace's characters, in their most luminous moments, are not 'desiring monads'. In using this term, I refer to the diagnosis of Best and Kellner of the 'contradiction of some postmodern theory': 'while theoretically it dispenses with the individual it simultaneously resurrects it in a post-liberal form, as an aestheticized, desiring monad' (1999, 284), stripped of 'moral responsibility' (291). Rather than being a desiring monad, Wallace's characters are lonely, and sad, and in need of something that would lift them from the 'cage of the self' – in Wallace's magnum opus *Infinite Jest* there are numerous references to this 'cage' (see, for example, 1997 [1996], 777). Paradoxically, this cage bars them not only from meaningful contact with something outside of the self, other people for example, but also from connecting to their own 'deep inside' – or, as Mark concludes in 'Westward': 'To be a subject is to be Alone. Trapped. Kept from yourself' (1989, 304). This paradoxical state is a very curious form of solipsism, a solipsism without a solipsist present (see also Timmer 2010, 116, 334, 352). Wallace's characters are characters or narrators who feel they have no true inner self. If the self is empty or merely a multi-layered shell of performative tactics, how is it possible to feel lonely? Or to phrase the question another way: where to situate feelings, if not deep inside?

Mark 'is revealed by me', the narrator in 'Westward' offers, 'to have professionally diagnosed emotional problems . . . he is troubled in relation to them, it's like he's denied access to them . . . I.e. either he doesn't *feel* anything, or *he* doesn't feel anything' (1989, 303; original italics). This paradoxical disturbance or pathology comes close to 'the *melancholic* structure of feeling' that Foster detected in 'recent intimations of postmodernism' in art (in the 1990s) – an oscillation between 'pure affect, no affect: *It hurts, I can't feel anything*' (1996, 165, 166; original italics). It is an inability to appropriate feelings, while feeling them nevertheless. These feelings are often the only 'real' existents in Wallace's fictions (where many a self regards himself or herself to be a fraud); these feelings are there, unavoidably present, overwhelming the self.

Such feelings have not, I believe, become 'free floating and impersonal', as for example Jameson once designated them to be when he outlined the difference between modern and postmodern art (1991 [1984], 16). Jameson believed that 'concepts such as anxiety and alienation (and the experiences to which they correspond . . .) are no longer appropriate in the world of the postmodern' because 'there is no longer a self present to do the feeling' (14, 15). There is, I believe, a crucial difference between experiences and conceptualisations of experiences that Jameson glosses over here; this difference or rift is exactly what is often highlighted in Wallace's oeuvre, and I will return to it in a short while. But for now, what is relevant is that even in the world of the postmodern, which still very much forms the background in Wallace's work (see Timmer 2010, 33–35), postmodern strategies of self-presentation do not have the effect of eliminating these good old modern-day human emotions (such as alienation, anxiety) that in theory, or Theory, were relegated to a pre-postmodern era. It is the *relation to* these feelings that is troubled; it hurts, and it is difficult to conceptualise how the type of self that is accustomed to posing as a self can be truly inflicted by this hurt. Adding another articulated layer of reflection makes these feelings only more ungraspable.

There appear to be two ways of perceiving the self still dominant in Wallace's fiction – or: Wallace draws from two different registers of presenting a self that are seemingly contradictory. These are what Foster has described as a 'psychologistic register' and a 'poststructuralist' register (1996, 168). The psychologistic register, informing popular culture, treats the self as 'witness, testifier' (168) to whatever troubles him or her (we could summarise that as 'I hurt therefore I am'). On the other hand, through the 'poststructralist critique of the subject' the position of the subject is 'evacuated' (168); this is, of course, the much-theorised death of the subject. If you combine them (as Wallace does in his oeuvre, informed by a keen sense of both critical theory and popular culture) you get a self which speaks from an empty, unstable subject-position, testifying 'it hurts'.

This specific expression can be interpreted differently than as simply signifying that feelings, hurt for example, have taken on an 'impersonal' quality. I will treat 'it' in 'it hurts' instead as an indexical sign, a gestural trace in language that may offer the necessary grip to form a new sense of self, which hinges on a particular experience of how the other (another person, fictional or otherwise) is perceived to be present, to partake in one's world – an experience that is often blocked, interrupted or disturbed in Wallace's fictional universes by the complex convergence of the two self-concepts mentioned earlier: a self driven to expressivity to testify to its existence, but for whom the means of expressivity have become a tiring or frustrating range of performative tactics 'manipulating [others'] view of me', in Wallace's already quoted words.

GHOSTLY FIGURES

Feelings of loneliness, alienation, insecurity cannot be addressed, nor appropriated, as long as they are conceptualised as the desire to be liked or loved. This is exactly what happens in much of Wallace's fiction (with full awareness). The source of this like or love is situated in an 'audience', which turns other persons into instruments of self-projection, or pieces of 'moral gymnastics equipment', as pointed out in 'Octet' (2001 [1999], 132). It gets pointed out often enough in Wallace's work, in usually very funny and clever ways, that such a performative self-reflectivity prevents one from truly connecting to another person, that it leads to a 'lonely' solipsism. What, though, is the solution, and is any such solution offered in Wallace's work? Perhaps not. What Wallace does succeed in is in atomising this audience, transforming the audience of other beings from an amorphous potential applaud-machine into a crowd of equally entrapped and distinct selves. This atomisation seldom happens within story worlds, but on the level of narration Wallace very elegantly makes clear that everybody has his or her own 'solipsistic delusions', that solipsism is what 'binds us together' (1989, 308, 309). The insight is sometimes attributed to one of the characters, but it is most obviously shown – by employing a technique difficult to imagine in real life, a melting or intermingling of two minds, of the narrator and a character, called free indirect discourse. Wallace excels in this.

Yet, narrator and character are, ontologically speaking, not part of the same world. A narrator is (potentially) in a position to know what is going on inside somebody else in a way that is not possible to achieve for characters, who remain entrapped in their own minds. This inequality can, from a logical perspective, not be dissolved, and thus Wallace sometimes resorts to ghost appearances (literally, ghosts appear). Not often, but when such a ghost-figure descends into the story world, it is able to 'use somebody's internal brain voice' (2001 [1996], 831). This happens in *Infinite Jest* (2001 [1996], and it happens in *The Pale King* (2011).

In a way these ghosts function as stand-ins for the kind of transcendent overview which is necessary to acquire the type of insights and experiences described by Wittgenstein, a view '*sub specie aeterni*', which is described in the *Tractatus* as view of the world 'as a whole – a limited whole. Feeling the world as a limited whole – it is this that is mystical' (2001 [1922], 88). In other words, the ghost-figures open up the possibility of ethical experiences. In Wallace's worlds, the ethical experience *par excellence* is that of 'interhuman sameness' (2001 [1999], 135). For example, wunderkind Hal Incandenza in *Infinite Jest* is 'struck by the fact that he really for the most part believes' (2001 [1996], 114) what he had just almost flippantly mentioned in a conversation with his friends, that: 'We're each deeply alone here. It's what we all have in common, this aloneness' (112). It is one thing to mention it; it is quite something else to actually experience it as such. This split, between experiences and the conceptualisations we construe of them, is also highlighted in 'Good Old Neon' when the narrator points out: 'As a verbal construction I know that is a cliché. As a state in which to actually be, it's something else, believe me' (2004, 175). To convey this state without getting entangled in verbal constructions (often amounting to clichés) is the hard part. It is as if you can only say 'Believe me', without explicating any further. This belief, or believing, hooks onto something larger, something that perhaps forms the background of everything you attempt to say, which motivates the *attempt*.

In the story worlds of Wallace, characters can only get struck by such insights; they don't have an intellectually satisfying explanation for them, or, like with Wittgenstein, they will disregard any such explanation of these types of experiences and insights on the grounds of their significance. It is as if the modern self cannot really signal this significance, or perhaps only in the way that I have found so moving while reading about dramatisation in pre-modern times. William Egginton, in his book *How the World Became a Stage*, explains that in the Middle Ages a 'dramatization creates the effect of an instantiation, a momentary entry into our senses of a timeless, immobile, and substantial truth' (2013, 50). He goes on to describe a practice of dramatisation in these days whereby 'the performers mimed actions and held placards over their heads with the words of speeches on them' (50). I picture many of Wallace's fictional human beings holding such a placard over their heads. It reads 'help'. But what is lost to them is the pre-modern or magical world view that has to accompany such a practice for it to be meaningful. Wallace's characters live in a disenchanted world.

The magic that does happen in Wallace's universe is that of the appearance of ghosts. Even if they may seem to be a minor detail in his work, making only the occasional appearance, I return to them because they fulfil a function that is sorely missed. These ghosts are like *dei ex machina*, descending on the staged drama from an elsewhere, from outside any rational-narrative framework of meaning and in a way that has nothing to do with the curtain pulling taking place in metafiction. They are supernatural, unlike dramatist and audience or author and reader. They are not embedded in time. In fact, they often have the utmost difficulty adjusting to the flow of narrative time (see, e.g., Wallace 2001 [1996], 830, 831). Rather, they appear; they are instantaneous. They are also self-effacing.

In *Infinite Jest* the most prominent feature of the ghost-figure is his capacity to use the brain voice of a character, to be inside an other person's head, to chat – sometimes experienced as some kind of 'lexical rape' (Wallace 2001 [1996], 832) – or offer advice. An even more advanced quality of the ghost, though, is his ability to be silent (very much in the spirit of Wittgenstein one could argue). In Wallace's notes to his posthumously published novel *The Pale King*, the function of one such ghost is described as 'being *with*' (2011, 542; original emphasis). The ghost-figure, especially in *The Pale King*, thus responds to an ethical demand, even if the character treated to a visit of such a ghost may not be able to formulate or articulate this demand clearly.

In a way, these ghosts are a bit of an emergency measure. It is almost as if they accentuate, make even more distressingly clear, that there appears to be no non-magical way to make manifest the 'something urgent and human'. Apart from the supernatural presence of these rare ghosts, being-with or being present to another human being occurs in Wallace's fictional universe almost exclusively on the level of articulation, 'chatting', on the level of a communicative exchange. Even then, on that level, the closest one can get to someone else is when speech acts merge, when thoughts intertwine. Although a distinction is made in *Infinite Jest* between communicating and 'interfacing' (whereby interfacing implies more intimacy and closeness), the focus often remains on ploughing through words, adding layers of reflection while attempting to peel them away. In 'Good Old Neon', this is a process which can be stopped only by 'saying, almost aloud, "Not another word"' (2004, 181).

Of course, we cannot really blame an author, or a narrator, for this preoccupation with verbalisation, but I am interested in getting closer to what is presumed to lie at the other side of the 'walls of our cage' – the walls of our cage that Wittgenstein identified as 'the boundaries of language' (1929, 10). There are instances in Wallace's writing when something happens, almost despite the verbal fire power, which allows a glimpse of what is beyond. I use the word 'instances' purposefully, because they are like the 'flash of light' that made Wittgenstein aware both of what is significant and the inability of language to express this significance.

I don't necessarily mean the type of instances that for example in 'Good Old Neon' are singled out and are framed as instances when language breaks down, when 'it's not English anymore' – like 'to cry in front of others, or to laugh, or speak in tongues, or chant in Bengali' (2004, 179). These temporary reliefs from the strictures of language, from the language of self-reflection, are not so uncommon. After all, a whole commercial industry has been built around offering such experiences. More difficult to achieve, though, is to find form for something that strikes you as truly important, which can only be gestured at, as in 'Octet': 'This thing I feel, I can't name it straight out but it seems important, do you feel it too?' (2001 [1999], 131). This approach requires that you're 'not just sincere but almost naked. Worse than naked – more like unarmed. Defenseless' (131).

DEFENSELESSNESS AND RELATIONALITY

Although some have come to see 'sincerity' as one of the most defining features of post-postmodern literature, I believe that something much more rigorous is at stake: defenselessness. A profound source for exploring further what this state of defenselessness could entail is, for me, the work of Emmanuel Levinas, who connects the 'risky uncovering of oneself, in sincerity' with 'the breaking up of inwardness and the abandon of all shelter' (1998 [1981], 48). This goes much further than a self signifying 'help' by sincerely offering this sign to someone else: holding a placard up above its head so to speak, for 'you' to read. Levinas clearly differentiates between 'the giving out of signs' and 'saying' (48). Saying is 'an expression of exposure' (49), and as such preconditions any form of communication (the inscription of meaning in 'tales', the 'circulation of information', the giving out of signs and the deciphering of them by another 'ego' [48]). I read it as a state, not bound by time or captured in thematization. It is a receptiveness, in Levinas's vocabulary a 'passivity' (47, 54), towards the other, through which being becomes 'vulnerability' (49, 50). This is not necessarily a pleasant state that carries only positive connotations. We could compare it to 'Octet', where there is mention of 'some nameless but inescapable "*price*" that all human beings are faced with having to pay at some point if they ever want truly "to be with" another person', 'like a kind of death' (2001 [1999], 132, 133).

The shift or transformation away from postmodernism does not necessarily align to a 'feeling better', or any sort of feel-good-form of empathy *per se*. Critchley's (2012) analysis of 'the Levinasian ethical subject' comes very close to what I think is at stake in the work of an author like David Foster Wallace. Critchley writes that for Levinas (2012, 61):

> The ethical demand is a traumatic demand, it is something that comes from outside the subject, from a heteronomous source, but which leaves its imprint within the subject. At its heart, the ethical subject is marked by an experience of hetero-affectivity. In other words, the inside of my inside is somehow outside, the core of my subjectivity is exposed to otherness.

From this more Levinasian perspective, the difficulty that the human figures in Wallace's fiction experience in relation to their feelings becomes like a first realization of this sense of exposure. It takes a very different view of subjectivity to come to grips with this realization, neither Foster's (1996) psychologistic nor a poststructural register will do (and perhaps no 'register' will do). In any case, the (unavoidable) proximity of the other, the radical exposure to the other, might be much more difficult, and might put a much greater demand on us, than the slippery just-out-of-reachness that characterised our dealings with other human beings (including all of our selves) within postmodern contexts.

A softer landing is suggested by, for example, John Shotter, who draws attention to the importance of '*momentary relational encounters*' for gaining a sense of self (1996, 387; original emphasis). Shotter emphasises (63):

> The expression of a thought or an intention, the saying of a sentence or the doing of a deed, does not issue from already well-formed and orderly cognitions at the center of our being, but originates in a person's vague, diffuse and unordered *feelings* – their sense of how, semiotically, they are 'positioned' in relation to the others around them. And the appropriate orderly expression of such feelings

is 'developed' in a complex set of temporally conducted transactions between themselves (or their selves), the feelings, and those to whom such expression must be addressed.

Feelings, however vague and diffuse, can thus function as orienting markers that situate a person in relation to other persons. Making sense is, from this perspective, no longer perceived to be a purely cognitive affair and the sole responsibility of a supposed autonomous subject; neither is the self in this view a subject passively imprinted by existing structures of meaning. Making sense is a transactional process that takes place within a specific situation. Shotter (also much influenced by Wittgenstein) introduces 'the situation' as a 'third agency that "calls out" reactions, spontaneously, from us' – 'there is something at work shaping our reactions', he argues, 'not in us as individuals, but, as it were, centred in the "space" between us and our circumstances' (1996, 402–3). The locus of meaning-making in this account has shifted from the individual (the individual's mind) to a difficult to define space, a 'relational-space' as Shotter labels it (404).

The relational space is difficult to define, I believe, because we are so used to conceiving meaning-making as a process that evolves through time and finds form in narratives, instead of in space (and instantaneously). In 'Octet', for example, the narrator struggles to bring across the more physical and spatial dimensions of sense-making, trying to compose 'palpations, feelers into the interstices of [the reader's] sense of something' (2001 [1999], 123), but he remains stuck on conceiving this sense-making as a 'something' which has to be brought across, that has to travel somehow from person to person, from one self-enclosed mind into another. The problem might be that this travelling has to happen through what Egginton calls 'empty space', that is how space is experienced in modern times, as empty versus 'full, impressionable and substantial' (2013, 37), an 'ever-present reality' as it was experienced in pre-modern times (55). 'Empty space' is a notion borrowed from the theatre, and that is exactly the point: 'the normative, modern mode of being' (28), according to Egginton, is characterized by 'theatricality' (29), whereby we always stand separated and in a representational relation to the realm of the physically real. This is in sharp contrast to being absorbed by what is already there, proximate and true 'whatever happens' in Wittgenstein's already quoted words.

CONCLUSION

In this chapter, I have traced the ways in which, throughout his fiction, Wallace attempts to convey a new sense of self, a self no longer alone and kept from itself but instead acutely aware of the proximity and presence of others, other selves which enrich but also disrupt the solipsistic experience worlds that his characters and narrators are so often encaged in by default. Wallace attempts to convey this new sense of self, but does he also succeed? Perhaps he succeeds because of the attempts plus failure to come to a solution, and in that sense he appears to be a perfect example of a metamodern artist, exemplifying in his practice a constant 'oscillation' between irreconcilable poles (Vermeulen and Van den Akker, 2010) – an oscillation, most notably, between two registers to articulate the self: a 'psychologistic' or diluted modern register and a poststructural (postmodern) register. Yet I cannot imagine Wallace's ambition was to be stuck in perpetual oscillation, and I think his failure to create a truly new register with which to articulate experiences of being human that somehow transcend the self-enclosed mind was painful and not a strategic choice. His attempts are stranded, significantly, at the exclamation 'not another word'.

In his book *Sources of the Self* – in which the development of our modern identity is traced – Taylor connects 'articulacy' with 'a particular ethical view': 'We aren't full beings in this perspective until we can say what moves us' (1989, 92). Wallace's characters and narrators, although very articulate, are not good at all at explicating what really moves them, what they truly value. It is this failure that lies at the heart of Wallace's fiction, and it is in this sense that his work calls out for a different ethical view, a view that is despairingly difficult to put into words, to 'say'. It is about being moved, being 'struck', but also: being the being that someone else is being-with. There is a certain passivity, an almost devotional receptivity and absorption in otherness involved in these instances, which might be hard to endure, particularly for beings expected to always 'articulate' themselves, with both the psychologistic and poststructural register. Yet it is exactly this element of radical defencelessness that has the potential to become a defining feature of the affective sensibilities of post-postmodern fiction, art, theory and life. I suspect it goes far beyond being sincere, as Wallace has shown in his work to be very much aware of as well.

Chapter 8

Contemporary Autofiction and Metamodern Affect

Alison Gibbons

Writing in 2009, Mortimer somewhat colloquially and somewhat polemically proclaims, 'Autofiction is front and center right now and shows no sign of giving up its ostentatious primacy' (2009, 22). Similarly, Rak speaks of the so-called memoir boom, which she ties to 'a period spanning roughly the first decade of the twenty-first century' (2013, 3). The contemporary trend for and upsurge in life writing can be read in two ways. On one hand, such works might be considered to inflate the self and magnify individualism (see Benn Michaels 2013). In this construal, the boom of life writing feeds into what Pine and Gilmore (2011 [1999]) have termed the experience economy, in which personal experience is a precious commodity and prized marketing tool. From this, it follows that the very notion of subjectivity is co-opted as an instrument of late capitalism (and by extension, of a neoliberal post-modernism) with the consequence that the signifying potential of personal experience, emotion and subjective identity is eroded into a constructed, commercial fabrication.

This reading, however, disappoints on three counts. First, it is based on the inevitable prevalence of the self rather than on the particularities of self-construction in contemporary life writing. Neglecting the latter means that all cases of life writing are seen as vanity projects, irrespective of content or historico-cultural grounding. Second, reading life writing as a major form of postmodern individualism prioritises the writing subject at the expense of readers. Benn Michaels, for instance, suggests that reading memoir is moti-vated not so much by a desire for 'the truth of what happened as the right attitude toward that truth' (2013, 922). That is, readers want to be told how they *should* feel about an event – ethically, socially, politically – in place of authentically feeling. Both the first and the second shortcomings fuel a post-modern account of subjectivity in which hermeneutic emotion is unfeasible and any claims to truth-value or ethico-political sentiment are worthless since they are seen to unavoidably produce a form of reality-kitsch which functions merely as self-aggrandisement.

Third and finally, the argument overlooks a contemporary shift in what Jameson calls 'emotional ground tone' (1991 [1984], 6): here, a shift from postmodern senses of ending to a 'structure of feeling' (Williams 1979) in which the interrelating axes of historicity, affect and depth reverberate once again in meaningful ways. This chapter pursues this alternative reading of contemporary autofiction by connecting the prosperity of the genre to metamodernism as a cultural dominant. In doing so, I am treading somewhat contested ground; the autobiographical mode has been inherently equated with postmodern, poststructuralist concerns, namely the fragmentation of the subject and the blurring of ontological boundaries between fact and fiction (cf. Gilmore 1994; Garber 1996; Gudmundsdóttir 2003; Saunders 2010). I contend that while contemporary autofiction incorporates stylistic tropes of postmodernism, it nevertheless departs from postmodernism's self-serving logic. To demonstrate this departure, I analyse two case studies, namely, Chris Kraus's (2006 [1998]) *I Love Dick* and Frédéric Beigbeder's (2004) *Windows on the World*. The analysis shows that, instead, the affective logic of contemporary autofiction is situational in that it narrativises the self, seeking to locate that self in a place, a time and a body. It also pertains to represent truth, however subjective that truth may be.

In the next section, I briefly outline Jameson's description of modernist and postmodernist affect. Further to this, I explore what situated metamodernist affect might entail, drawing on the post-positivist account of identity. After introducing autofiction as a genre, I consider two contemporary novels using situatedness as a conceptual lens through which to explicate their representations of subjectivity and affect.

SUBJECTIVITY AND AFFECT AFTER POSTMODERNISM

In Jameson's view, 'the waning of affect' (1991 [1984], 10) is inextricably allied with 'a new kind of flatness or depthlessness, a new kind of superficiality in the most literal sense' (9). Postmodern artworks do not articulate any hermeneutic reality beyond representation but instead are 'radically antianthropomorphic' (Jameson 1991 [1984], 34). Representations, humanity and the world more broadly are transformed into 'a glossy skin, a stereoscopic illusion, a rush of filmic images without density' (34). Correspondingly, poststructuralism and deconstruction flatten identity by dismantling the subject's claim to referentiality. While the poststructuralist 'death of the author' (Barthes 1977 [1968]) discredits textuality and critical, especially linguistic, meaning as inherently unstable and indeterminate, so too postmodernism abandons identity and affect by proclaiming the 'death of the subject' (Jameson 1992 [1988], 167).

For contrast, Jameson cites Edward Munch's (1893) painting *The Scream* to illustrate a prior, modernist conception of subjectivity. Jameson (1991 [1984], 11–12) explains that the image of the screaming human figure not only embodies affect in the form of 'alienation, anomie, solitude, social fragmentation, and isolation' but also:

> [t]he very concept of expression presupposes indeed some separation within the subject, and along with that a whole metaphysics of inside and outside, of the wordless pain within the monad and the moment in which, often cathartically, that 'emotion' is then projected out and externalized, as gesture or cry, as desperate communication and the outward dramatization of inward feeling.

The expression itself is symbolised not only in the image of the screaming figure but in the very texture of the painting too: 'The absent scream returns, as it were, in a dialectic of loops and spirals' that 'inscribe themselves on the painted surface in the form of those great concentric circles in which sonorous vibration becomes visible' (1991 [1984], 14). Thus, the textured surface of *The Scream* and the distorted gaping-mouthed figure demand an interpretation in terms of depth; they externalise inner torment – of the painter and of a depicted modernist subjectivity. In turn, this hermeneutic understanding implicates the viewer in an affective relation with the painting. In Buchanan's words, 'Ultimate truth is constructed by the viewer. It is a phenomenological truth rather than an ontological or epistemic truth, which is to say the truth of my experience, the truth *I* experience, but not a universal truth' (2006, 91).

In *The Forms of the Affects*, Brinkema speculates about the contemporary moment, 'Is there any doubt that we are now fully within the Episteme of the Affect?' (2014, xi). While her rhetorical question already implies an affirmative response, she continues by positioning the contemporary critical turn to affect as 'a post-poststructuralist or anti-poststructuralist response to perceived omissions in poststructuralism' (xi). Seen in this way, the affective turn is 'part of a larger reawakening of interest in problematics of embodiment and materiality in the wake of twentieth-century Western theory that, for many, was all semiotics and no sense, all structure and no stuff' (xi). Such a reawakening of, or turn to, affect is both expressed by and perceptible in contemporary autofiction. Nevertheless, contemporary autofiction does not reflect a straightforward, uncritical return to the affective subjectivity that defined modernism nor is it a complete rebuttal of postmodern disintegration but a vicissitude of both. Indeed, Brinkema notes, 'The affective turn in general is resonant with broader strains in what has been dubbed "metamodernism" as a "structure of feeling" that oscillates between modernist and postmodern relativisms' (xii).

A useful, critical discourse on contemporary subjectivity can be found in post-positivist criticism, in which identities are understood to be 'both real and constructed; they can be politically and epistemically significant, on the one hand, and variable, nonessentialist, and radically historical, on the other' (Moya 2000a, 12; see also Mohanty 2000 [1993]; Moya 2000b). Post-positivism collapses the polarisation to hold these two positions in tension. Thus, subjectivity can involve 'enabling, enlightening, and enriching structures of attachment and feeling' (Moya 2000a, 8) while being sceptical and self-reflexive about those attachments and feelings. Drawing on this, I suggest conceiving of metamodern subjectivity and affect as situated. In contemporary autofiction, subjects are shown to desire meaningful attachments with others and are susceptible to heartfelt personal experiences that may in turn shape their identities. Personal affect, though, is neither earnest nor individualistic; it is situational. The represented subject seeks to situate or ground their self corporeally in the world, including in relation to others (see also discussions of relationality: Moraru 2011; Gibbons 2016; Timmer, this volume). Thus, affective subjectivity involves ongoing emotional and cognitive effort. While value is assigned to situated personal and interpersonal – including emotional – experiences, identity is also acknowledged as a social category that is constructed by subjects and by larger structures of social power.

Through this brief discussion, I have advocated a rethinking of affect beyond the flattened subjectivity that characterises postmodernism affect. While I have explored metamodern representations of contemporary experience and selfhood elsewhere (see Gibbons 2015, 2016), herein I now turn to two works of contemporary autofiction. My analyses demonstrate that we find in contemporary autofiction not a postmodern waning of affect but rather a revival of affect. Representations of subjectivity in contemporary autofiction resonate instead with the notion of a situated subjectivity that can be considered metamodern.

CONTEMPORARY AUTOFICTION

Autofiction is an explicitly hybrid form of life writing that merges autobiographical fact with fiction. The autofictional mode is not restricted to writing; it has been observed in the visual arts, cinema, theatre and online (e.g. see the special issue of *Image [&] Narrative* edited by Masschelein 2007; Kjellman-Chapin 2009). However, literature is the dominant form.

The term 'autofiction' was coined by French critic and novelist Serge Dou-brovsky in 1977 when it appeared on the back cover of his novel *Fils*: 'Fic-tion, of facts and events strictly real, if you prefer is called *autofiction*, where the language of adventure has been entrusted to the adventure of language in its total freedom' (Doubrovsky 2013, 1; original italics). The term described Doubrovsky's own novels and an emergent trend in 1970s France. The form was originally considered to share postmodernist concerns about the per-formance of selfhood and questioning of any unique style. It is telling, for instance, that Roland Barthes's *roland BARTHES par roland barthes* (1975) is counted among initial examples of French autofiction. Even Doubrovsky has claimed: 'One could say that all this [autofiction] is a postmodern version of autobiography' (2013, 2).

Although it maintains a privileged status in France, autofiction has spread globally since the 1970s. Thus, Doubrovsky writes, 'Autofiction: A weird word, is now being used around the world' (2013, 1). There is also a growing consensus that contemporary autofiction expresses a sentiment that is beyond the postmodern. Sadoux claims that 'it is undeniable that *autofiction . . .* is a resilient attempt to deal with notions of self and subjectivity in writing in an age of multiple crisis' (2002, 177; original italics), while Sturgeon (2014) argues:

> The self is no longer drowned in a system of disinformation, paranoia, and entropy, in the vein of Pynchon and DeLillo. Nor does the self get washed away in an ocean of hyperreality or unreality, in the (Baudrillardian) style of Ballard. Nor is it beholden to the logic of late capitalism, at least not entirely. We're wit-nessing instead the induction of a new class of memoiristic, autobiographical, and metafictional novels – we can call them autofictions – that jettison the logic of postmodernism in favor of a new position.

This is because, Sturgeon contends, autofictions 'redistribut[e] the relation between self and fiction. Fiction is no longer seen as "false" or "lies" or "make-believe"' (2014). Rather, Sturgeon believes that autofiction 'eschews the entire truth vs. fiction debate in favor of the question of how to live or how to create' (2014). Sturgeon's words already suggest a fit between contempo-rary autofiction and the situated model of affect discussed earlier in that – like the post-positivist position and the oscillating dynamics of metamodern-ism – he argues that autofictions disrupt polarising accounts of ontology, self-hood and truth.

Narrowly defined, autofictional texts identify as fiction to a greater or lesser extent, and the central character or narrator bears the name of the author. Autofiction is, to my mind, a broad genre, containing novels that conform to this strict definition, but also other forms in which the central character does not take the author's name (e.g. at all, they take a variation of the author's name, or they remain nameless), such as the related modes of fictional autobiography and fictional memoir as well as autobiographical fiction. Examples of contemporary autofiction in the strict sense are Dave Eggers's (2001) *A Heartbreaking Work of Staggering Genius*, Damon Galgut's (2010) *In a Strange Room*, Will Self's (2010) *Walking to Hollywood*, Sheila Heti's (2013) *How Should a Person Be*, Ruth Ozeki's (2013) *A Tale for the Time Being*, Ben Lerner's (2014) *10:04* and Karl Ove Knausgaard's *My Struggle* series (2013 [2009] – forthcoming). Broader examples of autofictions are *Every Day Is for the Thief* by Teju Cole (2014 [2007]), *Shanghai Dancing* by Brian Castro (2008), *Jeff in Venice, Death in Varanasi* by Geoff Dyer (2009), *Leaving the Atocha Station* by Ben Lerner (2011), *Kapow!* by Adam Thirlwell (2012) and *The Wallcreeper* by Nell Zinc (2014).

This chapter takes two autofictions as central case studies, namely Chris Kraus's (2006 [1998]) *I Love Dick* and Frédéric Beigbeder's (2004) *Windows on the World*. Autofiction is a feature throughout both these authors' oeuvres. I have selected these texts specifically because although they have been considered postmodern, my analyses demonstrate that, instead, Kraus and Beigbeder write out of a postmodernist formulation of fragmented, fictitious, textual identity and towards a metamodern affect, whereby subjectivity is linked to an external reality through personal connection and situatedness.

I Love Dick

Chris Kraus's *I Love Dick* has been heralded as 'a postmodern memoir of obsession' (Johnson 2008). Such a description is not entirely erroneous. Yet, *I Love Dick* goes beyond postmodern fragmentation and presents instead the cognitive, emotional effort of the central character, as proxy for the author Chris Kraus, trying to realise a sense of selfhood that is anchored in personal experience and affective response. First published in 1998, *I Love Dick* was reprinted in the United States in 2006 and in the United Kingdom in 2015, and has become a feminist cult classic. It is written in two parts with 'Part 1: Scenes from a marriage' structured as diary entries. The first entry, dated 'December 3, 1994' begins: 'Chris Kraus, a 39-year-old experimental film-maker and Sylvère Lotringer, a 56-year-old college professor from New York, have dinner with Dick _____' (Kraus 2006 [1998], 19). Herein lies the premise of the book: the story focuses on Chris's growing romantic obsession with her husband Sylvère's friend and fellow cultural critic Dick after their first meeting in December 1994.

The diary entry style grounds the fiction seemingly in real time. The names of the characters are also not coincidental. There is, of course, an onomastic correspondence between author and character Chris Kraus, but the facts of the story also serve an autobiographical agenda. 'Dick' is known to be cultural theorist Dick Hebdige, and between the late 1980s and late 1990s, the real Kraus was married to the literary critic Sylvère Lotringer. Furthermore, Lotringer founded Semiotext(e) where *I Love Dick* was originally published and where Kraus was responsible for launching the Native Agents series, devoted to publishing fiction by women. In interview with Schwarz and Balsamo, and speaking before *I Love Dick*'s appearance, Kraus described the series as presenting 'a very public "I." The same public "I" that gets expressed in these other French theories' (1996, 214). She adds, 'It's like this personal "I" that is constantly bouncing up against the world – that isn't just existing for itself' (214). Her description, with its reference to French theory and its emphasis on a first-person subject occupying a space between public and personal, intimates an awareness of French autofictional practice. It also suggests an attempt by contemporary female writers to reclaim the first-person, and by extension literary subjectivity, in a way that connects an internal self to an external world.

After the fictional character Chris meets Dick, she cannot stop thinking about him. Her first response is to channel her obsessive energy into a short story, substituting Dick's name for 'David Rattray', a 'reckless adventurer and a genius and a moralist' (Kraus 2006 [1998], 23), another name that has real-world reference. This in itself seems recursively postmodern: a character with the same name as the author writes a short story based on a previously narrated event and transparently substitutes the characters' names. In fact, much of part 1 of *I Love Dick* feels decidedly postmodern. Chris shares her feelings about Dick with Sylvère, and together they start to write love letters to Dick that are included in the text. These letters are knowing, with the characters coming to think of them as an art project; they are self-reflexive, commenting on the project's (and thus, the book's) own status or as Sylvère fictively writes, 'these letters seem to open up a new genre, something in between cultural criticism and fiction' (2006 [1998], 43).

There is no reply from Dick to Chris's and Sylvère's letters (though he does purportedly speak to them on the phone) and thus, instead, he appears to haunt part 1, like a Derridean 'trace' (Derrida 1982), notably felt by his absence. Dick's identity, therefore, is inscribed textually. Indeed, in a letter dated 'Tuesday, December 13, 1994', Chris and Sylvère write: 'Last night we thought we had it nailed, and in a sense we do. There's no way of communicating with you in writing because texts, as we all know, feed upon themselves, become a game. The only way left is face to face' (2006 [1998], 73). Despite the ludic superficiality of these letters to Dick as a fabricated but unfulfilled identity, this final sentence points beyond the text. A witty quip about the reflexive surface of postmodern textuality ends with a statement preferentially gesturing towards hermeneutic, interpersonal actuality.

The diary entries that frame the letters in part 1 are written in third person. Thus, despite the autofictional nature of *I Love Dick*, the author and character – Chris Kraus – is a less imposing presence in the text. Her identity is defined by her feelings for Dick, as expressed in the letters, and by her marital relationship to Sylvère, her letter-writing co-author. This idea is considered in the diary entry also from 'December 13, 1994', which features a lengthy rumination on the representation of female identity, particularly within literary contexts (2006 [1998], 71–72; original italics):

> Because most 'serious' fiction, still, involves the fullest possible expression of a single's person's subjectivity, it's considered crass and amateurish not to 'fictionalize' the supporting cast of characters, changing names and insignificant features of their identities. The 'serious' contemporary hetero-male novel is a thinly veiled Story of Me, as voraciously consumptive as all of patriarchy. While the hero/anti-hero explicitly *is* the author, everybody else is reduced to 'characters'. Example: the artist Sophie Calle appears in Paul Auster's book *Leviathan* in the role of writer's girlfriend. . . . – but in *Leviathan* she's a waif-like creature relieved of complication like ambition or career.
>
> When women try to pierce this false conceit by naming names because our 'I's' are changing as we meet other 'I's', we're called bitches, libellers, pornographers and amateurs.

Kraus's words here again insinuate a departure from postmodern representations of subjectivity and affect. She cites Paul Auster's work as an example of the ' "serious" contemporary hetero-male novel', and Auster's poststructuralist games, in which he often appears as a character throughout his oeuvre, are also well known. Kraus's argument is that the game or the playful artifice of (male-dominated) postmodernist fiction is damaging, especially to (female) subjectivity ('everybody else is reduced to "characters" '). In *I Love Dick*, there is instead an insistence on depth (she wants 'to pierce this false conceit') and an acknowledgement that identity and subjectivity develop through personal, situated, lived experience ('our "I's" are changing as we meet other "I's" ').

Comments such as those already discussed mark *I Love Dick* as a text in transition, a literary work on the cusp of the postmodern moving towards a metamodern sensibility. In part 1, having just raised some intertextual references, Chris asks, 'Does analogy make emotion less sincere?' (2006 [1998], 70), a rhetorical question which intimates the oscillating characteristics Vermeulen and van den Akker attribute to the metamodern, oscillation 'between a modern enthusiasm and a postmodern irony, between hope and melancholy, between naïveté and knowingness, empathy and apathy, unity and plurality, totality and fragmentation, purity and ambiguity' (2010, 5–6). Part 1 culminates in a fight between Sylvère and Chris. Identity is at its heart: ' "Who's Chris Kraus?" she screamed. "She's no one! She's

Sylvère Lotringer's wife! She's his "Plus-One"!' (2006 [1998], 116). Part 1 ends (117):

> 'Nothing is irrevocable', Sylvère said. 'No', she screamed, 'you're wrong!' By this time she was crying. 'History isn't dialectical, it's essential! Some things will never go away!'

> And the next day, Monday, January 30, she left him.

The final sentence is foregrounded by it positioning on the page, a few lines of blank space preceding it, while the conjunction 'And' implies causality: Chris has left Sylvère as a means of reasserting her self-identity. The reference to history is also intriguing. Earlier, Chris writes to Dick, 'Everything is true and simultaneous' (2006 [1998], 87) and the ending of part 1 articulates a similar point. Chris is not only reclaiming herself but also history. History, like identity, is not a narrative construct that can be constantly rewritten. The emotional force of Chris's outburst intimates that history can have continued personal resonance. In opposition to the playful plasticity of postmodern a-historicism and a-personal intensities, history – whether personal or public, and including our own engagements with it – does set the parameters for and work to shape subjectivities in some way.

In 'Part 2: Every Letter Is a Love Letter', the third-person diary entries have been removed. Thus, Chris Kraus, character and author, finds the first-person 'I' and her letters to Dick are solely authored by her. Chris initially writes that she feels 'torn between maintaining you [Dick] as an entity to write to and talking with you as a person', but she decides 'Perhaps I'll let it go' (2006 [1998], 129–30). As a result, part 2 feels like a secession and a liberation from postmodern textuality and subjectivity. This is most clear when Chris explicitly reflects on the change from her previous failure to write using the first-person 'I' (138–39):

> I'd even made up art theories about my inability to use it. . . . I couldn't ever believe in the integrity/supremacy of the 1st Person (my own). That in order to write 1st Person narrative there needs to be a fixed self or persona and by refusing to believe in this I was merging with the fragmented reality of the time. But now I think okay, there's no fixed point of self but it exists & by writing you can somehow chart that movement. That maybe 1st Person writing's just as fragmentary as more a-personal collage, it's just more serious: bringing change & fragmentation closer, bringing it down to where you really are.

Kraus's reference to 'art theories' is a nod to poststructural models of text and self, while her sense of 'the fragmented reality of the time' which denies 'a fixed self' contextualises Kraus's words within the cultural dominant of the postmodern. Her emancipation, though, comes from realising a post-positivist, situated sense of selfhood: 'There's no fixed point of self but it exists & by writing you can somehow chart that movement'. Kraus's own writing in *I Love Dick*, now in the first person, is therefore 'more serious'. It acknowledges fragmentation as a postmodern insight but tries nevertheless (perhaps in vain) to integrate it with a grounded sense of self, a necessary thinking, feeling subjectivity in search of meaningful identity.

Tellingly, it is also in part 2 that Chris finally has her rendezvous with Dick. The latter does not, ultimately, become the epic romance that Chris or readers may have hoped for. The failing of the romance is beneficial though, since it leads Chris to an understanding of her emotions: 'No woman is an island-ess. We fall in love in hope of anchoring ourselves to someone else, to keep from falling' (2006 [1998], 257). Even Kraus's closing words in the final letter hold irony and sincerity in tension. They are tinted with postmodern intertextuality in their reference to John Donne's famous phrase ('No man is an island'), but nevertheless insist on situated and affective attachment.

Windows on the World

Frédéric Beigbeder's *Windows on the World* was first published in French in 2003, with the English translation appearing a year later. The novel imagines the final living moments of those in the Windows on the World restaurant in the North Tower of the World Trade Center on 1 September 2001. Temporality is therefore central to the narrative, both in terms of its focus on the event and in terms of structure: each chapter of the book is assigned a time between 8:30 and 10:29am – spanning fifteen minutes before the first plane hit the North Tower (at 8:46) to a minute after it fell (the South Tower having already collapsed at 9:59). As such, *Windows on the World* resurrects history and unlike postmodern resistance to narrative closure, the narrative and the event at its heart has an inevitable conclusion.

At 8:30, then, the novel begins: 'You know how it ends: everybody dies. Death, of course, comes to most people one day or another. The novelty of this story is that everyone dies at the same time in the same place. Does death forge bonds between people?' (Beigbeder 2004, 1). The rhetorical question raises another important issue of the novel, the idea of collective memory, mourning and shared affect. The structural conceit of *Windows on the World* also engages with affect, since the chapters alternate between two narrators: an extratextual counterpart of the author Frédéric Beigbeder who is self-consciously writing about 9/11 and Carthew Yorston, a Texan divorcee in the Windows on the World restaurant with his two sons Jerry and David. As such, the book mixes genres or, in Brandt's words, it is 'a contemporary mash-up of autofiction and hyperrealism' (2015, 1).

Hyperrealism, as a genre indicator here, obviously calls up Baudrillard's postmodern conception of the hyperreal, 'the meticulous reduplication of the real' (1993 [1976], 71). Baudrillard posits that the hyperreal 'effaces the contradiction of the real and the imaginary. Irreality no longer belongs to the dream or the phantasm, to a beyond or a hidden interiority, but to *the hallucinatory resemblance of the real to itself* (72; original italics). Furthermore, in terms of selfhood, Baudrillard claims that hyperrealism constructs 'a void around the real, to eradicate all psychology and subjectivity from it in order to give it a pure objectivity' (72). Both Baudrillard (2003 [2002]) and Žižek (2002) have analysed the hyperreal nature of 9/11. It is also a term Beigbeder himself employs to describe *Windows on the World*. Beigbeder does so, however, in a way that seems to invert the relationship between real and imaginary: 'Writing this hyperrealist novel is made more difficult by reality itself. Since September 11, 2001, reality has not only outstripped fiction, it's destroying it. It's impossible to write about this subject, and yet impossible to write about anything else. Nothing else touches us' (2004, 8). It is not that the real appears as a fictive simulation, like Jameson's 'rush of filmic images'. Rather, the magnitude of 9/11 as an event in recent human history pierces fiction; the real insistently infiltrates fiction to assert its epistemic imperative.

Returning to the alternating narrative voices of *Windows on the World* and their function in relation to subjectivity and affect, the ironic narrative mode of Beigbeder's autofictional chapters is ultimately undercut by their relation to the so-called hyperreal chapters. That is, despite the extreme self-reflexivity of Beigbeder as author-character, the self-conscious literary project of *Windows on the World* is ultimately and intimately driven by a desire for affective connection. As Beigbeder writes, *Windows on the World* 'isn't a thriller; it is simply an attempt – doomed, perhaps – to describe the indescribable' (2004, 57). Beigbeder's authorial character persistently strives to vicariously experience Carthew's last living moments in the North Tower, and by extension those of the real victims of the attack. Doing so is a relational endeavour, since it ruptures the divisions between public and private and seeks to give shared meanings to personal experiences. It also implies that while the fictive imaginary is not a substitute for reality (or indeed, vice versa), it can offer hermeneutic insight into ourselves, others and our relationships to and in the world. As Brandt affirms, 'Beigbeder's dual protagonists in *Windows on the World* serve to expose the relationship between collective identity politics and personal experience within times of national crisis' (2015, 4).

Interconnectedness and situated identity is also emphasised in Carthew's chapters. At 9:03, an SMS news alert makes it apparent that the plane crash is part of a terrorist attack. Carthew realises (2004, 111–12):

> And so it happened: all those things I didn't understand, that I didn't want to understand; the foreign news stories I preferred to switch off, to keep out of

my mind when they weren't on TV; all these tragedies were suddenly relevant to me; these wars came to hurt me this morning; me, not someone else; my children, not someone else's; these things I knew nothing about, these events so geographically remote suddenly became the most important things in my life.

The references here to TV and foreign news stories are further reminders of the hyperreality of postmodern culture. However, Carthew's affective realisation is that his treatment of them as simulations or filmic images empties them of meaning. Their newly found sudden relevance is, of course, due to the tragic extremity of Carthew's circumstances. Nevertheless, Beigbeder's writing here uses frequent repetitions to foreground the global interconnectivity and significance both of human life in the world and of human history.

Despite the pursuit of authentic experience through personal imagination, Beigbeder is careful not to assume or assert that Carthew's narration is a faithful account. Indeed, he avows, 'Even if I go deep, deep into the horror, my book will always remain 1,350 feet below the truth' (2004, 124). It will always be divorced from the reality of 9/11 because that reality is eventually unknowable. Thus, despite the fact that *Windows on the World* presents an objective, real-world event though two fictionalised subjective viewpoints, the postmodern tricks it employs (irony, knowingness, self-reflexivity) deliberately show up the artifice of the endeavour. In Beigbeder's words, 'I had a credibility problem, everything I said was unreliable, even the truth' (89). In fact, the narrative styles of Carthew and the fictionalised Beigbeder are almost indistinguishable as are some of their biographical details – in particular, their status as divorced middle-age men, now in tumultuous relationships with younger girlfriends. The foregrounding of artifice, though, is not part of a postmodern project of simulation or textual entrapment; it is a staging of artifice in order to address the real, however impossible that may be. This is clearest around half-way through the novel, when the two characters metaleptically address each other. At 9:16, Beigbeder considers what drove people to jump from the towers, concluding that it is a rational response to the realisation of inevitable death. At 9:17, Carthew interjects, 'Bullshit, my dear Beigbeder. If somewhere between thirty-seven and fifty people threw themselves from the top of the North Tower, it was simply because everything else was impossible, suffocation, pain, the instinct to survive, because jumping couldn't be worse than staying in this suffocating furnace' (153). At 9:18, Beigbeder responds, 'Okay, Carthew, if you're going to be like that, I'll go to New York' (155). By travelling to New York, Beigbeder seeks out a meaningful, lived experience in relation to the historical event. Moreover, while the unnatural metaleptic address that prompts his journey is almost painfully postmodern, Beigbeder's crass employment of the device is purposeful. The characters' disagreement displaces any notion of *Windows on the World* as an accurate or didactic account and instead privileges situated subjective or phenomenological truth.

Windows on the World is inevitably a poignant novel, and readers are likely to engage emotionally with it, but Beigbeder tries to avoid being excessively moralistic. As the event gets closer to its conclusion, at 10:08, Beigbeder informs readers (2004, 276):

> From here, we can penetrate the unspeakable, the inexpressible. Please excuse our misuse of ellipsis. I have cut out the awful description. I have not done so out of propriety, nor out of respect for the victims because I believe that describing their slow agonies, their ordeal, is also a mark of respect. I cut them because, in my opinion, it is more appalling to allow you to imagine what became of them.

The adjectives 'awful' and 'appalling' and the nouns 'agonies' and 'ordeal' do communicate an unmistakable evaluative stance to readers. Still, in the succeeding Carthew chapters, Beigbeder does leave narrative gaps and empty white space on the page, the implication being that readers' own cognitive and imaginative effort is a vital means of subjective engagement with the event and with its victims.

Brandt claims that it is through autofiction that '*Windows on the World* suggests one way in which subjectivity is understood and lived as a physical body in a particular moment in history' (2015, 14). More than this, the interaction between the autofictional and hyperreal modes works to stimulate a situated form of subjectivity. The postmodern tropes in *Windows on the World* may be self-conscious or even self-indulgent, but they are continually undercut by or used in pursuit of a deeper hermeneutic engagement, an emotional attachment that recognises that the real victims of 9/11, like Carthew, 'died for you and you and you and you and you and you and you and you' (2004, 300). In both *I Love Dick* and *Windows on the World*, the fragmented and constructed postmodern mode of being is shown to be inadequate precisely because it fails to account for lived experiences. In both novels, forms of artifice – such as metatextual or hyperreal representations – are employed not to loosen the subject from the grip of time, place and selfhood. On the contrary, the fictional counterparts of Chris Kraus and Frédéric Beigbeder seek ways to ground themselves – whether through travelling to New York or explicitly narrativising the self using the first-person *I*. By locating the embodied self in an external socio-political world, such grounding has ethical force: it reinforces the corporeality of bodies, of the self in the body and in connection with others, and the potentiality of personal affective experience.

CONCLUSION

While Jameson argued that postmodernism was characterised by a waning of affect, the analyses in this chapter suggest that affect has re-emerged, re-awoken. Specifically, contemporary autofictions show that affect as a possibility has revitalised within a situated model of subjectivity. In doing so, autofictions attempt to ground the inner self in an outer reality – in time, space and corporeal being. Examining two works of contemporary autofiction – Chris Kraus's *I Love Dick* and Frédéric Beigbeder's *Windows on the World* – this chapter has demonstrated that while the postmodernist sense of subjectivity (as fragmented, socially constructed and textually fabricated) persists, it does so alongside a renewed desire to recognise personal feelings and interpersonal connections.

Contemporary autofictions do not only narrativise the self, but they also thematise the sociological and phenomenological dimensions of personal life such as how identities relate to social roles, how time and space are lived and how experience is often mediated by textual and/or digital communication. It is in this sense that metamodern affect is situational; it is ironic yet sincere, sceptical yet heartfelt, solipsistic yet desiring of connection. Most of all, it is experiential. Autofictions may also ruminate on global concerns such as terrorism and the environment or place the self in relation to conflicts, thus exploring an individual's ethical responsibilities to and affective engagements with socio-political events. This is because contemporary crises have reformed affective sensibilities. Recent events such as the terrorist attack of 11 September 2001 and the global financial crash of 2008 have shaken the stronghold of postmodernity, its antianthropomorphism, its cool detachment. Indeed, scholars of the contemporary have noted both a renewed 'affection for affect' (Brinkema 2014, xiv) and a prevailing sense of anxiety which 'has surely returned with a vengeance' (Beasley-Murray 2010, 126; see also Lipovetsky 2005; Woodward 2009; Mack 2014). In a crisis-ridden world, subjects are once more driven by a desire for attachment to others and to their surroundings (wherever boundaries are drawn between in-group and out-group or between inside and outside). In such a fragile and fragmentary reality, the decentred self reasserts itself by grounding its subjectivity in lived experience as well as in the interactions between our bodies and our environments. The affective turn in autofiction, and in the humanities more generally, has a common thread: in Brinkema's words, 'ethics, politics, aesthetics – indeed, lives – must be enacted in the definite particular' (2014, xv).

Chapter 9

The Joke That Wasn't Funny Anymore: Reflections on the Metamodern Sitcom

Gry C. Rustad and Kai Hanno Schwind

When the hosts of the BBC's successful motor-themed programme *Top Gear* (BBC, 2002–present) indulged in some racist comments about Mexican culture (e.g. 'Mexican cars are just going to be lazy, feckless, flatulent, over-weight, leaning against a fence asleep looking at a cactus, with a blanket with a hole in the middle on as a coat'), most people stopped laughing. The joke wasn't funny anymore. In his commentary on the incident, British comedian Steve Coogan argues (2011):

> It's not entirely their fault, of course. Part of the blame must lie with what some like to call the 'postmodern' reaction to overzealous political correctness. Sometimes, it's true, things need a shakeup; orthodoxies need to be challenged. But this sort of ironic approach has been a licence for any halfwit to vent the prejudices they'd been keeping in the closet since *Love Thy Neighbour* was taken off the air.

Debates about the offensiveness of humour and comedy on television are as old as the medium itself. It seems, however, that in recent years, the past decade in particular, a shift in the tone of comedic discourses is evident across the spectrum of televisual formats and genres. From the racist jokes of British stand-up comedian Bernhard Manning in the 1970s, via what might be termed the 'decade of irony' in the 1990s, to the ascent of embarrass-ment humour in the 2000s through programmes such as *The Office* (BBC, 2001–2003), mediatised forms of humour now seem to be more interested in 'laughing with' rather than 'laughing at' the butt of the joke.

The shift in taste from 'laughing at' to 'laughing with' seems to emerge most manifestly in American television comedy. In the early twenty-first century, American sitcoms like *Community* (NBC 2009–2015), *Parks and*

Recreation (NBC 2009–2015) and *Louie* (FX 2010–2016) represented a markedly different tone of humour from postmodern shows. They also seem to mark a new trend in the American sitcom. Showrunner Mike Schur has continued his exploration of human kindness in *Brooklyn Nine-Nine* (FOX 2013), which treats the cops it is about as decent albeit goofy do-gooders and *The Good Place* (NBC 2016–) a high-concept science fiction that even poses the questions: 'What does it mean to be a good person?' Louis CKs *Louie* has been quite influential, and we can trace the tendency to be 'laughing with' in the Louis CK–produced semi-biographic anthology comedies *Better Things* (HBO 2016–) and *One Mississippi* (Amazon 2015–). In these two comedies the viewers are invited to laugh with Pamela Aldon and Tig Notaro, respectively, and their everyday lives. *Community*'s live action aesthetics has perhaps not been as influential but can be found in *Son of Zorn* (FOX 2016–) where animated characters are mixed with real actors in order to dwell on the alienated relationship between father and son. We can also trace this development of 'laughing with' in other Anglo-American countries like the British sitcom *Catastrophe* (Channel 4 2015–) and Australian *Please Like Me* (ABC 2013) which both are 'laughing with' their flawed and deeply human characters in their search for human connection.

If this new generation of sitcoms is compared with some of the comedies of the late 1990s and early 2000s, a subtle shift in tone becomes apparent. Instead of the blank parody in shows such as *Family Guy* (FOX 1999–present) or the self-conscious superficiality and cynical resentment in *Seinfeld* (NBC 1990–1998), *Parks and Recreation*, *Community* and *Louie* encompass a human warmth often missing in their predecessors and are often characterised by a sincere yearning for meaning. There are still plenty of stylistic and formal similarities with postmodern practice, and it is not like the 'new' comedy can't be parodist, self-conscious or cynical, let alone superficial; they still appear, though, to signify a distinct change in the overall tone in humour. But what does this new tone of television humour entail? We understand tone in accordance with Pye, as 'the complex but seemingly automatic process which enables us to understand the kind of film we are watching and how it wants us to take it' (2007, 7). Tone thus lies in a film or, in our case, sitcom's address and how it communicates with its viewers.

This chapter explores the shift in sitcom tones and aesthetics from a postmodern to what we will argue is a metamodern comedic sensibility, and asks what this new metamodern tone and aesthetic of television humour might entail. We conceptualise what we take to be representative for the metamodern sitcom by investigating two different aesthetic categories, namely style and tone. These categories are interrelated: a programme's tone is inflected by its choices in style, but tone also encompasses how a programme communicates with its viewers through choices in narrative, dialogue, performance and music. Furthermore, we consider how choices in style and tone facilitate a distinct thematic sentiment. This metamodern sensibility is explored in detail by analysing three contemporary American sitcoms as follows: (1) *Community*'s style and how it seems to represent a metamodern sitcom aesthetics; (2) the performance tone and temperature of *Louie* which is located in a historic context of the stand-up as performer sitcom; and (3) the narrative scope and socio-cultural trajectories of *Parks and Recreation*. The latter analysis enables a discussion of a metamodern sitcom discourse and themes. Finally, these new shows are juxtaposed with two dominating postmodern sitcoms *Family Guy* and *Seinfeld*. We will focus on *Community*, and in particular *Louie* and *Parks and Recreation* because of their influence on current Anglo-American comedies.

SITCOM: HUMOUR, GENRE AND SOCIETY

In his study of contemporary sitcom, Antonio Savorelli asserts (2010, 176):

> Even some less conspicuous shows may have relevant roles as pressure valves, as fields of debate, as sources of inspiration. The public's mere need for laughter could not explain the success of a genre that remained for decades, if not unchanged, at least firmly anchored to its own productive principles.

In trying to identify a shift of tone within the sitcom genre, the question arises: how does situation comedy reflect the socio-cultural agenda(s) of the *zeitgeist* or, put in other words, how does humour take societies' temperature?

The vast and interdisciplinary field of humour studies proposes three main theories in order to explain what makes people laugh and why we experience jokes, performances and situations as funny: superiority, incongruity and relief. Without exploring these theories in detail, they all point to the fact that humour occurs as a result of social interaction between individuals and social groups. Hence, the kind of humour chosen reveals something about the values, codes and hierarchies prevailing within that certain group. Following out of that, we argue that humour in one of its most dominating mediatised forms, situation comedy on television, reflects on the social norms and taboos, as well as a general cultural *status quo* of (Western) society. Thus, we can assert 'a remarkable parallel between the themes of successful situation comedies and the social history of modern society' (Paterson 1998, 66).

No doubt, humour's volatile nature has influenced the sitcom genre throughout the past decades – from the anti-authoritative, feminist and politicised spirit of the 1970s, visible in shows such as *The Mary Tyler Moore Show* (CBS, 1970–1977) and *M*A*S*H* (CBS, 1972–1983), via the dichotomy of domestic conservativeness and subversiveness in 1980s sitcoms such as *Family Ties* (NBC, 1982–1989), *The Bill Cosby Show* (NBC, 1984–1992) and *Roseanne* (ABC, 1988–1997) and the postmodern irony of the 1990s in *The Simpsons* (FOX, 1989–present) and *Seinfeld* (NBC, 1989–1998) to the 00's excesses of mockumentary embarrassment in *Curb Your Enthusiasm* (HBO, 1999–present) or *The Office – An American Workplace* (NBC, 2005–2013) and intertextual play and self-reflexivity in live action sitcoms *Scrubs* (ABC, 2001–2010) and *30 Rock* (NBC, 2006–2012). Just as society changes, humour changes. In the next section, we turn our attention to one of the most recent tonal shifts of humour in a more detailed analysis of three contemporary sitcom formats: the intertextual and self-reflexive live action *Community*, the stand-up–based genre-defying *Louie* and the mockumentary *Parks and Recreation*.

FROM AN AESTHETIC OF FARTS TO HEARTS

Community, a comedy created by Dan Harmon, is about a group of different misfits attending Greendale community college. They end up in the same study group and eventually become friends. It centres on the hipster lawyer Jeff (Joel McHale); the overachieving, young girl with a former addiction to Adderall Annie (Alison Brie); the political correct idealist and buzz-kill Britta (Gillian Jacobs); the stupid jock Troy (Donald Glover); the divorced housewife turned student Shirley (Yvette Nicole Brown); the old, racist pig (Chevy Chase); and the borderline Asperger, pop-culture geek Abed (Danny Pundi).

The programme is often heralded for its clever self-reflectiveness, intertextual play and meta-referentiality (see, e.g., Emily Nussbaum's top ten list of 2010, *Entertainment Weekly*'s list of the top twenty-five Cult Shows from the past twenty-five years). *Community* has episodes spoofing everything from Louis Malle's (1981) film *My Dinner with Andre* ('Critical Film Studies' 2:19), Ken Burns documentaries ('Pillows and Blankets' 14:3) to spaghetti Westerns ('A Fist Full of Paintballs' 23:2) and zombie movies ('Epidemology' 6:3). With its use of parody, pastiche, intertextual play and irony – identified as some of the central characteristics of postmodern aesthetics by the likes of Eco (1993), Huyssen (1986) and Jameson (1991) – *Community* can, at first glance, be conceived to be a postmodern sitcom. Indeed, *Community* shares many aesthetic similarities with other live action comedies like *Scrubs* and *30 Rock* and animation comedies like *Family Guy*, with their excessive use of popular cultural references, irony, pastiches, parodies and throwaway jokes. Of these, *Family Guy* appears the most postmodern in style and will therefore serve as a point of comparison in our analysis of *Community*.

Crawford contends *Family Guy*'s use of parody, irony and pastiche results in a kind of magic realism and should be understood in light of the 'concerns of the postmodern age' (2009, 63). Drawing on Jameson's argument about postmodern aesthetics and culture she continues: 'The fact that *Family Guy* and many other prime time sitcoms are so sophisticated intertextually is due to the anxieties that the postmodern writer experiences. The postmodern writer feels there is nothing left to say' (63). *Family Guy* has translated this postmodern notion into an aesthetic often criticised for being blank and empty. Certainly, Trey Parker and Matt Stone have, for instance, criticised *Family Guy* for relaying too much on gag humour that has nothing to do with the story (Gillespie and Walker 2006). Crawford continues to argue that the pleasure of *Family Guy* lies in its aesthetic deconstruction.

The aesthetic function of *Community*'s intertextual play and use of parody and pastiche, however, does not appear to be deconstruction. It rather appears to function as an aesthetisation of the characters' quest for friendship and community. Take, for example, the episode 'Contemporary American Poultry' (21:1). The entire episode is more or less a pastiche on *Goodfellas* (Martin Scorsese, 1990) from the (freeze) framing and camera movements to the doo-wop music and the voice-over. The plot centres on something as silly as chicken fingers. The student-cafeteria's chicken fingers are immensely popular and run out fast. *Goodfellas*-style, the study group takes control of the production and distribution of the chicken fingers, turning it into a neat black market operation. As Abed states in his voice-over: 'The entire campus is controlled by our group. Our group is controlled by chicken and the chicken is controlled by me'. However, not everyone is happy with Abed obtaining so much power as the chicken finger cook/mob-leader. Jeff, the study group's unofficial leader starts to sabotage Abed's operation. In the inevitable comedown between the two, the episode takes an unexpected turn. The episode is revealed to depict something as real and raw as Abed's struggle with his un-diagnosed Asperger syndrome; Abed and Jeff share an incredibly sweet moment, deepening the characters' relationship and their emotions for each other. As such, what at first seemed like just another *Goodfellas* pastiche transcends into a character-developing vehicle for Abed and highlights Abed's struggle to connect to other humans. Indeed, the episode also resonates on a more general level, as it exposes and thematises the struggle to make genuine human connections and communities, thus connecting with the viewers emotionally.

Community's articulation of emotion and affect through parody and pastiche, and herein lies its difference to *Family Guy*, is perhaps most visible in the sitcom's animated episodes and sequences. In 'Foosball and Nocturnal Vigilantism' (3:9), the programme featured an anime-styled sequence of Jeff and Shirley playing foosball as they work through their childhood trauma

of being, respectively, the bullied and the bully. As the game is at its most
dramatic, the scene switches to animation and Shirley and Jeff are, during
their game of foosball, transported to the top of a dramatically drawn moun-
tain cliff in the style of Japanese anime. At once, the animation visualises
the emotional drama underlining each angry scream and emotion, as well
as distancing the spectator from the characters' human selves. Similarly, in
the episode 'Abed's Uncontrollable Christmas' (11:2), Abed is only able
to process his feelings towards his absentee mother when he and the other
characters are turned into stop motion animation figures and transported to
a nostalgic, fantasy winter wonderland, indicating that he has to go back in
order to move forward. In 'Digital Estate Planning' (3:20), the group is turned
into eight-bit game animated characters, as they play to help Pierce win a
game his dad made before he died as a battle for his inheritance. During the
game, both Peirce and his father's assistant, revealed to be his brother, come
to terms with the passing of their father.

The animation sequences are interesting because they disrupt and distance
the viewers from the physical actors. The animation indeed allows for a kind
of magic realism but, unlike *Family Guy*, the magic realism does not function as deconstruction. The choice in animation style visualises and under-
scores the characters' emotional states and the themes of the episode. The
use of animation simultaneously creates aesthetic distance as well as a space
wherein real emotional connections occur. Thus, *Community*'s use of parody
and pastiche cannot be understood as empty and blank. Rather, it endows
the programme with emotional realism and meaning. If, as Jameson argues,
postmodern aesthetics' main characteristic is emptiness and blankness, *Community* cannot be postmodern.

If *Community*'s use of pastiche, parody and irony is not postmodern, it
should be conceptualised in the context of what follows postmodernism,
namely metamodernism. Vermeulen and van den Akker argue that we have
arrived at a stage where postmodernism can no longer explain certain tendencies in the arts and culture. Their account of irony, in particular, seems apt
to describe *Community*'s use of aesthetics. They write: 'Metamodern irony
is intrinsically bound to desire, whereas postmodern irony is inherently tied
to apathy' (2010, 10). *Community* does bestow its use of parody, pastiche
and intertextual play with ironic knowingness, but at the same time, perhaps
because intertextuality and irony have – after decades of postmodernism
– become so common, our desire to obtain connections, affect, feelings of
sincerity and empathy has to be articulated through popular cultural parody
and pastiche.

What this analysis of the use of style in *Community* demonstrates is that the
metamodern comic sensibility is not so much a question of a distinct style,
but is rather defined by the tone of the humour and the meaning the stylistic

tropes are imbued with. Thus, a metamodern sitcom is perhaps in particular defined by a specific comic tonality. Therefore, to conceptualise this shift in the sitcom genre we will now turn our attention to what appears to be a change in tone by comparing two on the surface very similar yet incredibly dissimilar sitcoms, and contextualise them more broadly in terms of the history of sitcom performances and humour.

PERFORMING COLD AND WARM: *SEINFELD* VS. *LOUIE*

There is an interesting moment in the HBO special *Talking Funny* (2011), in which four of the world's most well-known comedians (Ricky Gervais, Chris Rock, Jerry Seinfeld and Louis CK) engage in a conversation about their careers, comedy and humour. Jerry Seinfeld re-tells one of his favourite jokes by Louis CK. CK, watching in awe, concludes: 'That's a completely Seinfeld-ed version. You really polished it up'. Leaving the specifics of this particular joke aside, the little episode strikingly illustrates the fundamental differences between the comedians, as performers, as crafters of jokes, indeed as representatives of different comedic trajectories.

Jerry Seinfeld started out as a stand-up comedian on New York's comedy circuit in the late 1970s before gradually establishing himself as one of the most influential comedians on a global scale culminating with the sitcom *Seinfeld* (NBC, 1989–1998). Seinfeld created a unique comic voice based on his observational humour about the inanities of the everyday life faced by mostly white urban middle-class Americans, developing a comedic discourse about nothing. Interestingly, over a decade later, CK has had a similar ascent from the comedy clubs of New York City to the world of television sitcom. His humour, though equally observational, nevertheless has a more straightforward, personal, edgier, perhaps even tragic feel to it. For the purpose of this chapter, we will now juxtapose the performance styles as part of the comedic trajectory of both sitcoms, locating them within different historical camps with varying temperatures and identify them as representatives of respectively a postmodern and a metamodern humouristic tone.

Seinfeld: Romantic Love Is Not an Option

Whether *Seinfeld* can be described as the sitcom defining the 1990s is a tedious argument. Instead, it seems more appropriate to include it in a cluster of formats such as *Frasier* (NBC, 1993–2004), *Friends* (NBC, 1994–2004), *The Larry Sanders Show* (HBO, 1992–1998), *Everybody Loves Raymond* (CBS, 1996–2005), *Will and Grace* (1998–2006) and *The Simpsons* (FOX, 1989–present), which successfully illustrate the *zeitgeist* of the 1990s and represent the last heyday of successful sitcom programming on American network television before the arrival of the digital broadcast age. For instance, NBC's Must-See TV Thursday night line-up (1981–2014), which combined episodes of various sitcoms back-to-back into one generic televisual text, can be regarded as one of the most successful examples of attaching an audience to a particular slot of television programming. What *Seinfeld* did, however, was to carve out a distinct kind of humour, which interestingly contradicts many of the basic rules of trying to attach an audience to a television sitcom format and, as a consequence, established a postmodern notion of cynical detachment.

In the show, we encounter stand-up comedian Jerry Seinfeld playing a fictional version of himself, as well as his friends George (Jason Alexander), Kramer (Michael Richards) and Elaine (Julia Louis-Dreyfus). There are various plots the characters engage in, seemingly meaningless activities triggered by the urban experience of a life in Manhattan, with memorable plots such as a contest of who can withhold masturbation the longest ('The Contest' 11:4), an encounter with a bossy soup salesman ('The Soup Nazi' 6:7), a frustrating wait for a table in a restaurant, presented in real time ('The Chinese Restaurant' 11:2) or the desperate search for a parked car in a multilevel shopping mall car park ('The Parking Garage' 6:3). The storylines are framed by excerpts of Jerry Seinfeld performing routines as stand-up comedian, which often take up the themes of the episode.

The series successfully established a functioning world for its characters to exist in. However, *Seinfeld* neither actively tried to attract the largest audience possible nor play up to a lowest common denominator sitcom humour. Indeed, as Hurd suggests, 'The show actively resisted popularity: it even openly invited network disapprobation in its flagrant contempt for the firmly entrenched sitcom conventions so revered by network executives as indicators of commercial success' (2007, 763). It did so by refusing to indulge in the many possible options of soap opera narratives. Even though Jerry and Elaine have been dating in the past, there is no overarching narrative or plotline trying to get them back together in contrast to, say, *Friends*' Ross and Rachel, and they actually seem quite happy to not be together anymore ('The Note' 1:5, 'The Mango' 1:5). Even more so, all romantic relations of the main characters seem to have the single purpose of being objects of ridicule or serve as battle grounds for the protagonist's quirks, ticks and social anxieties – from Kramer's long line of bizarre dates – in 'The Puffy Shirt', Kramer dates a woman who is a 'low talker'; he converts a lesbian to heterosexuality ('The Smelly Car'); and dates a woman whose sole personification is that she has long fingernails ('The Pie') – via George's ill-fated engagement to Susan, which results in her death ('The Invitations' 24:7) to the portrayal of Jerry's parents whose depiction is first and foremost a parody of Jewish pensioners living in Florida. As O'Brien suggests, 'Seinfeld is defined by a series of refusals. Romantic love is not even a possibility' (1997, 13).

The series, again unlike *Friends*, does not necessarily opt for the 'friends as substitutes for family or partners' approach either. Rather, it presents its main protagonists as a group of highly neurotic people randomly stuck together and, possibly out of laziness and convenience, not bothering to move on to other personal relationships or indeed to, socially and psychologically, develop themselves. One could argue, of course, that this facet is mostly a result of the genre's elliptic nature denying its protagonists a true sense of growth and character development.

There is another aspect where the series is deliberately trying to avoid an audience's deeper emotional attachment or to encourage any kind of serious interest in the notion of empathy when engaging with its (main and supporting) characters: the aspect of cold performance. Mills, in his attempt of theorising sitcom performance, hints at this phenomenon when he admits (2005, 92):

> I find *Seinfeld* virtually unwatchable, and know I'm in a minority for saying so. Yet my problem with the programme has nothing to do with its politics, setting, characters, or any other of a number of factors; I just think it's really badly performed, with an overeager excessiveness that feels like the programme is trying too hard to demonstrate its funniness.

Even though there seems to be a general tendency to accuse Jerry Seinfeld in particular of 'bad' or 'slack acting' in the series (in fact, there are numerous websites dedicated to his tendency 'to corpse' in scenes and reacting with genuine laughter to the joke deliveries of his fellow actors), it seems more appropriate to ascribe the performance concept of *Seinfeld* to a constant desire to foreground the jokes and punch lines, and by no means to engage in an authentic portrayal of characters and behaviour. It thereby creates a 'cold performance style', which, in turn, reflects the cynicism and detachment of the series' comedic trajectory. Hence, *Seinfeld* was playing to an audience in the 1990s which was aware of the potential 'meaninglessness' of its everyday lives and which, through the series, was able to reconcile its fragmented and postmodern existence with the generic workings of a sitcom on prime time network television. In the words of Hurd (2007, 771):

> The world of *Seinfeld* is an aesthetic one, in which the meaning lies in each well-made episode and the show's thematic negation of the world of work its viewers are bound to. Rather than minutely dissecting 'the real world', as is often supposed in discussions of the meaning of 'nothing', *Seinfeld* transforms it into humour.

Thus, *Seinfeld* is indeed drenched in postmodern ironic apathy where the humour is first and foremost observationally distanced, highly judgmental and very often serves as an end in itself.

Louie: Drunk, Angry and Humanly Imperfect

If, then, the humour performed in *Seinfeld* is 'cold', we argue that the humour of *Louie* (FOX, 2010–) might derive from a cold world but is nevertheless performed with warmth. Louie CK has developed two sitcom formats to date: *Louie* and *Lucky Louie* (HBO, 2006). The latter, which only ran for one season before being cancelled, tried to combine the traditional multi-camera sitcom look, recorded in front of a live audience, with adult themes and language. *Louie*, CK's second attempt at the genre, proved more successful. In itself, it would be an interesting task to compare the comedic discourses of both of CK's sitcoms to determine why his first attempt failed to find an audience, but it extends the scope of this chapter. In this section, we juxtapose the aesthetics, narrative and performance style of *Louie* with our previous analysis of *Seinfeld*.

Louie is produced as a single-camera hybrid sitcom. A hybrid sitcom abandons the traditional generic features of sitcom, such as the laughter track, multi-camera shooting style and theatrical setting. On an aesthetic, narrative and performance level, it successfully borrows from other genres, such as television drama, soap or reality TV. The premise of *Louie* reads like a sibling to *Seinfeld*. Louie CK plays a fictional version of himself, a quite successful stand-up comedian living in New York City, divorced and sharing custody for his two daughters. There are a few recurring characters, most notably his daughters, his friend and, at times, love interest Pamela (Pamela Adlon). Although they are not featured as regular recurring sitcom characters, the sitcom also includes his brother Robbie (Robert Kelly), his shockingly young-looking agent Doug (Edward Gelbinovich) and his ex-wife Janet (Susan Kelechi Watson). The plots and storylines do not follow a linear structure; instead, the episodes are fragmented, consisting of bits and sequences, similar to a stand-up comedian's dramaturgy. Just like in *Seinfeld*, actual footage of Louie CK performing in comedy clubs frames most of the episodes. However, *Louie* is less a show about 'nothing', but much more about CK's own fictionalised accounts of how to reconcile his divided 'single-dad'/'stand-up comedian' personas. Explorations of the latter especially feature various meta-narratives commenting on the world of comedy with many actual comedians playing fictionalised versions of themselves.

On an aesthetic level, *Louie* departs significantly from the traditional sitcom-ness of *Seinfeld*: instead of laughter track or single camera shooting style, *Louie* opts for a sophisticated mixture of mockumentary arbitrariness and the cinematic mise-en-scene of the more recent films of Woody Allen (Susan E. Morse, Allen's regular editor, co-edits the series). In a way, the series' intro sequence perfectly encapsulates this dichotomy: it captures Louie CK on his way to work, ascending from the metro stop at Washington Square, walking to the streets of Chelsea and grabbing a slice of pizza before descending the stairs to the Comedy Cellar. CK's demeanour is passive, thoughtful, even world-weary and contradicts the chirpy cheerfulness of Jerry Seinfeld in his series. Similarly, the theme song, a re-recording of Ian Lloyds 1970s song 'Brother Louie' (an excerpt from the lyrics: 'Louie, Louie, Louie you're gonna cry/Louie, Louie, Louie you're gonna die!') sets the tone for the melancholic, often lethargic tone of the series and could not be further from *Seinfeld*'s slap-bass happiness.

Despite *Seinfeld* and *Louie* fictionalising the same world – the life of a stand-up comedian in New York City – their depictions could not be more different. Where the experiences of *Seinfeld*'s protagonists are drenched in sitcom wackiness and populated by artificial characters who mostly serve as targets for the distanced and cynical mockery of Jerry and his friends, the world of *Louie* consists of gritty New York streets and apartments, the shabby and narrow backstage areas of comedy clubs, populated by 'authentic' people. The tonality of the series is fuelled by its main protagonist's feelings of oscillation between personal doubt and self-loathing on the one hand and a desperate search for love and human kindness on the other.

Returning to our analogy of performance temperature in the sitcom genre, *Louie* serves as a striking example of what Mills identifies as the switch between serious and comic modes of sitcom performance, arguing that 'sitcom performance is not purely comic performance, just as all comic performance, in theatre, stand-up, film and radio, often uses a variety of interpretive modes' (2005, 90). To illustrate the length to which *Louie* is willing to go to display the serious mode of performance with the sitcom genre and how this influences the comedic tonality of the show, we would like to single out a sequence of the episode 'Eddie' (9:2). Here, Louie runs into his old friend and fellow comedian Eddie (Doug Stanhope) whom he has not seen in years. The two started out together as young comedians, before Eddie got jealous of Louie's success and broke with him. Now he is back and invites Louie to take a nightly drive. Louie soon realises that Eddie has truly hit rock bottom: he is living out of his car and is an alcoholic. When they stop at an open mike show in a small club in Brooklyn, Eddie goes on to perform and actually delivers some funny material, but on their way back to the car, with the Brooklyn Bridge looming in the background, he reveals to Louie that he is thinking of ending his life. He indulges in a rant of self-pity where he claims: 'I don't want anything. I don't want anybody. That's the worst part. When the want goes, that's bad'. Louie, visibly disturbed by the entire encounter, then delivers a monologue in which he reflects on Eddie's failures and general outlook on life:

> Fuck you, man. I got my reasons to live. I worked hard trying to figure out what they are, I am not just handing them to you . . . ok. You want a reason to live? Have a drink of water, and get some sleep, wake up in the morning and try again like everybody else does . . . You know, you're laying this shit on me . . . *(a couple, loudly arguing walks by and interrupts them)* . . . Listen man . . . I . . . I haven't seen you in twenty years, and you're right, I don't think much about you . . . I hope you don't kill yourself . . . I really do . . . but I gotta go home. I gotta pick up my kids in the morning.

After the fragmented nature of the episode's plot up to this point and Louie CK's performance as passive observer, among other things subtly playing out how his fictional self struggles with drinking too much cheap booze out of a bottle – a nuanced, but nevertheless sitcom(ic) moment – he then switches mode into serious acting and grounds his character in a way which used to be unthinkable for this genre only some years back, delivering the speech with a humble sense of bewilderment that his character is confronted with these thoughts, at this hour, in this place. *Louie* compared to the apathy of Eddie (and *Seinfeld*) is filled with a detached desire for life. As TV critic James Poniewozik observes (2011):

> It would be so easy for the scene to become preachy. It would be easy to deflate it, to lower the stakes and puncture the tension, to assure us that, nah, Eddie not really going to off himself in a crappy motel in Maine. Instead, Louie never relents on the idea that this is a dead-serious moment, and it has the character Louie make the case for life in a drunk, angry, humanly imperfect way.

This kind of acting, then, which refuses to sacrifice all of a characters' frictions and contradictions for a joke or a laugh (like the more postmodern *Seinfeld*), and is primarily interested in portraying authentic emotions in realistic human beings, is metamodern and what we call 'warm performance style'.

PARKS AND RECREATION: TAKING ON THE TOWN

The transition from cold to warm performance style, we argue, signifies a shift from a postmodern to a metamodern tone and sensibility. *Community* and *Louie* both represent a warmer tone of humour that we would term metamodern. The metamodern tone of humour seems to encompass a certain sentiment and world view, and like the metamodern discourse seems to be 'inspired by a modern naïveté yet informed by postmodern scepticism, the metamodern discourse consciously commits itself to an impossible possibility' (Vermeulen and van den Akker 2010, 5).

This sentiment – and the constant oscillation between naïveté and scepticism, and the commitment to the impossible possibility – is perhaps particularly evident in NBC's critically acclaimed mockumentary comedy *Parks and Recreation*, created by Greg Daniels and Michael Schur. It centres on the life of the employees of the Parks and Recreation Department in the small fictional town Pawnee, Indiana. Through six seasons, viewers have been able to follow the main character, dedicated civil servant and the assistant director of the Park Department Leslie Knope (Amy Phoeler), fight to fill a hole and turn it into a park, organise a Harvest Festival, run for city council and fight to keep her city council seat under the threat of a recall vote.

What sets *Parks and Recreation* apart as a comedy is its focus not only on the core group of colleagues but also on political process and the town of Pawnee. For a sitcom to focus on an entire town's politics is quite unique; usually, sitcoms focus on the family, a group of friends or a workplace. The situations in the sitcom usually arise in a domestic or a workplace setting; thus the fictional world of the sitcom has traditionally been limited to the family, the family of friends or the work place family (Mills 2009). Often, characters seem to only interact with the core ensemble with some recurring characters and guest stars. *Parks and Recreation* with its focus on local government has a rather unique all-encompassing world view. Schur has even compared his sitcom to the expansive socio-political urban drama *The Wire* (HBO 2002–2007) in terms of scope (see Rosenberg 2012). Like *The Wire*, the bureaucracy in *Parks and Recreation* is sometimes treated as surreal, irrational and – as Leslie's libertarian boss would argue – a giant waste of money. Unlike *The Wire*, though, bureaucracy and civil servants are mostly represented with sincerity and as something positive.

Take, for example, the episode 'Sweetums' (15:2). The Park department has struck a deal with the local candy factory, Sweetums, and is supposed to start selling its energy bars from concessions stands. When it turns out that the energy bars only contain high fructose corn syrup and are extremely unhealthy, Leslie and her friend the nurse Ann (Rashinda Jones) try to stop the deal by hosting a town meeting to inform the public of the health risk. However, during the town meeting it becomes clear that the citizens of Pawnee are happy eating sugar, as one of the citizens argues: 'If sugar is so bad, why did Jesus make it taste so good?' Even after Leslie and Ann have explained how bad the energy bars are, the citizens still vote to let the 'heartless corporation, Sweetums stuff [their] children with sugary "crap"'. After being defeated Leslie mutters: 'We did our job, we informed the public, that's all we can do'.

Leslie's idealistic spirit is often crushed by the citizens of Pawnee, but she still continues fighting for the best of its citizens, whether they want her to or not. The season six storyline – where angry citizens want a recall of the city council election because, among other things, Leslie fought for a law banning enormous soda cans – is telling precisely because Leslie fights for the citizens' best interests, even though if she ultimately loses her job. What separates the postmodern *Family Guy* and *Seinfeld* and the metamodern *Parks and Recreation*, *Community*, and *Louie* lies in a difference of sentiment informing the tone of humour and style.

Postmodernism is often associated with the death of meaning and grand narratives, a disbelief in progress and reason, and the idea of linear progress is replaced by deconstruction, irony, nostalgia and nihilism. This sentiment was in the late 1980s first translated into a handful of dysfunctional family sitcoms like *Married with Children* (FOX 1987–1997), *Roseanne* and *The Simpsons*, and eventually into the blank and entirely cold *Seinfeld* and *Family Guy*. The characters in *Community*, *Parks and Recreation* and *Louie* seem to live by a 'this is going to hell, but in the end at least we tried' mentality. It is particularly visible in *Parks and Recreation* because of its grand scope and focus on politics, but it is also apparent in how *Community* tends to end every episode with all the characters rallying to help each other establish a tiny community. It is also apparent in *Louie* and how, despite being tough, he always seems to lose the girl or the job; he is still aiming to be a good comedian, friend, boyfriend (material), lover and dad. The characters Eddie and Louie in the scene discussed earlier are perhaps the perfect manifestation of postmodern and metamodern sentiments, respectively. Where Eddie has lost all desire, Louie has also struggled with finding 'a reason to live', and knows that he has to pick up his kids tomorrow. These characters seem to be defined by their commitment to impossible possibilities.

CONCLUSION

Tracing tendencies in the sitcom is difficult because of the wide variety of (often-conflicting) formats, styles, temperatures and sentiments that characterise both the history of the genre and the contemporary American sitcom. Our case studies – *Parks and Recreation*, *Louie* and *Community* – are contemporaries of other comedies, including (to mention a few): the very Seinfeldesque *The League* (FX 2009–2016); many traditional multi-cam sitcoms like the somewhat 'cold' *Two and A Half Men* (CBS 2003–present) and the 'warmer' *The Big Bang Theory* (CBS 2007–present); a 'cold' cynical animation sitcom like *Archer* (FX 2008–present) and a 'warm' one like *Bob's Burgers* (FOX 2010–present); and warm mockumentary sitcoms like *Modern Family* (ABC 2009–present). However, *Community*, *Louie* and *Parks and*

Recreation stand out in their balancing acts, constantly oscillating between parody and sincerity, apathy and desire, naïveté and scepticism.

The shift in tone from the coldness of *Family Guy* and *Seinfeld* to the warmth of *Community*, *Louie* and *Parks and Recreation*, as well as their distinct world view and discourse indicates that a shift in comedic tone is prevalent. As *Parks and Recreation* and *Community* ended in 2015 and *Louie* is on hiatus, their legacy is as mentioned continued. *Parks and Recreation*'s focus on human idealism is continued in *Brooklyn Nine-Nine* where the cops portrayed come across as the idealised version of cops – true civil servants. *The Good Place* drives this exploration even further focusing on the afterlife. The answer to what constitutes a good person seems to be that there are no really good people just flawed ones who do their best. *Louie*'s search and longing for genuine human connections is continued in *Better Things* where viewers follow Pamela Aldon's everyday struggles as a single mom and aging actress and *One Mississippi* as Tig Notaro's return to her home town to deal with the passing of her mum. Like *Louie* these two programmes focus on felt everyday situations, like a the death of a parent or the struggles of single parenting facilitate an affective feeling of lived-in-ness not found in the postmodern sitcoms

These situation comedies feel metamodern because they derive from a specific cultural logic within Western capitalist societies (van den Akker and Vermeulen, this volume) in which sitcoms as products of television entertainment merge the mode of production with their distinct mockumentary aesthetics and focus on everyday life. It is here that a clash between irony and authenticity emerges, reconciling audiences with flawed and complex, but ultimately lovable characters.

Section III

DEPTH

iii. Metamodern Depth, or 'Depthiness'

Timotheus Vermeulen

In her introduction to the second section of this book, my co-editor Alison Gibbons invokes Jameson's discussion of Vincent Van Gogh's painting *A Pair of Boots* and Andy Warhol's photo print *Diamond Dust Shoes* to exemplify the distinction between modern and postmodern affect – between sensation and euphoria – as well as to set up the discussion for a third modality of thinking about affect, one that we would call metamodern: postirony, an informed naivety, or rather still, perhaps, a hypocritical sensitivity (less affect than affectedness) towards self and others. I, too, would like to draw on this discussion about shoes to construct the book's final argument about the resurfacing of depth. For if Jameson's discussion of Van Gogh and Warhol's shoes differentiates between two modes of feeling, it also – and relationally – distinguishes one approach of perceiving from another: what Jameson calls the 'depth-model' (1991 [1984]) – whereby the world that appears to us, the world that we see, is a reflection, an expression, a symptom of what you might, with some liberty, call 'noumena', an invisible realm behind or beneath it, a hinter- or nether-world – and the 'surface-model', in which what you see is what you get.

As Gibbons noted, Jameson's assertion about these pairs of shoes is that Van Gogh's *A Pair of Boots*, painted in thick, 'hallucinatory' colours and with 'raw materials' (1991 [1984], 7), intimates a lived context outside the painting – the artist's state of mind, for instance, or the 'brutal', 'backbreaking' (1991 [1984], 7) agricultural reality of the farmer – whereas Warhol's nondescript monochrome photo print betrays neither authorial voice nor a definitive or at least traceable reality behind the screen. Indeed, as Jameson points out, this picture lets on so little that it could just as well depict the cover of a glossy magazine, a 'pile of shoes left over from Auschwitz or the remainders and tokens of some incomprehensible and tragic fire in a packed dance hall' (1991 [1984], 8). Van Gogh's painting pulls the viewer into the world it depicts, extends our gaze beyond the paint, behind the canvas. Warhol's print, by contrast, pushes us back, cuts short the 'hermeneutic gesture' (1991 [1984], 8) to suggest, as the artist would later himself explain, that 'there is nothing behind it' (Berg 1989, 56). To put it in so many words: Van Gogh's shoes are worn-out sandals, his feet register every rain drop, each little bump in the road. Warhol is wearing the latest Nike Air Max, if you will, the advertised 'Air' a buffer between feet and ground, dulling the sensations. This does not mean he is actually floating, that the ground no longer exists; what it means is that it no longer matters what the ground is made of – grass, stones, fire: Warhol does not feel it all that much, he is not himself burdened by it.

The chapters in this section each suggest that current artists, writers and activists have stepped into another footwear trend, to stick with the metaphor, one which neither allows contact with an ultimate ground nor negates it, but instead performs it. To be more precise: this trend draws on the techniques of Warhol, of Air Max, to portend, to pretend, the effect of Van Gogh's peasant shoes. The shoes that Irmtraud Huber and Wolfgang Funk, Sam Browse, and Raoul Eshelman describe and perform the outside, the rain drops and the bumps in the road, to such an extent that it is a reality we could imagine walking in: not the 'brutal' reality but a brutal(ised/isable) reality.

In his contribution to *Metamodernism: Historicity, Affect and Depth after Postmodernism*, Eshelman – one of the pioneers in the study of post-postmodernism and, though we disagree on a number of issues, a major influence on our own thinking – writes about unity in performatist photography and speaks of pictures 'creating an impression' of a 'source' that is itself 'not directly accessible'. This impression is 'the effect of transcendence – a transcendence that is formally palpable'; the underlying causes remain ultimately out of reach – and thus, unsubstantiated. Similarly, discussing authenticity in Ali Smith's novel *How to Be Both*, Huber and Funk contemplate the responsibility imparted onto the reader to affectively 'delineate' depth even though – or precisely because – it 'cannot be mapped in any objectively meaningful way'. Finally, Browse takes on the phenomenon of post-truth politics, contrasting the postmodern 'mimetic' sincerity of Tony Blair, in which one's persona is mirrored on the watching audience in front of him, to Jeremy Corbyn's 'curated' earnestness, which suggests it selects from the experiences of the public behind him.

As I am sure the reader will find, there is far more to these essays than the single strand I reduce them to here. They elaborate and question, diversify and move on. Above all, also, they express differing opinions, from one another as well as, in some instances, the view of the editors. This, I think, makes the semblance all the more striking. If, in Jameson's words, the nineteenth and early twentieth-century depth-model was premised on the presumption that surfaces reflect depth – Van Gogh's shoes reflect the toil of the land, bodily symptoms reflect psychological conditions, actions reflect an authentic soul – and the postmodern repudiation of that model insists on simulacra – the short circuits of Warhol's photographs, but also Venturi's hotchpotch architecture, and the so-called nostalgia films, flattening a rocky, potholed history to a smooth, glossy glaze, discourse theory with its emphasis on social conditioning over interiority – each of the authors in this section, in spite of their individual approaches and indubitable differences, suggests that contemporary artists, activists and writers feel that appearances may well inspire sensations of an outside, of an elsewhere – even if the existence of that elsewhere is by no means certain, often even unlikely or impossible. You could also say: the modernists excavated depth from the surface, the postmodernists flattened it by means of the surface, the metamodernists apply depth onto the surface. The phenomena, movements and debates not described in this section that could be theorised in the same terms are manifold, from the popular post-positivism Gibbons contemplates in her chapter of this book to the speculative art history that Sjoerd van Tuinen pursues in his chapter, to object oriented philosophy (Wolfendale 2014), to the frankly frightening populist mythmaking of the alt right and other demagogic movements in politics (see Heiser, this volume).

A few years ago, in an essay on surfaces in contemporary art published in *E-Flux*, I described a sensibility very similar to the one theorised here with a wink as the 'new depthiness' (2015). As I explained in that essay, the notion of depthiness is a composite of Jameson's depthlessness and comedian Stephen Colbert's gimmick of 'truthiness' (2006), a term that connotes a sense of truth established not through empirical research or rational reasoning but through the affective register of the 'gut': regardless of what the facts suggest, or even common sense, if it feels true, to you, in your belly, it may well be true, for you. Depthiness in this sense is the establishment of depth not as a shared epistemological reality but as one among many personally performed (im)possibilities – which is, to be sure, not to say they cannot be shared, but rather that they are by no means necessarily shared.

If metamodernism as we conceive it here can be summarily described as the return of historicity, affect and depth, it is a return that should be understood above all as a desperate but wishful attempt to think, feel and perceive historically, spatially and corporeally. This may well be effective – and even considered necessary – in the short run but, given its irreconcilable tensions, it seems to me entirely unsustainable in the long haul. That is, it is an assault, sure, on the feedback loop of late capitalism, but also, not unlikely, a by-effect of another stage of capitalism, a stage characterised less by the short-circuiting of the present than by a Marty McFlyesque dissolution of the certainties of the past and the present into increasingly atomized – and indeed, intangible, simulated rather than experiential, logical rather than rational – speculations about the future (see Avanessian 2016b).

What is needed therefore, and what the following chapters offer, is an exploration of the nature of depthiness (or depthinesses), its possibilities and its limitations, its inner logic, if there is one, and its ethos. These chapters map this metamodern territory of hitherto uncharted – and, to be sure, existent only in the performance – spaces and the implications it holds for our larger semiosphere.

Chapter 10

Reconstructing Depth: Authentic Fiction and Responsibility

Irmtraud Huber and Wolfgang Funk

Ho this is a mighty twisting thing fast as a
    fish being pulled by its mouth on a hook
        if a fish could be fished through a
            6 foot thick wall made of bricks or an
        arrow if an arrow could fly in a leisurely
    curl like the coil of a snail or a
star with a tail if the star was shot
    upwards past maggots and worms and
        the bones and the rockwork

In this poetic beginning of one part of Ali Smith's novel *How to Be Both* (2014: 3/189),[1] depth is literally dragged to the surface: the fish pulled up from the deep, the star shot upwards out of the earth, the dead past brought up into the present. At the same time, meaning also manifests on the surface of form in the twisting coil of the typesetting, while the insistent assonances and consonances of the passage emphasise its formal structure in their phonetic playfulness. Attention is drawn to the text as text, carefully composed and presented on the surface of the page. Nonetheless, this part of the novel introduces a highly colloquial (and in its diction, insistently oral) first-person narrative voice: the ghost of the Renaissance painter Francesco del Cossa, who for some reason is called up from the dead into the present day of the year 2014 to witness the novel's other protagonist, teenaged George, cope with the premature and unexpected death of her mother and with the first experiences of love. Like the ghost of Hamlet's father in Derrida's (1994) evocative interpretation, this ghost, oscillating between past and present, absence and presence, effects a foreclosure of conclusion and demands engagement. The editors of this volume have identified oscillation as a crucial characteristic of that particular contemporary 'structure of feeling' they identify as 'metamodernism'. While metamodernism, as the editors explain in the introduction, necessarily and programmatically remains vague and general, our approach in this chapter and beyond focuses on specific aesthetic forms and draws on narratological categories. We thus propose and outline the term 'reconstruction' for the form of engagement which is induced by the oscillation of the artwork, an engagement which appeals to the reader's authentic responsibility in their encounter with the text. We offer *reconstruction* as a complementary, more specifically formal approach to understanding the encouraging in-betweenness (*metaxy*) of the metamodern paradigm.

RECONSTRUCTION

At first glance, *How to Be Both* has many features that might mark it as a prime example for a postmodernist aesthetics of playful self-consciousness and subversive criticism of master narratives. Throughout, it remains highly conscious of its textual status, and it presents a non-linear, fragmented plot-line, with interchangeable parts, one of which is narrated by a ghost who gives voice to a historical figure about whom next to nothing is known today. Historical authority is contrasted with the highly individualised and subjective vision of fiction. Protagonist Francescho (who, departing from the 'official' spelling, refers to herself with an additional 'h') is imagined as a cross-dressed woman, thereby implying a reason for the painter's obscurity while at the same time counteracting the historical silence. Both the novel's protagonists continually renegotiate and undermine gender distinctions and most of the depicted love relationships defy heteronormativity in one way or the other. Even the novel's title *How to Be Both* recalls the frequent characterisation of postmodernism as favouring a stance of 'both/and' as opposed to a modernist 'either/or' (Hutcheon 1988: 49).

It is precisely this proximity to a postmodernist aesthetics and agenda that makes the departure from postmodernism in novels like *How to Be Both* most striking. Smith's novel shifts its focus from a postmodernist emphasis on depthless surfaces to an attempt to acknowledge and sound the depths of human relationships and the role of art. Instead of deconstructing surfaces to reveal the absences gaping beneath, glimpses are offered of a depth that is full of meaning and relevance, even if it may not be directly accessed. In this sense, the title of the novel may also be brought in relation to Vermeulen and van den Akker's suggestion that metamodernism relates to its predecessors modernism and postmodernism in 'a 'both-neither' dynamic', in a 'double-bind . . . of a modern desire for *sens* and a postmodern doubt about the sense of it all' (2010).

We take *How to Be Both* to be exemplary for a wider development in recent literature, which is characterised by a shift away from postmodernism and which has been variously called metamodernism (Vermeulen and van den Akker 2010; Gibbons 2015), post-postmodernism (McLaughlin 2012), performatism (Eshelman 2008; this volume) and renewalism (Toth), among others. With our focus less on questions of literary periodisation and more on the effects and practices of the recent shift, we prefer to speak of a *literature of reconstruction*. We thus offer our observations in this chapter as a literary case study, a specific aesthetic formation indicative of a literary trend which contributes to the new cultural moment metamodernism strives to come to terms with. The focus in our respective work has been the ways in which recent narratives take their cue from postmodernist insights and deconstructive impulses, but explore the ways in which fictionality and meta-referentiality may serve in the endeavour to reconstruct some kind of meaning that allows for intersubjective communication, for human connection and for a paradoxical authenticity. Funk (2015) explores various reconstructions of authenticity by way of the formal procedure of metareferentiality in works by Dave Eggers, Julian Barnes, Jasper Fforde and Jennifer Egan. Huber (2014) considers the role of embedded fantastic stories in recent novels by Jonathan Safran Foer, Mark Z. Danielewski, David Mitchell and Michael Chabon, in which the potential of fiction to reconstruct communication and meaning is gauged in spite of a persistent postmodernist scepticism towards the possibility of representation.

Like its significant other, deconstruction, reconstruction should not first and foremost be seen as a neutral signifier that can or cannot be applied to a given text. It should instead be understood as both a configuration that is inherent in a literary text qua its very specific formal organisation and as a mode of answering and addressing the challenge presented by this textual surface. It represents what Derrida calls a 'performative interpretation, that is, . . . an interpretation that transforms the very thing it interprets' (1994: 51). Literature, as seen through the prism of reconstruction, cannot but appeal to the response-ability of the reader, and the subjective form that the individual responses will take vouchsafes for the authenticity of the individual literary encounter. Reconstruction is thus a strategy of reading as well as a potential that literary texts may activate to a varying degree by means of specific aesthetic and formal features.

In order to account for the nature of this authenticity and thus for the aesthetic principle on which our understanding of reconstruction/responsibility/reciprocity rests, we propose the importance of a critical attention to form. We understand form not as a static container that may be filled with meaning, but rather as a dynamic challenge, as, in the words of Attridge, 'performed mobility, as a performance of reading answering to a performance of writing'

(2004: 111). Literature is thus conceived as a 'formal act-event' (2004: 111) which both conditions and appeals to the reader's response-ability, a challenge in which 'to respond fully to a literary work is to be responsively and responsibly aware of [its] otherness, and of the demands it makes upon us' (2004: 120). We now want to address more specifically the issues of how the necessary formed-ness of literature is, and at the same time also in*forms*, the framework for a text's impact and interpretation. Based on this, we will show how the paradigmatic changes that we have subsumed under the heading of 'reconstruction' can and need to be analysed as formal features and effects of the literary works in question.

FORM, THE FICTIVE AND READER RESPONSE-ABILITY

This insistence on the foundation of reconstructive effects in primarily formal features is all the more imperative, since the principal terms on which our analysis of such tendencies in contemporary literature is based – authenticity and responsibility – are notoriously hypothetical and intuitive. An enquiry into the strategies of reconstruction entails an exploration of the various ways in which a literary text subverts its own inescapable constitution as a mere surface, or in other words, how it paradoxically writes back against its ineluctable depthlessness by performatively pricking, indenting or displacing the surface boundary that separates the text from its reader.

The presence of form in any kind of art is very lightly taken for granted; after all, any artwork must assume some form in order to be appreciated. Leighton (2007) reminds us, however, that the essence of form transcends its function of rendering matter perceptible, of introducing order into reality. Form, she argues, connects and disrupts, situates and unsettles; it 'is a go-between, an interval, an interrupter, breaking the norms of representation and obstructing the passage from thing to name' (2007: 20). Being other than thing or name, it refutes both the logic of pure materialism and symbolic representation (2007: 21). It hints at a depth beyond the surface of representation and, crucially, this interstitial quality comes with an exhortation to mind, and mediate, the gap between the thing and its representation, to attend to the traces of all that form is not, cannot be.

At this point, Leighton's concept of form can be fruitfully related to Iser's (1993) understanding of the constitution of the fictive in fictionalising acts. Iser's concept is based on a triadic structure in which the fictive as process negotiates between the determinacy of the real and the indeterminacy of the imaginary: 'Just as the fictionalizing act outstrips the determinacy of the real, so it provides the imaginary with the determinacy that it would not otherwise possess' (1993: 3). The fictionalising acts – which Iser names as selection, combination and self-disclosure – are thus, in essence, processes of giving form. At the same time, however, they introduce a play space by their inherent structure of doubling. Selection and combination always emerge against the background of what has been excluded, while self-disclosure functions in the dual logic of the 'as if' (Iser 1993: 13 and passim), in which readers are forced to both apply and question their natural attitudes towards the presented world. Thus, 'the doubling structure of these fictionalizing acts creates the area of play by holding on to everything that has been overstepped, thus making it a partner in the game of countermoves' (Iser 1993: 229).

From this perspective, literature (which Iser equates with the fictive), itself paradoxically invested both in reality and in the imaginary, figures as the objective correlative of form in Leighton's sense, as it is 'neither an unreferential pure play nor an ideologically coded impure play. It is a play between the two . . . in which things are not obviously quite useful or known, and where their meanings might not be quite what we expect – which is not to say that there is no meaning at all' (Leighton 2007: 123). Literature does not have form, it is form; but, 'because it exceeds what is, [it] is imbued with an intention that can never totally control what it aims at' (Iser 1993: 230–31). Short-circuiting Iser and Leighton in this way thus highlights the way in which both intentionality and reader response-ability emerge in form, a potential that a novel like *How to Be Both* activates by way of the various reconstructive endeavours to which we attend below.

AUTHENTICITY, DEPTH AND METAREFERENCE

While in common understanding both form and the fictive could be seen as standing in contradiction to a notion of authenticity, they are both, at a closer look, implicated in its central paradox, which presents itself in what Culler calls the 'dilemma of authenticity' (1988: 164) – that, by definition, authenticity escapes any attempt at definition. 'To be experienced as authentic', Culler suggests, something 'must be marked as authentic, but when it is marked as authentic it is mediated, a sign of itself, and hence lacks the authenticity of what is truly unspoiled, untouched by mediating cultural codes' (1988: 164). Authenticity, in other words, aspires to unformed immediacy and non-fictive truth but can only ever manifest in and as fictive form (for a comprehensive archaeology of authenticity, see Funk 2015: 13–66).

As far as literary discourse, and our argument here, is concerned, authenticity's foundational paradox of 'mediated immediacy' (*vermittelte Unmittelbarkeit*; Zeller 2010: 8 and passim) finds its formal correlative in the aesthetic procedure of metareference, which we define as a textual strategy of self-reference that results in fundamental epistemological ambiguities or ontological paradoxes which cannot be resolved within the surface structure of the text itself (Funk 2015: 87). Metareference thus deliberately foregrounds and amplifies the effects of doubling and dual-countering which Iser identified as fundamental to all fictionalising acts. It seems important to emphasise that a reconstruction of authenticity by means of metareference operates beyond and independent from questions about the possibility of truthful representation. Instead, reconstruction puts its focus on the potential of fictionality as a communicative strategy which aims towards an activation of the reader's response-ability, an endeavour which is related to the reciprocal trust between author and reader at the base of Hassan's notion of 'fiduciary realism' (2003: 9).

The metaphorical deep structure which results from the response-ability necessitated by attending to such metareferential disruptions of textual logic conflates the (post)structuralist surface separation of author, reader and text as distinct entities and, in doing so, dissolves the text as surface and renders it an immersive site. With a nod to Vermeulen's image of the snorkeler as the explorer of a new metamodern 'depthiness' (2015), we suggest that some examples of contemporary literature imagine and bring into form a kind of authentic depth, which cannot be mapped in any objectively meaningful way but which is nevertheless delineated by the reader's responsibility.

Leighton claims that form, if imagined visually, can be understood as 'the distribution of space caused by edging one thing against another, so that each calls attention to the other' (2007: 16). In addition to this spatial doubleness, in which form emerges as 'both a container and a deflector' (Leighton 2007: 16), Luhmann emphasises the temporal duplicity of what he calls the 'Paradox of Form' (1999: 19):

> From a structural point of view, the two-sided form only exists in the temporal mode of simultaneity; operationally considered, however, the two-sided form can only be actualized in consecutive operations since operations that proceed from one side exclude operations that proceed from the other side. The form is the simultaneity of sequentiality.

When, in what follows, we read *How to Be Both* as a case in point for a reconstructive tendency in contemporary fiction, we argue that Smith's novel can be seen as an attempt to engage with this temporally and spatially two-sided form. Protagonist George herself reflects on the challenge inherent in such a palimpsestic *Gestus* of simultaneous and simulated sequentiality, when she muses that 'if things really did happen simultaneously it'd be like reading a book but one in which all the lines of the text have been overprinted, like each page is actually two pages but with one superimposed on the other to make it unreadable' (2014: 10/196). This courts postmodernist thoughts about unreadability in which meaning is lost with the difference between surface and depth. *How to Be Both* resists this unreadability, however, by constantly pointing the reader beyond its textual surface. In what could be understood as a performative enactment of Luhmann's simultaneity of sequentiality, the textual surface continually opens up towards what it excludes, even while it ultimately resists the attempt of conclusively bringing depth to surface.

RECONSTRUCTING *HOW TO BE BOTH*

The formal features of *How to Be Both* that invoke this doubleness, this harnessing of form in the novel's multifaceted exploration of how to be both, occur on the level of the *histoire* as well as the *narration* and also pertain to the *Gestalt* of the book as published artefact.

The Book as Artefact and Material Object

The monolithic singular outline of the textual surface is disrupted by the spatial doubleness of the novel's two print versions (cf. endnote 1). The precise form of the text that the individual reader encounters (whether they read Francescho's or George's story first) constitutes a prima-facie meditation on the form of form itself, as it both irrevocably configures the individual reading experience, while at the same time triggering an (objectively futile but imaginatively conducive) reconstruction of the road not taken in the reading of the novel. Always present beneath the specific textual surface a reader encounters, it is the content of the text one did not read, the non-formalised sequence of the two sections of the book, the matter beyond form as it were, which demands the reader's response.

The bipartite narration is mirrored in the two images of exactly equal size which adorn back and front of the book jacket, one a detail from a fresco by Francesco del Cossa from the Palazzo Schifanoia in Ferrara, showing a young androgynous figure, the other a photograph of two young French singers from the 1960s, identified on the back cover of the novel as Sylvie Vartan and Françoise Hardy. Linking the two images to the two main characters, the novel suggests a likeness of Francescho to the figure in her fresco (2014: 111/297) as well as a likeness of George to one of the photographed singers (2014: 274–75/88–89). As one of the many connections between the two parts, these two images enter into a complex relation of gazes and layers of meaning, in yet another play on surface and depth. Intermediaries in many senses, they 'can be both life and death at once and cross the border between the two' (2014: 158/344), as Francescho claims of pictures generally.

Both images are described from different perspectives in the two parts of the novel. On their surface, Francescho's and George's gazes thus meet the gaze of the reader, as the various ekphrastic descriptions challenge the reader to return to the jacket and reconsider the images in view of what has been said about them. At the same time, the images serve as a visual arbiter between reality and fiction. Physically marking off the fictional space of the novel by their position on the jacket, they feature both as an integral part of the fictional story and as a reference to the historical reality in which the novel is placed. Liminal figures joining the past to the present and the surface to its background, they point to the depth of the story developing between them in the pages of the book and to the historical depth beyond the novel, as well as to their own material manifestation as fresco and photograph, respectively. Positioned on the jacket to mirror each other, the images challenge the reader to look for points of connection and similarity, while at the same time serving as a visual reminder of the immense temporal distance of roughly 500 years as spanned by the 372 pages of the novel evolving between them.

Narrative Form

Such a perpetual oscillation between proximity and distance, similarity and difference, simultaneity and sequence also characterises the novel's narrative form. On the metaphorical level, this finds expression by reference to the technique of fresco painting, in which the surface painting can sometimes differ significantly from the underdrawing on which it is based. A conversation between George and her mother once more points to the temporally paradoxical relation of surface and depth which also applies to the novel's own narrative structure, and indeed to the placement of the images on its jacket (Smith 2014: 289/103):

> But which came first? her mother says. . . . The picture underneath or the picture on the surface?
>
> The picture below came first, George says. Because it was done first.
>
> But the first thing we see, her mother said, and most times the only thing we see, is the one on the surface. So does that mean it comes first after all? And does that mean the other picture, if we don't know about it, may as well not exist?

This question of primacy, or superimposition, simultaneously involves the question of whether the work of art is realised in its production or its reception, whether to emphasise intention or effect and in what relation they stand.

Such questions of primacy, and of the ontological status of what is narrated, inform the juxtaposition and combination of the different narrative perspectives of the two parts, which once again play out in terms of surface and depth. On what one could call its surface realism, the novel is meticulous in its numerous historical and particularly ekphrastic references. Several of the surviving paintings by Francesco del Cossa are described in detail, and the few facts known about the painter's life are faithfully adhered to. Furthermore, the novel frequently references popular culture, especially music, and clearly defines the setting of its narrative present (Cambridge and London, 2013–2014). At the same time, the narrative perspectives complicate this picture.

George's part of the narrative draws heavily on free indirect discourse and presents her as the sole focaliser of events. Towards its end, however, its fictional status is clearly exposed in a metareferential gesture, which unveils its extradiegetic perspective (Smith 2014: 368/182; our emphasis):

> This is the point in this story at which, according to its structure so far, a friend enters or a door opens or some kind of plot *surfaces* . . .; this is the place in this book where a spirit of twist in the tale has tended, in the past, to provide a friendly nudge forward to whatever's coming next.

The narrative voice that emerges here displaces itself in terms of space and time. It oscillates between the surface that is constituted by the novel's plot and an imaginary depth, or reservoir of potentialities, from which potential twists are to be conjured up (by whom: by the author? the narrative voice? the characters? the reader?).

At the same time, the novel both fulfils and thwarts the expectations raised by the passage quoted earlier. Only a couple of paragraphs later someone does enter, a former acquaintance and quite possibly lover of George's mother called Lisa Goliard, and the narrator even gives a brief summary of what is going to happen next: George will leave the gallery in which she is right now looking at one of Francesco del Cossa's paintings, follow Lisa and resolve to keep surveillance over her home. George's own narrative, however, stops at this point. The plot which potentially surfaces with the appearance of Lisa Goliard is obliquely taken up in Francescho's story, where it serves as little more than a background to the painter's own narrative. Her ghostly voice, entering as 'a mighty twisting thing' (Smith 2014: 3/189), provides precisely the 'spirit of twist' from the past which the narrative voice calls for in the afore-quoted passage. Just as it is displaced in space, the narration of George's part appears thus to be suspended from a definite position in time, as, towards its very end, it anticipates (or recapitulates, as the case may be) much of the events which Francescho observes taking place in the novel's other half, only to return to George's narrative present with the words: 'But none of the above has happened. Not yet, anyway. For now, in the present tense, George sits in the gallery and looks at one of the old paintings on the wall' (2014: 371–72/185–86). With an ambiguous gesture, which anticipates further plot developments and nevertheless attempts to deny a moment of closure, George's part of the novel ends with an emphasis on the urgent yet undetermined moment implied in this particular act of seeing, which is suspended between past, present and future, between surface and depth: 'It's definitely something to do. For the foreseeable' (2014: 372/186).

The narrative voice in the other part of the novel likewise oscillates between the here and there and the then and now. Although its first-person narrator Francescho endeavours to establish the immediacy of oral discourse in her colloquial, elliptic style and her use of the present tense, her part is insistently textual in its layout, much more so than George's in fact. At both its beginning and end, the distribution of text on the page calls up the verse structure of poetry while at the same time suggesting the twisting shape of a DNA double helix, another symbol of significant doubleness that recurs throughout the text. Moreover, in Francescho's part, clauses are often separated by a colon, a punctuation habit which, we find out, she took over from her mother (2014: 151/337). Both emphatically oral and textual, Francescho's act of narration takes up an underdetermined position with regard to her location in time and space. She figures as a ghostly observer, called up from the dead and thrown into a contemporary world which makes little sense to her and in which her presence remains entirely unnoticed: 'I'm a painter, dead (I think, though I remember no going), placed here for my many prideful sins in this cold place that has no horses to watch unseen unheard unknown the back of a boy in the kind of love that means nothing but despair' (2014: 45/231). A variation on the question what comes first, Francescho's voice is called into George's present from the past by George's act of looking at one of her paintings, a gaze that Francescho is given the chance to return. While the painter's narrative thus precedes George's part historically – materially manifested in the picture that is the object of George's gaze – Francescho's narration chronologically follows that of George (irrespective of what its actual position in the novel might be), even while it is anticipated by the proleptic passage at the end of George's part mentioned earlier.

In spite of their exposure to the constructedness of the narrative form, the questions posed by these various metareferential challenges, however, do not aim primarily to question the novel's relation to reality. Neither do they serve the obvious purpose of commenting on and defamiliarising the present from a historical perspective, in spite of Francescho's initial brief humorous references to the sad absence of horses. Instead, they self-consciously expose the fictionality of the novel and thus performatively throw the suspension in time and space, between surface and depth, back at the reader. Abandoned by the guidance of a stable narrative perspective, the reader faces similar questions as the characters themselves: what are the connections between George and Francescho? In what relation do the two narratives stand? What are the consequences of the simultaneous sequentiality of these two parts, whose metaphorical deep structure exceeds the sum of their surfaces?

It is precisely this ineluctable openness and ambiguity, the impossibility of establishing unequivocal temporal, spatial and causal relations between the different parts of the novel, which elicits an authentic reader response. As Funk (2015: 51–55) has described elsewhere, authenticity can be regarded as an emergent phenomenon, not merely in the traditional Aristotelian sense of the whole being more than the sum of its parts – even though this is patently relevant as well – but also in so far as the authenticity engendered by an act of literary communication cannot be attributed to a distinctly designated interplay between author, text and reader but rather results from practices of reconstruction. These reconstructive procedures are both intrinsic to the novel in its form and have to be realised by the reader in the process of reconstructing, however transitorily and open-endedly, these relations. Transposing Goldstein's observation that emergence can be conceived as a 'self-transcending system' (2005: 64) to a literary key, we claim that reconstructive texts such as *How to Be Both* can be said to transcend themselves as they employ the undecidability written into them qua their simultaneous sequentiality, not in order to confound any attempts to establish meaning but to call up and demand the reader's response-ability, which in turn engenders an emergent and authentic literary encounter.

Histoire

The dialectics of surface and depth also feature heavily on the level of the novel's *histoire*. Whether it is the two protagonists' gender performances, the ubiquitous use of puns and linguistic ambiguities or various anachronistic misconceptions, all over *How to Be Both* appearances may deceive and perceptions seem to mislead. In various shapes and forms, the novel invites reflections on the question and instruction, which is its title and provides guidelines for how to perform, sustain and embrace ambiguity. As a *Bildungsroman*, George's part summons the reader to retrace George's journey from her initial certainty of 'Past and Present? . . . Male or female? It can't be both. It must be one or the other' (2014: 194/8) towards the non-binary world represented by Francesco del Cossa's images, which her mother exults in: 'Male, female, both, ... Beautiful, all of them, including the sheep' (2014: 238/52). The frescos open up the hard surface of the wall towards layers of depth, echoing the aesthetic programme of the novel itself: 'It is like everything is in layers. Things happen right at the front of the pictures and at the same time they continue happening, both separately and connectedly, behind, and behind that, and again behind that. . . . The picture makes you look at both – the close-up happenings and the bigger picture' (2014: 239/53).

In the course of her development, George eventually learns to appreciate such duplicity of looking at both, surface and depth, foreground and background. The process of working through her loss after her mother's sudden death thus culminates in George's avowal that 'in honour of her mother's eyes, she will use her own' (2014: 371/185).

Meanwhile, throughout the novel, the act of seeing insistently unites aesthetic and ethical perspectives, in a shift from, as George's mother puts it, '[w]hat we see' to 'how we see' (2014: 290/104), for example, when George's mother draws parallels between the layered frescoes and the relation between a surface of present perception and the awareness of historical depth: 'We are sitting here having our supper . . . and looking at everything that's round us. . . . If this was a night seventy years ago . . . we'd be sitting here watching people being lined up and shot against that wall. Along from where those seats for the café bar are' (2014: 289/103). The ability to generate depth beyond the surface of the present, George's mother implies, in itself becomes an ethical responsibility. Applying this instruction to a different form of seeing through surfaces, George habitually watches a video depicting the apparent rape of a young girl on her tablet device. On being confronted about this by her father, she explicitly presents this practice as an act of bearing witness, so as 'to remind herself not to forget the thing that happened to this person' (2014: 223/37). The repeated act of seeing constitutes an attempt at an ethical response, even while George is painfully aware that every time someone watches the video of the rape 'it happens for the first time, over and over' (2014: 224/38). In the act of seeing, the absent is fused with the existent, the past with the present, the living and the dead, the surface of what is seen with the depth of what is remembered. In the evocation and acknowledgement of such ghostly presences, the act of seeing becomes necessarily an ethical act. So, in fact, does reading the novel.

Francescho's practice of seeing is more hands-on. As a painter, she equates seeing with feeling with painting: 'It is a feeling thing, to be a painter of things' (2014: 42/228). If George's acts of seeing emphasise the responsibility that lies in distance, Francescho's seeing almost always translates into touch and expression. In an appropriate symbolic reference to these two different versions of seeing, George's part of the novel is introduced with the icon of a surveillance camera, while Francescho's part is preceded by the image of the flower-stem with disembodied eyes which del Cossa's *St Lucy* holds in her hand (see figure 10.1).

In spite of the disembodied saintliness implied here, seeing and painting for Francescho almost always come with an erotic charge. In one of the most striking examples, Francescho recalls 'the time I was seen, entered and understood by someone I was acquainted with in my life for 10 minutes only'

Figure 10.1.   Francesco del Cossa, *St. Lucy* (ca. 1473–1474), Washington National Gallery of Art. Image from Wikicommons.

(2014: 96/282). During one of her travels on the road she encounters an 'infidel' worker, who calls after her in a language she does not understand (2014: 97/283). The word he calls her with, so he subsequently explains, means 'you who are more than one thing. You who exceed expectations' (2014: 98/284). Recognition in this case, and in more than one sense, is not generated on the surface of linguistic exchange but results from the non-verbal reciprocity of visual perception, as he 'sees me see this beauty in him and it makes his nature rise' (2014: 285/99). Like the form of authenticity at the base of reconstruction, this reciprocity is not a consequence of rational comprehension but of ambiguity and paradox, and it emerges rather than results: 'It was all : it was nothing : it was more than enough' (2014: 99/285).

George's disembodied and distanced acts of seeing are juxtaposed with Francescho's erotic and creative ones, even while both are paradoxically combined when the disembodied eyes of pure seeing come to stand for the body/the self itself: 'All we are is eyes looking for the unbroken or the edges where the broken bits might fit each other' (2014: 59/245). Faced with the shattered surface of representation offered by the novel, the reader is challenged to translate these acts of pure seeing into acts of responsible reading and to reconstruct an 'unbroken' depth, where the fragments shored against postmodernism's ruins might once again reconnect.

CONCLUSION

While tantalisingly suggesting such reconnections and parallels, between the two images on its jacket, its two parts, the protagonists and even the historical moments in spite of their distance and difference, the novel never provides its reader with clear answers to any of the questions it raises. Temporal and spatial distance is emphasised as much as similarities and meaningful echoes are hinted at, but never fully emerge. Nevertheless, while meaning may thus remain elusive, this does not suggest that the endeavour to find it is futile or impossible. Quite the contrary, *How to Be Both* emphatically exposes itself as a formal act-event, metareferentially celebrating its own fictionality and constructedness, precisely in order to appeal to the response-ability and responsibility of the reader, who is challenged to make their own sense of the complexities the novel offers. Very much in the vein of the mother figures featuring in its story, the novel itself prefers to pose unsolved conundrums leaving its reader 'twisting . . . with the dilemma of it' (2014: 61/247).

Figure 10.2.   Detail from Francesco del Cossa, *March*, Il Salone dei Mesi, Palazzo Schifanoia, Ferrara. Image from Wikicommons.

The questions posed by the formal and aesthetic challenges that constitute *How to Be Both*'s *Gestalt*, narration and *histoire* (and their complex interplay) do not, in modernist fashion, concern the nature of representation as such. Nor do they partake in a deconstructive mission to endlessly postpone or even entirely disqualify meaning. Rather, they are reconstructive in their endeavours to engage the reader's response-ability in an encounter with the text that interrogates the way in which fiction may serve to suggest meaning beyond the surface of representation. In a gesture that is equally ethical and aesthetic, they constitute a withdrawal that doubles as a new departure towards the possibility of authenticity. This is where our concept of reconstruction suggests a somewhat different view on the 'depthiness' which Vermeulen ascribes to the metamodern work of art. The aesthetic depth which had been flattened in postmodernism is not only re-applied by the conscientious author figure (as Vermeulen indicates in the preface to this section), but it is formally activated in the act of reading itself. The half-hidden face that looks straight out at the observer from the *March* fresco at the Palazzo Schifanoia (see figure 10.2) – a face that may or may not belong to Francesc(h)o himself or herself (2014: 168/354) – does convey the unfathomable depth of the past onto the present surface of the walls. The novel, in similar fashion, performs this exploration of imaginary deep space when, at its very end, Francescho's narrative literally spirals off from the plot's surface into the abyss of form, where binaries (old, new) collapse and meaning is always ever in the process of being made (2014: 186/372):

> hello all the new bones
> hello all the old
> hello all the everything
> to be
> made and
> unmade
> both

NOTE

1. Since the novel has been printed in two versions, with its two parts in different order, this may either come at the beginning or in the middle. All subsequent references to the novel will give page numbers for both versions, the first one always referring to the edition that starts with Francescho's narrative.

Chapter 11

Between Truth, Sincerity and Satire: Post-Truth Politics and the Rhetoric of Authenticity

Sam Browse

I once had an argument with my grandfather that ended – decisively – in him saying, 'I know my opinion; don't confuse me with facts'. (Although my grandfather did not mean to joke, the comedian, Stewart Lee (2007), similarly quipped, 'you can prove anything with facts'.) There is probably no better phrase to sum up an attitude that scholars and media pundits have called 'post-truth politics'. The term 'post-truth' originates in Keyes's (2004) book, *The Post-Truth Era: Dishonesty and Deception in Contemporary Life*. It was later applied explicitly to politics by a journalist, David Roberts, in an article written for the environmental news and opinion website, *Grist*, in 2010. Since then, it has been taken up by scholars from various disciplines to describe the contemporary political *zeitgeist* (see Fish 2016; Harsin 2015; Parmer 2012; Tallis 2016). Roberts himself defines post-truth politics as 'a political culture in which politics (public opinion and media narratives) have become almost entirely disconnected from policy (the substance of legislation)' (2010). Thus in post-truth politics, the veracity of what one says matters far less than the extent to which one sincerely believes it. The comedian Stephen Colbert (2016) sums up this attitude succinctly in his skit to the White House correspondent's dinner:

> Do you know that you have more nerve endings in your gut than you have in your head? You can look it up. And now some of you are going to say: I did look it up and that's not true. That's because you looked it up in a book. Next time look it up in your gut. My gut tells me that's how our nervous system works . . . I give people the truth unfiltered by rational arguments.

Vermeulen (2015) discusses this quote in the context of what elsewhere Colbert calls 'truthiness'. The things that 'my gut tells me' have the ring of truth about them – a 'truthiness' – that facts simply do not. Post-truth politics represent the triumph of 'truthiness' over truth.

Vermeulen (2015) goes on to relate the notion of 'truthiness' to the idea of 'depth', or what he calls 'depthiness':

> 'Truthiness' expresses the production of a 'truth' according to emotion instead of empiricism; 'depthiness' articulates the creation of 'depth' as a performative act as opposed to an epistemological quality. . . . Truthiness puts the truth into question; depthiness raises doubts about depthlessness. Truthiness abandons the reality of truth as a legitimate register of signification; depthiness restores the possibility of depth as a viable modality for making meaning.

Related concepts, here, are authenticity and sincerity: the performance of 'depthiness' is the performance of both. Indeed, throughout their discussion of metamodernism and utopia, Vermeulen and van den Akker (2015, 59) frequently run these terms together. Thus, insofar as the proofs of classical rhetoric are concerned, the appeal to ethos is the argumentative *modus operandi* of the post-truth politician; they are plain-speaking, gutsy and authentic.

Although the post-truth epithet is most often applied to politicians and causes of the political right (in the United States, Trump; in the United Kingdom, Brexit and Nigel Farage), in this chapter I argue that post-truth rhetoric – in Britain at least – has its origins in the social-democratic, Third Way politics of the late nineties. In the following section, I suggest that, like post-truth politicians today, the rhetoric of Tony Blair's Labour Party demonstrates the same pre-occupation with authenticity. I label Blair's particular strategy of appealing to his own authenticity and political conviction *mimetic authenticity*. In order to gauge the reception of this rhetorical appeal, I examine the representation of the New Labour government in the British satirical show, *The Thick of It*. If *The Thick of It* illustrates a widely held attitude towards New Labour, it also demonstrates a particularly negative attitude towards the way in which Labour politicians of the noughties performed political conviction. Vermeulen and van den Akker (2010) identify the collapse of the Third Way as an important factor in the development from a post- to metamodern cultural sensibility. At the heart of such a shift is a renewed emphasis on depth and authenticity in the cultural sphere (see Vermeulen and van den Akker 2015). Given this political and cultural dynamic, I describe how it is that the current (at the time of writing) leader of the Labour Party, Jeremy Corbyn, employs a new and different means of appealing to authenticity, naming this new rhetorical strategy *curated authenticity*. In doing so, the chapter seeks to trace the stylistic realisation of what Vermeulen (2015) calls 'depthiness' in the rhetoric of the British Labour Party from 1997 to today.

FROM *DIEGESIS* TO *MIMESIS*: TONY BLAIR AND AN EMERGENT RHETORIC OF SINCERITY

In 1997, Tony Blair led a rebranded British Labour Party to a landslide electoral victory. Blair's 'New' Labour was the British expression of a global ideological realignment of the centre-left. While some hailed this 'Third Way' as transcending the old divisions of 'left' and 'right', in reality the new social democratic politics inflected a liberal attitude to issues of race, gender and sexuality with a neoliberal faith in markets as the fix-all solution to social problems. In Britain, the rightward shift was accompanied by changes in the presentation of policy. New Labour placed 'a premium on form over content, on photo-opportunity rather than debate', and was 'committed to the view that presentation is part of the process of policy formation' (Franklin 1998, 4; see also Franklin 1994).

Part of this new presentational strategy and rebranding of the party involved an emphasis on Blair himself. In his analysis of a 1997 Labour Party election broadcast, Pearce suggests that prior to 1997 there had been 'no established tradition of political parties using their leaders' biographies in election campaigns' (2001, 211). Certainly, Blair played an unprecedentedly important part in the 1997 election campaign. Youthful and messianic images of the party leader featured prominently in Labour's election posters (see figure 11.1), and a whole party election broadcast was given over to a biography of Blair.

Leaders of the party had, however, played a prominent role in campaigning materials before. For instance, ten years previously in the 1987 election, the Labour Party had run an election broadcast about Neil Kinnock, dubbed 'Kinnock the movie' by its detractors. While there are similarities between the two short films, it is instructive to examine their differences. Although 'Kinnock the movie' can be seen as a precursor to the 1997 broadcast – it featured interviews with the Labour leader and his family, personal anecdotes and biographical stories from Kinnock's life – it did not collapse what Wodak (2009, following Goffman 1959) has called the 'front' and 'backstage' of politics to the same extent as the 1997 election broadcast. While the production values of the 1987 film are relatively high with anecdotes from Kinnock's family, friends and colleagues given in a 'talking heads' format, the 1997 film is shot in a 'fly on the wall' documentary style. Blair is seen chatting to camera in the backseat of a car, on a train and in his own kitchen (which at different stages in the interview is also occupied by his children). In 'Kinnock the movie', we learn biographical details about Kinnock, but they are conveyed with polished cinematography, lighting and music. Conversely, in the 1997 election broadcast, Blair tells us about himself seemingly between meetings or public

Figure 11.1. 1997 New Labour election posters. *Left*: http://www.phm.org.uk/our-collection/object-of-the-month/may-2017-because-britain-deserves-better-poster-1997/; *right*: http://nottspolitics.org/2013/05/29/picturing-politics-the-1997-labour-manifesto/.

engagements (as in the car and train shots) or before and after work (as in the kitchen scenes). The 1997 short film is thus an apparently 'real', behind-the-scenes portrayal of Blair, whereas the 1987 film had no such pretensions.

In fact, as Pearce (2001) notes, the tension between front and backstage political spaces is highlighted by Blair himself in the 1997 broadcast. It begins with Blair being interviewed in the car, then cuts to a scene in which Blair is standing in front of a crowd of photographers and campaigners signing the poster bearing the head-shot picture shown in figure 11.1. Over this scene, Blair's voice from the car can be heard saying 'and there is a part of you that wonders whether it's worth staying in politics because of all the rubbish you have to do'. In self-consciously thematising the tension between front and backstage – and scorning 'all the rubbish you have to do' as part of the everyday staging of politics – the 1997 broadcast attempts to construct an 'authentic' image of the 'real' Blair. As Blair himself says, 'What I keep saying to people is "get behind the image"'. This is exactly what the 1997 broadcast invites its audience to do. Of course, it also happens to be the case that the man 'behind the image' is a totem of the New Labour brand.

Blair's biography is recruited throughout the broadcast as a propaganda tool for the rebooted party. Pearce (2001, 223; original italics) notes:

> For Blair it seems that the new Labour 'project' is to unite the 'best' features of the Conservative and Labour traditions: you *can* have a dynamic free market

and social justice. Blair presents his own biography and personality as a symbol of this synthesis. He is vigorous, active, driven – the attributes of a successful business leader; yet he is also compassionate and caring – traditional social democratic qualities.

Blair's life story is used as a symbol for the political project; 'every facet of Blair's personality and every detail of his background [is] turned to political advantage' (Pearce, 2001, 213). This is all the more potent because these are anecdotes – disclosures, even – told in intimate, seemingly authentic moments over the kitchen table or travelling between political engagements. In 'Kinnock the movie', we should vote for Labour because Kinnock's friends and family tell us that he is a good, honourable man. In the 1997 broadcast, however, we should vote for *New* Labour because despite 'all the rubbish [he] has to do' as a politician, after work and between meetings Blair is like us; our values are his values, and by extension our values are the same as those of the party he leads. Kinnock only told us he was a good man; Blair showed us. Kinnock's was a *diegetic* authenticity, Blair's *mimetic*.

This notion of mimetic – perhaps another word for it is 'performed' – authenticity is also evident in Blair's rhetorical style. One of the distinctive features of this style is what Fairclough (2000, 99) has called the 'public construction of normalness'. Fairclough (2000, 95–118) outlines a variety of stylistic features that Blair uses to perform 'normalness'. I have summarised these linguistic forms in table 11.1. All serve to personalise Blair's rhetorical style. They combine with Blair's use of body language – for example, he smiles frequently – to project an image of personable, middle-class authenticity. As Fairclough (2000, 99) puts it, 'Blair's political performances are inflected by the language and communicative style of Blair "the normal person"'. Thus, the backstage, 'ordinary guy' of the 1997 party election

Table 11.1. A summary of linguistic strategies that Blair uses to perform to 'normalness' (c.f. Fairclough 2000).

Linguistic structure

Glottaling – Using the non-standard [ʔ], rather than the standard [t] in words like butter.
Northern pronunciation of first-person singular pronoun, 'I' – using the non-standard [æ], rather than the standard diphthong, [aɪ].
Frequent use of generic 'you'.
Frequent use of the first-person singular pronoun, 'I', even when talking about the party.
Frequent use of the discourse marker, 'I mean'.
Use of epistemic modality (relating to knowledge, e.g. 'I think') and boulomaic modality (relating to desire, e.g. 'I want').
Emphasising consensus – using nominalisation and passive sentence structures to background division and conflict.
Using pauses, hesitation and repetition to suggest thoughtfulness, 'rather than a politician reeling off prepared answers' (Fairclough 2000, 2013)

broadcast remains visible in the frontstage politician delivering the Labour leader's address from the platform in the conference hall.

A corollary of this continuity between backstage and frontstage politicians is that in addition to being authentic, Blair seems like a conviction politician; his performance of authenticity extends into a performance of sincerity. Like his authenticity, this sincerity is not simply diegetic, it is mimetic. Blair does not only tell us he is a man of deep conviction; he shows us with his rhetorical style. Fairclough (2000, 14) suggests that the main way he performs political conviction is through his use of body language and vocal delivery. According to Fairclough (2000, 14), his furrowed brow, gestures and use of intonation are all ways in which Blair indexes sincerity. These indices are joined by his emphatic use of rhetorical questions and boulomaic modality (verbs relating to desire, such as 'I want') to demonstrate his strongly held political beliefs. Paradoxically, then, given New Labour's spin-savvy focus on the presentation of policy, authenticity and sincerity were key motifs of Blair's rhetorical performance.

TRUTH, SINCERITY AND SATIRE: *THE THICK OF IT* AS AUDIENCE RECEPTION

Although the party would govern for thirteen years, the 1997 high point of the New Labour project soon turned to steady decline. Between the first landslide victory and electoral defeat in 2010, the party gradually lost six million votes. To get some idea of how New Labour was received throughout this period, it is worth considering how the government was represented in British culture. In this section, I focus on one particularly influential representation – Armando Iannuci's BBC television show *The Thick of It*, which first aired on 19 May 2005. The show was critically lauded by the Royal Television Society, the Broadcasting Press Guild Awards and won multiple BAFTAs. In what follows, I do not provide a comprehensive summary of the views of the British public regarding the New Labour government, but rather one particularly prominent attitude to New Labour in power – an attitude that I nonetheless suggest has influenced the rhetorical landscape of contemporary political debate.

As Fielding (2014, 258) notes, *The Thick of It* 'constituted a running critique of New Labour and to a lesser extent of David Cameron's modernized Conservative alternative' (2014, 258). Fielding (2014, 258) provides a good summary of the show's satirical parallels:

> While the party in power is never named, disputes between the Prime Minister's Office and the Treasury echoed those between Blair and Brown, the outgoing premier's obsession with his 'legacy' called to mind Blair's, and his successor

shared many of the characteristics attributed to Brown. More importantly, the style of government evident in *The Thick of It* (specifically the obsession with spin) evoked what many thought of New Labour.

Fielding suggests that one of the show's satirical targets was New Labour's 'style of government' and it's 'obsession with spin' (2014, 258). Throughout the show, the relationship between spin and reality is thematised. Basu writes that in *The Thick of It*, 'the political parties are all the same, and neither the politicians nor the journalists are interested in telling the truth or doing good for society' (2014, 92). Similarly, Fielding states that '*The Thick of It* is ultimately a highly moral series concerned to explore how politicians and others obscure the ideal of Truth' (2014, 9).

The following scene from Series 1, Episode 1 (2005) is exemplary. Malcolm Tucker, the prime minister's foul-mouthed Director of Communications and political enforcer, is talking to the minister for the (fictional) Department of Social Affairs, Hugh Abbott. In a press conference earlier in the day, Abbott wanted to make a new policy announcement but was vetoed by Tucker at the last moment. With nothing to report to the assembled journalists, Abbott desperately gropes for a newsworthy story. Finally, he settles on the announcement that everything at the ministry is running smoothly and berates the journalists for their relentless negativity. In this scene, Tucker has come to tell Abbott that actually the prime minister liked the policy and that Abbott – now scorned by the Whitehall press pack – should announce it:

Abbott: What, um, what are we going to do now?
Tucker: You are going to completely reverse your position.
Abbott: Hang, hang, hang on a second. Malcolm, it's not actually that, um – that's actually quite hard, really.
Tucker: Yes, well, the announcement that you didn't make today, you did.
Abbott: No, no, I didn't and there were television cameras there while I was not doing it.
Tucker: Fuck them.
Abbott: I'm not quite sure what level of reality I'm supposed to be operating on.
Tucker: Look, this is what they run with – I tell them that you said it and people believe that you said it. They don't really believe that you said it, they know that you never said it.
Abbott: Right.
Tucker: But it's in their interests to say that you said it because if they don't say that you said they're not going to get what you say tomorrow or the next day when I decide to tell them what it is you're saying.

Tucker acknowledges that the press 'know[s] that you never said it', but considers the truth to be of secondary importance. What matters, then, is that Tucker will deny the journalists political access if they fail to print what he says. As Basu writes of the show, 'Politics and news media are shown to comprise one enormous complex – an *apparatus* – and there is no salvageable space within it' (2014, 92; original italics).

In *The Thick of It*, the press packs and political class conspire against reality in pursuit of their own interests. What was actually said is subordinated to how it is reported; the medium supplants the message. Abbott's anxiety over 'what level of reality [he is] supposed to be operating on' represents a disquiet with this postmodern primacy of mediation. For Abbott, 'reality' is a malleable concept – he sees that it operates on 'levels' – but the spinning into existence of a policy he never announced is an ontological step too far. Tucker later illustrates the trick by reference to the adultery committed by his friend – the friend would come home after the affair and 'flick a switch' in his head that meant, in Tucker's formulation, it 'never happened'. This adds an explicitly moral dimension to Tucker's negation of reality, putting Tucker, the press and Abbott in the same category as adulterers.

In a foreshadowing of contemporary post-truth politics, this glib approach to reality extends to expert advice. Just as reality is bent out of shape, distorted or substituted for fiction in the service of a political agenda, expert opinion in *The Thick of It* is not marshalled for its intrinsic value, but for the way in which it corroborates the policy agenda of the government. In the following scene from Series 2, Episode 3 (2005), Tucker and Abbott are arguing over the government's education policy for students with special educational needs (SEN). Following advice from an expert and his own political advisor – Glenn Cullen, the father of a SEN child – Abbott believes SEN students should have their own separate special needs schools. However, the government's position – and therefore Tucker's – is that SEN students should be integrated into mainstream schools.

Abbott: Before I went away I consulted an expert, Mark Ryan.
Tucker: The LSE education guy?
Abbott: Yeah.
Tucker: And what did that sandal wearing nonce have to say?
Abbott: What he said was that closing down special needs schools and putting needy kids in mainstream education is a lousy idea.
Tucker: Yeah, but I've got an expert who will deny that.
Abbott: And SEN parents want the special needs schools kept open.
Tucker: Yeah, well my expert would totally oppose that.
Abbott: Who is your expert?
Tucker: I have no idea, but I can get one by this afternoon. You see the thing is, you have spoken to the wrong expert. You've got to ask the right expert, and you've got to know what an expert's gonna advise you before he advises you. Hugh, whether you like this or not, you are

going to have to promote this bill so what I'm gonna do is, I'm gonna get you another expert, yeah?

Abbott: Okay.

Once again, reality suffers. In *The Thick of It*, experts are used by politicians to add credibility to the policies they are already pursuing, not to get to the truth of what constitutes the best policy for the people for whom legislation is written. Indeed, this perception that experts are used for cynical, instrumental purposes rather than for the knowledge they bring to debate arguably laid the ideological groundwork for Michael Gove's infamous remarks in the Brexit debates, that 'Britain has had enough of experts'. The flippant recourse to expert views as *post hoc* justification for *any* opinion is bound to foster wary – weary, even – attitudes to those with technical or professional expertise.

Despite the opinion of his own expert and protests from Cullen, Abbott goes ahead with supporting the government's position. Later in the episode, Abbott is forced to give evidence in a public inquiry about the reasons behind his support for the policy. In a cringe-inducing moment – Cullen is sat beside him, looking aghast and furious – Abbott recruits Cullen's experiences of raising a SEN child to justify his support for the policy, despite Cullen's repeated advice throughout the episode that 'inclusion is an illusion'. Abbott uses Cullen's (made-up) biographical experiences in much the same way as Blair in the 1997 party election broadcast. The personal anecdote is mobilised as a propaganda resource in the pursuit of political support. In *The Thick of It*, we know that the anecdote is a fabrication – worse in fact, it is the complete opposite of the truth. Abbott's performance of authenticity comes at the expense of Cullen's (truly authentic) experiences and at the expense of their friendship (although they later make up). The message, here, is not simply that politicians owe some fidelity to the truth, but that just as the New Labour brand of spin is personalised, it is personally corrupting; it pollutes personal relationships by instrumentalising them in the service of policy. Abbott's performed sincerity hollows out any meaningful relationship he may have had with Cullen, rendering him morally abject.

The projection of authenticity and ordinariness is exposed as fraudulent throughout *The Thick of It*. In Series 1, Episode 2 (2005), Tucker reveals that the only reason the prime minister seems 'to be so clued up' is because of what his special advisors have dubbed 'the zeitgeist tapes' – video tapes that provide a brief digest of the week's popular culture. The prime minister does not actually watch television or listen to popular music; his normality is a cheat. Amusingly, the characters in the show are unable even to identify a 'normal' person. In the same episode, Abbott employs a number of focus groups to test the popularity of a new policy proposal. One particular woman in the focus group meetings is very enthusiastic about the policy so Abbott, Cullen and Ollie Reader (another of Abbot's special advisors) dismiss the other group members, farcically reducing their focus group to a member-ship of one. However, it transpires that the person they had assumed was an ordinary middle-class single mother is actually an actor and was recruited to pad-out the group and provoke discussion. Thus the demographic to whom the policy is supposed to appeal is also a fiction. This satirical targeting of New Labour's focus group policy formulation is an implicit critique of the middle-class normality performed by Blair in the 1997 election broadcast; his performance is the performance of another performance, a simulation in Baudrillard's (1983) sense. There is no 'ordinary' middle-class single mother to whom the cosy kitchen chats and the candid car seat conversations will appeal, only an actor playing the role they have been asked to play. Following the logic of *The Thick of It*, Blair is performing an illusion of his own making.

Insofar as it thematises the motifs of authenticity and sincerity characteris-ing the rhetoric of New Labour, *The Thick of It* speaks to the 'structure of feeling' (Williams 1977) experienced by some of those living through the Blair years. The show represents a dissatisfaction and impatience with the skin-deep performances of sincerity and authenticity. Indeed, the characters are loathsome because they hate the 'normality' they perform. For example, in Series 2, Episode 1 (2005), Abbott calls the 'real' electorate a 'different species' with 'beady eyes and sneering, mean mouths'. The show not only expresses distaste for spin and the mimetic authenticity accompanying it, but also weariness. Yet the tired performance goes on, maniacally orchestrated by Tucker; it is a surface without much pretence of depth. In this regard, *The Thick of It* represents an attitude or current of opinion concerning New Labour's communications strategy. Vermeulen's (2015) comments on Col-bert's notion of 'truthiness' and his own concept of 'depthiness' are relevant here. If *The Thick of It* tells us anything about the rhetoric of New Labour and its reception, it is that Blair's mimetic authenticity was – is – experienced by some as depthless – a surface ringing hollow. Whatever the initial potency of New Labour's 'performative acts' of depth, to use Vermeulen's (2015) expression, in delivering a landslide election result, at some point they fail, at least for Ianucci and the audience members who share his perspective (elsewhere I have provided a more complex account of the satirical meanings different audiences attach to *The Thick of It*: see Browse forthcoming). There are multiple ways in which one might explain the development of this cyni-cism towards mimetic authenticity by reference to Labour's record in power. Unfortunately, there is not the space to do this properly here. Given my analysis of the critique of New Labour implied in *The Thick of It*, however, it is fair to say that this way of styling authenticity and sincerity had become potentially toxic to the party in at least some quarters of the electorate. In the next section, I outline the changing political landscape on the British left and how it led to a new way of performing depthiness or what I will call 'curated authenticity'.

THE NEW RHETORICAL 'DEPTHINESS': JEREMY CORBYN AND 'CURATED AUTHENTICITY'

In August 2015, to the surprise of everyone across the political spectrum, the veteran left-wing Labour Member of Parliament (MP), Jeremy Corbyn, became the odds-on frontrunner in the Labour Party leadership election. After Blair's resignation in 2007, Gordon Brown assumed the leadership of the Labour Party and the country. The global commodities boom that had sustained New Labour, making it possible for the party to invest in public services at the same time as being 'intensely relaxed' about people getting 'filthy rich' (as Peter Mandelson, a key architect of the Third Way, put it), came to a crashing halt in the 2007/2008 global financial crisis. In the wake of the economic maelstrom, the 2010 general election removed Brown from office and replaced the Labour Party with a Conservative/Liberal Democrat coalition. The new coalition government's response to the economic crisis was to implement a dramatic programme of austerity, delivering swingeing cuts to public services, investment and social security. The Labour Party countered by electing Ed Miliband – the 'soft'-left leadership candidate. Miliband repositioned the party to the left of his predecessor – he denounced the decision to go to war in Iraq and attacked 'predatory' capitalism. This repositioning was contradictory, however – for example, at the same time as condemning the government's cuts for going 'too far and too fast', the Labour Party accepted the coalition spending envelope for the next parliament. Although the polls predicted a second hung parliament or a narrow win for Labour, in the 2015 general election the Conservatives won an outright majority.

It was in this context that Corbyn stormed the 2015 Labour leadership, taking an unprecedented 59.5 per cent of the vote. After a rebellion of Labour MPs in 2016 followed by a second leadership challenge, he increased his mandate even further, beating the challenger, Owen Smith, with 62 per cent of the vote. Notwithstanding the opposition from Labour parliamentarians, it is fair to say that in the wider Labour Party Jeremy Corbyn is very popular. Corbyn began his political career as a trade unionist. After winning his Islington parliamentary seat in 1983, he became a prominent supporter of the left-wing icon and erstwhile MP, Tony Benn, and joined the socialist 'Campaign Group' of MPs. He was a prominent opponent of the Iraq War and a key figure on the British anti-imperialist left. As such, he represents a very different type of politician to Blair and his election a decisive break with the politics of the Third Way (one of his campaign slogans was 'a new kind of politics').

Corbyn's rhetorical style is also very different from Blair's as is his way of 'doing' sincerity. In fact, one of the reasons Labour Party members give for their support of Corbyn is that unlike leaders who came before him, he is authentic – he seems to believe what he says and has a campaigning record to prove it. In what follows, I examine how Corbyn performs authenticity, or depth, and contrast this with the mimetic authenticity that characterised the New Labour years. My analysis suggests that this new way of performing authenticity is a contributing factor to Corbyn's electoral success in the Labour Party, especially when framed in relation to the mimetic authenticity that preceded it. Indeed, Vermeulen and dan den Akker (2010, 2015) suggest that the 2007/2008 economic crisis, the failure of Third Way politics and collapse of the political centre ground were central to the development of a new metamodern *sens*. One can interpret the rhetorical shifts I outline, then, as expressions of this transition from post- to metamodern sensibility.

Whereas Blair's mimetic authenticity emphasised his own feelings, Corbyn demonstrates a general reluctance to talk about his emotions at all. Take, for example, this exchange from an interview with the BBC journalist Andrew Marr (*The Marr Show*, 2016). The interview was given shortly after the rebellion of Labour MPs that triggered the second leadership ballot.

Marr:	You have been under enormous personal pressure, you must have talked about this with your family and there was talk that there was a period when you did have a bit of a wobble. You thought, 'is it really worth it? Can I carry on, personally, doing this'?
Corbyn:	Andrew, you read too many newspapers, you really do.
Marr:	It's all I do.
Corbyn:	It's all you do, read newspapers!
Mar:	Yes, all I do.
Corbyn:	Can I tell you something? There's no –
Marr:	Can I ask, is it true?
Corbyn:	No, absolutely untrue. There's no wobbles. There's no stress. There's no depression. I'll tell you what real stress is: real stress is when you can't feed your kids; real stress is when you don't know if you'll get a job next day; real stress is if your landlord is gonna evict you from your home. That's what real stress in our society is. Our job, our job as politicians and public representatives is to recognise the real stresses people face in society and try and bring about a society that deals with those issues.

Marr provides Corbyn with an opportunity to emote – to say that, yes, he *is* personally affected by the rebellion. Instead, he briskly negates his own feelings ('no wobbles', 'no stress', 'no depression') and changes the subject to what 'real stress' is. In this enumeration of what constitutes 'real stress', his use of generic *you* generalises these stresses to an everyman subject. This is the opposite of the personalisation in Blair's style. Rather than recruit how he feels to make a point about the contemporary political situation, Corbyn's response is to imply that how he feels does not matter because other people – the generic *you* experiencing 'real stress' – are much worse off. I call this rhetorical strategy 'curated authenticity', 'curated' because Corbyn is presenting somebody else's experience rather than his own, and 'authenticity' because – on the one hand – that experience is presented as one that authentically exists (these are 'real' stresses), and – on the other – because those experiences clearly resonate with Corbyn himself – he feels strongly about them (which is evidenced in his emphatic triadic listing of 'real stresses', and his use of the word 'real', which acts as both an adjective – it denotes 'realness' – and an intensifier in this instance).

Where mimetic authenticity involved performing depth by recourse to one's own feelings and aspirations (or, rather, mimicking in one's own emotional performances what one imagines the demos to feel or aspire towards), curated authenticity is about presenting and empathising with the 'real' experiences of others. Probably the best example of this is Corbyn's use of crowd-sourced questions. Instead of asking his own, he frequently invites supporters to send him theirs, which he reads at the dispatch box. This is a curation of other people's experiences – a bricolage of authentic anecdotes from 'real' electors. As a stylistic strategy, bricolage is often associated with postmodernism and the pleasure taken in 'the production of production' rather than the product itself (Deleuze and Guattari 1983, 7). Bricolage is about 'surface' form – about rearranging 'fragments continually in new and different patterns or configurations' (Deleuze and Guattari 1983, 7). In this example, though, the 'stuff' of the bricolage – the experiences of real people – is used to construct a sense of depthiness. The effect is to take Corbyn out of the rhetorical picture, so to speak; the rhetorical appeal is not to his own ethos, but the authority of the (struggling and suffering) demos. Yet, paradoxically, this strengthens his own appeals to authenticity and sincerity – the sense of depthiness surrounding him – because he selflessly promotes other people's concerns above his own; the political cause comes before self-interest.

This is echoed in the insistence from supporters that their admiration for Corbyn is about more than support for a leader, but a movement. Corbyn's frequent use of the first-person pronoun *we* reflects this style of movement politics. This extract from a leadership election fundraiser video entitled *Powered by People* is a good example (Corbyn 2016):

We've been travelling all over the country to rallies and meetings, a message of hope, a message of involvement, a message of how politics can be exciting and done very differently. We don't have lots of money, we don't have big donations, and really, we're not looking for big donations. People that give us £5, £10, through the website or on their mobile phone, help us get more people involved in the most exciting time in politics for a very long period, so that nobody and no community is ever left behind.

Rather than make a personal appeal to supporters to donate money to the campaign, Corbyn speaks on behalf of a collective 'we'. At the end of the video, the camera cuts to a town square filled with Corbyn supporters dressed in red, waving Corbyn banners. The suggestion is that Corbyn and the crowd comprise the *we* for whom he speaks. The focus of the campaign video is on including more people in this *we* category – getting 'more people involved in the most exciting time in politics'. Importantly, too, the *we* that Corbyn represents does not have 'lots of money' or 'big donations'. This coheres with the ethos of Corbyn's 'new politics' – just as Corbyn's performance of authenticity involves curating the experience of other people, so his campaign, or 'the movement', is powered by them.

There is some degree of similarity, here, with Blair's rhetoric. As Fairclough notes, 'Blair's form of conviction politics is the claim to be in tune with the people' (2000, 115). Blair used epistemic and boulomaic modals such as 'I *sense* that the British people demand . . .', 'I *could sense* confidence returning', or 'you *know* what I *want*', which all serve to invoke 'a mythical narrative . . . of how the leader at the moment of assuming leadership enters into a mystical communion with the people' (Fairclough 2000, 115, emphasis mine). Contrastingly, Corbyn's use of *we* positions him with the people, rather than as someone intuiting their feelings and wishes. These differences map onto the differences between mimetic and curated authenticity: in the former, the politician interprets the experience of the demos with their own emotional (and political) intelligence (and, in doing so, they perform their own *separate* egocentric authenticity); in the latter, the politician authentically reproduces those experiences (and, in doing so, demonstrates their *unity* with the demos).

Corbyn is, also, himself the object of curation. He does not perform conviction mimetically in the same way as Blair, but his public speeches are often framed by his political allies (and even enemies) with reference to his ethos. For example, the slogan of the first leadership campaign was 'honest, straight-talking politics'. There is a sense, then, that what the audience already knows about Corbyn contributes to their perception of him in the discourse event itself (see Browse forthcoming): he has been a principled socialist who has stood for roughly the same values since his entry into parliament. Rather than invoke it himself, this record is instead used by other people to frame his public speeches. For example, in the introductory segment immediately before his interview with Corbyn during the 2015 leadership campaign, Owen Jones, a Corbyn supporter and journalist at the liberal *Guardian* newspaper, said, 'I'm backing [Corbyn] because I think he's a man of principle, a courageous man who stands up for his principles' (Jones 2015). Such framing devices in many ways make it unnecessary for Corbyn to perform sincerity in the same way as Blair. He is often offered as an example of principle and conviction before he even opens his mouth to speak.

CONCLUSION

What has been characterised as 'post-truth' politics revolves around notions of conviction and authenticity – of sincerely feeling something 'in your gut'. This chapter has argued that authenticity was thematised in the language of New Labour and the transition from diegetic to mimetic forms of 'doing' sincerity. However, if *The Thick of It* can be read as indicative of the 'structure of feeling' – to borrow Williams's (1977) term – experienced by at least some of those living under the Blair government, it is clear that the mimetic strategy soon wore thin. It is perhaps unsurprising that the mimesis involved in the rhetoric of New Labour would become the subject of cynicism and satire. While attempting to appeal to a metamodern concern for authenticity, its 'fronting' of the backstage of politics – and the supposedly 'normal' people populating that space – simply projected another depthless surface. Vermeulen (2015) suggests we have seen a transition from a postmodern experiential register that, like the surfer, skates over surface waters, towards a metamodern register of experience more similar to the snorkeler, who 'imagines depth whilst never experiencing it'. To stretch, by his own admission, Vermeulen's (2015) already taut metaphor, the curator in this arrangement is one who points to important or interesting features of the underwater vista and in demonstrating their knowledge of the depths below, takes on something of their depthiness. Rather than the mimetically authentic politician who (apparently) reveals all and in doing so creates yet another surface, the curator's performative act of 'pointing' to someone else's experiences, combined with the dismissal of their own, is a tacit claim to their authenticity; they may be here on the surface with you now, but their authority stems from having been deeper and seen further into the oceanic depths below.

Chapter 12

Notes on Performatist Photography: Experiencing Beauty and Transcendence after Postmodernism

Raoul Eshelman

For many years, art photography was dominated by ironic, detached perspectives and flat, trivial or repelling representations of reality. As typical examples one could point to the work of such renowned photographers as Lee Friedlander, William Eggleston, Diane Arbus, Boris Mikhailov, Thomas Ruff or Nan Goldin. This photographic approach to reality is not an individual whim of the artists involved but is typically postmodern. It is postmodern in the sense that it abandons the modernist strategy of revealing beauty in the everyday world using rigorous technical means – the sort of photographic high art once produced by Edward Weston or Ansel Adams. Such postmodern photography generates continual visual irony by demonstrating that the art form which is best suited to representing reality directly is also least suited to transcending the banality and contingency of that reality. As Barthes notes in his seminal essay *Camera Lucida*, the photograph never transcends its subject matter for the sake of something else (1981 [1980]: 4); it always leads us back to the objects it refers to and into a 'flat death' (1981 [1980]: 92).

From the postmodern point of view, there is no way out of this ironic bind. As Susan Sontag (1990), among others, has suggested, to do so would be to return to the illusions of photographic modernism (which heroically thought it could change us by revealing hidden beauty through technical rigor) or to those of photographic humanism (which sought to promote understanding through a positive identification with appealing, apolitical representations of the 'family of man'). It follows from this historical experience that we must maintain a profound scepticism towards any images that seem to convey any higher sensation of beauty, order or transcendence or to try to prompt a positive identification with the human. Since critics influenced by postmodernism tend to equate any deviation from irony with a restoration of humanism and/or modernism, they have great difficulty grasping photographic art in anything other than their own irony-steeped terms. Even critics sceptical of postmodernism offer little in the way of an alternative. Michael Fried's (2008) *Why Photography Matters as Art as Never Before* – the most ambitious attempt to conceptualise present-day trends in photography – advances brilliant individual arguments but is incoherent as a whole. Fried tries to define a new historical trend in photography based on a universal opposition between theatricality and anti-theatricality/ absorption that he developed in the wake of his famous article on 'Art and Objecthood' (1967), which was directed against postmodernist minimalism. Having set up his categories, Fried then wilfully goes on to ignore them, lumping together theatrical ironists such as Thomas Struth or Rineke Dijkstra with anti-theatrical aestheticians such as Andreas Gursky and Thomas Demand (for a critical perspective on this confusion, see Kelsey 2009).

In the past few years, the ironic, deadpan approach to the world peculiar to postmodernism has become increasingly tired and predictable. This has caused a new generation of photographers to follow paths that are no longer postmodern in the sense noted earlier but are also not repetitions of previously occurring humanist or modernist positions. Instead, we now find pictures that confront us with visual images holding forth the possibility of a higher, aesthetically transmitted value. This kind of photography does not work by startling us into seeing the world anew or by appealing to wishful thinking about the human. Rather, its starting point is much the same as in postmodernism, in the sense that it starts off with unappealing, banal objects or situations. The crucial difference is that this type of photography forces us to identify with these things aesthetically and formally in such a way that their banality is overcome. This affirmative, forced movement towards beauty and transcendence *per formam* – through form – corresponds to similar strategies in literature, film, painting and architecture. This general development, which I call performatism, is gradually replacing the ironic strategies and anti-aesthetic attitude of postmodernism (see Eshelman 2008: 195–227; 2010). In this chapter, I provide a short theoretical introduction into how performatism operates in photography and examine six photographers whose work exemplifies this new artistic approach.

PERFORMATISM IN PHOTOGRAPHY: DOUBLE FRAMING

Just how does performatism work in photography? The crucial technique of performatism is what I call double framing. In photography, this means that a 'lock' or 'fit' must be established between the formal givens of the photographic work (the inner frame) and the authorial agent organising them (the outer frame). At first, one could object that this distinction is trivial or self-evident, for even postmodern works (no matter how chaotic their subject matter or deadpan their perspective) are organised by a higher agent or author of some kind who is acutely aware of what he or she is doing. The difference is that in performatism both the inside and outside frames work together to force us to perceive whatever is being photographed as an aesthetic unity rather than as anti-aesthetic disorder. Instead of producing an endless regress of ironic references or confronting us with a Barthesian 'flat death' (1981 [1980]) that reminds us of our own materiality and mortality, the photograph creates a binding, palpable feeling of unified order that seems to transcend the immediate subject matter of the picture.

This creation of unified order solves certain problems but raises other ones. Above all, the question arises as to who or what is responsible for this unity. Is it coincidence that the photographer discovered this unified order, or was this order willed upon the picture arbitrarily by a God-like photographer-author? While the question of how much order and/or beauty is desirable is hardly new to photographic criticism (see Sontag 1990: 101), performatism answers it in an entirely different way than did modernism and postmodernism. Performatism uses the direct or indexical relation of photography to reality to suggest that banal or everyday things are charged or loaded with some higher form of order (whose origin remains unknown). The will of the photographer and the formal givens of the picture – the human and the natural – work together performatively to create the impression of a higher, transcendent unity but at the same time block ultimate access to the source of that unity. This stands in direct contrast to postmodernism, which undermines unity through ironic scepticism, and to high modernism, which claims to uncover the dynamic order of the world directly with technical means. Performatism might be thought of in historical terms as reversing the disordering, critical scepticism of postmodernism while not returning to the modernist conceit that natural, dynamic order can be directly revealed through art. The goal of performatist photography is to create what one might call the effect of transcendence – a transcendence that is formally palpable but whose source is not directly accessible to the viewer.

While it is possible to reject this performatist unity after the fact (the postmodern viewer will certainly want to do so), the viewer cannot escape the formal intuition of unity forced upon him or her by the work of art. The totalising gesture of the photograph gives the viewer but little choice: take it or leave it. This gesture also repeats itself on a higher, historical level. Together with many other such events, the individual performance or event of the photograph helps establish the end of postmodernism and the beginning of a new epoch that returns numinous value to the world through art, rather than devaluing it through a Neo-Nietzschean perspective that flatly rules out the transcendent and ironically relates that which seems alive and real to the grim materiality of death.

The new trend is certainly not universal or even dominant in art photography. Only time will tell whether this particular direction will assert itself as massively as did the modernist new way of seeing or as did postmodern irony. In the following brief analyses, I show how the new aesthetic works and why it must be thought of as part of a unified field. To do so, I have selected six very different photographers whose work demonstrates similarities in their approach to the world. The photographers – Nicholas Hughes, Alina Kisina, Mike Perry, Nikita Pirogov, Mike Sinclair and Kurt Tong – are, variously, from the USA, England, China, Ukraine and Russia; they range in age from their early twenties to their mid-fifties and in biographical terms have little or nothing in common. Although they use very different techniques and address very different themes, these photographers share a common aesthetic vision that offers an affirmative, though not untroubled, approach to the contemporary world.

ALINA KISINA

Alina Kisina was born in Kiev, Ukraine, in 1983 and has lived in the United Kingdom since 2003. Her pictures (see http://alinakisina.co.uk), which she takes almost entirely in her Ukrainian homeland, range from the dramatic to the contemplative. A favourite technique of hers is to use reflections that

Figure 12.1. *City of Home III, 9 –* Alina Kisina.

confront us with forms and planes that draw us involuntarily into her pictures and then dissolve into dynamic, unexpected dimensions resisting everyday definition or description, as for instance in *City of Home III*, 9 (figure 12.1) and 6 (For all *City of Home* images discussed in this chapter, see: http://alinakisina.co.uk/City-of-Home). In spite of the difficulty of distinguishing between up and down, in and out, fore and back, these and similar pictures convey a feeling of higher, inscrutable order rather than of rampant irony.

In *City of Home III*, 9, this sense of order is confirmed by the slightly slack wire stretching across the photo. Higher order is suggested in this particular case by the division of the photograph (which resists description in terms of normal spatial coordinates) into two roughly equal halves. The wire, which is ordinarily a photographic mistake to be avoided at all costs, exemplifies the metaphysical optimism that is operating in a great deal of performatist art: even errors or flaws work to heighten a sense of greater order.

Another of Kisina's photographs – *City of Home*, 1 – features the Kiev skyline and appears to be directly numinous; shafts of perfectly parallel light stream oddly onto a cityscape from above. The otherworldly effect was achieved through an accident that neatly demonstrates the ineffable interplay of authorial and natural order mentioned earlier. The mysterious shafts of light were caused when the artist's film stock was run through the X-ray machine at Kiev airport; the damage to the film created a feeling of order that accidentally corresponded to precisely the sort of numinous effect that Kisina (who does not normally manipulate her images) was looking for in the first place.

Kisina rarely photographs people. *City of Home*, 19 is an exception that juxtaposes the minuteness of a human figure with the vast, but not empty or motionless, expanse of water spread out before and above it. Nature here is neither sublime nor beautiful, but rather a barely marked tabula rasa suggesting, but not fulfilling, its enormous potential. The human subject in the photo remains anonymous and small, but he is also the crucial feature that keeps the large, slightly rippling expanse of water from becoming a mere abstraction. Here, we find an apprehension of nascent, but unfulfilled sublimity that organises and unifies man and nature within the frame of the photograph. In an image in the series *Dacha* (http://www.alinakisina.co.uk/Dacha), Kisina uses the accidental order created by the greenish-blue colour marking the lawnmower, the shirt and the ceiling to create an effect of numinous unity; the strong foreshortening of the floor beams and the ceiling draw us inexorably into the picture, and the coiled wire wrapped around the lawnmower and connected to the wall creates an antipodal moment of tension to the receding horizon lines. As in much postmodern photography, the subject is emotionless and expressionless; in contrast to postmodern photography, she appears empowered by the aesthetically mediated order around her rather than diminished by it.

Kisina's return to her homeland is neither nostalgic nor hypercritical. It is worth comparing her work to the postmodern vision of Eastern Europe conveyed by Boris Mikhailov, perhaps the best-known contemporary photograph in the Russian-speaking world (Mikhailov is Ukrainian by nationality). Mikhailov's approach continues a typically Russian line of thought: in the early nineteenth century, the renegade thinker Pyotr Chaadaev characterised Russia – in his (1969) *Philosophical Letters* as a kind of cultural and historical tabula rasa – as a backward, empty land that was all the better suited for radical social and spiritual renewal by virtue of its utter cultural barrenness. Following in the long indigenous tradition that grew out of Chaadaev's thought, Mikhailov implies with his repellent, staged images of mostly naked or half-naked homeless people that his photos, which draw on Russia's extreme material deprivation, are best at conveying the kind of 'flat death' that Barthes (1981 [1980]) thinks is at the core of all photography.

Kisina's pictures, by contrast, while not allowing easy identification with her subject matter (which consists for the most part of drab urban scenery), offer a metaphysical way out of this drabness using formal or compositional means. Her photography always implies that there is some kind of higher order at work within her bleak, superficially unattractive cityscapes, and that this order works through clarified form and not through brute, deadly matter. This perspective is global. It arises because Kisina, though physically distant from her homeland, is able to return there freely to examine it without false sentimentality or nostalgia. This makes her work difficult for both East and West to identify with, but it exemplifies a kind of planetary or global perspective that conflates genuinely felt nearness to a 'city of home' with a higher, outside vision of order.

NIKITA PIROGOV

Nikita Pirogov is a young photographer from Petersburg, Russia, who creates magical harmonies out of quotidian material. In an image from the series *The Other Shore* (figure 12.2), a girl's face, which is almost literally cut out of its surroundings by the thin grey line surrounding it, seems to exist on a plane of its own before the almost palpably liquid surface of the water. It is this dissociation from the background that makes her utterly normal expression into something enticing and luminous: it is a face so open and receptive that you can almost only fall in love with it. Rather than being intimidated by the point of view of the photographer (who is after all directly pointing the camera at her face from above) the face turns the tables on him and enchants us as viewers.

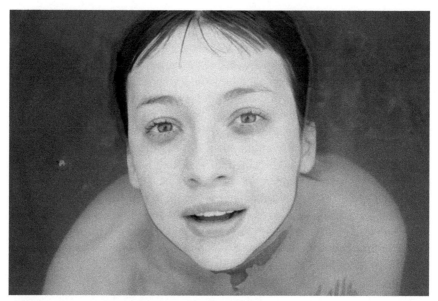

Figure 12.2. From *The Other Shore* – Nikita Pirogov.

For those familiar with goings-on in contemporary art photography, this picture must appear as a deliberate rebuttal to the work of Thomas Ruff. Beginning in 1986, Ruff began taking flat frontal portraits of expressionless people staring directly back at the viewer. These dreary-looking images confront us with an object of the greatest curiosity – a human face – and then block that curiosity as drastically as possible. In its place, we are given the feeling that we are being looked at by the inert, dehumanised image that is the photograph. It is as if Barthes's (1981 [1980]) 'flat death' would come to life and gaze ominously back at us. Pirogov's photo returns life to the girl's face and to us, but through a numinous, and not a merely human identification: the disembodied face emerging from the water presents itself to us as a formal totality that we cannot resist.

Another image from *The Other Shore* depicts a perfectly centred black hole in the midst of the textured earth surface. The hole appears nonetheless more as a point of promise than as an empty threat; both the twigs on the ground and the distortion caused by the camera work to create a sense of order in the midst of what seems to be nothing much at all. In a further work from the series, a snow-covered street leads into a misty, but nonetheless temptingly lit centre. We are guided into this centre by buildings on the right and trees on the left; the golden glint on the buildings gives a hard edge to the fuzzy point of promise situated in the picture's midst. In yet another image, a frame of trees leads us deep into the picture to a brightly, artificially coloured slide that nonetheless seems in perfect harmony with its natural surroundings: the slide is framed by the trees, and the tree branches softly repeat the diagonal of the slide. We are still aware of the difference between nature and culture, but they seem to complement one another without ironic conflict. In a final image from the series, reflections and colour on water's surface bestow a shimmering, ethereal multidimensionality to an everyday scene, which seems to rise out of its different material components to form a new whole.

Pirogov's metaphysically optimistic project (collected in his aptly named series *The Other Shore*) is directly comparable to Kisina's; the difference is that his search for order and value works from inside the country – it is literally much closer to its subject matter (faces, holes in the ground, puddles, etc.) than is Kisina's and therefore less abstract and more sensual in its stylization of that reality. Pirogov is a resident and Kisina a returning visitor to Eastern European venues that are grasped in terms of numinous potentiality rather than in terms of thematic disillusionment.

NICHOLAS HUGHES

The work of Nicholas Hughes (see http://www.nicholas-hughes.net) has a strong painterly, abstract quality that conflates natural order with the artificial vision of the photographer in both harmonious and dramatic ways. The photos cited here employ an abstract visual language using yin-yang oppositions that vary in depth (deep in *Field Verse III, Image # 7*, flat in *Edge Verse II, Image # 2*) and colour (monochrome in *Field Verse III, Image # 7*, intense and punctuated by a numinous red circle in *Field Verse I, Image # 1*). Although lacking subject matter in the usual sense of the word, these pictures convey a sense of balance and harmony, of depth and directedness. Rather than leading us into a void or flattening the world à la Barthes, they open new horizons in an aesthetically unexpected, inimitable way. Once more, we cannot say for sure whether the order is natural or artificial, willed or accidental. The formally experienced inability to decide on the status of this order, however, gives it a transcendent or numinous feel. This realm of opaque but unified order conveys an intuitively felt premonition of transcendence that is the main effect of what I call the double frame.

The opening of a new horizon occurs most dramatically in *Field Verse 1, Image # 5* (figure 12.3), where our gaze follows the sweeping arc of tire tracks across a coarse earthen field leading towards a blank sky. The dreariness of the theme is more than transcended by the whiteness reflected in the water of the tracks, which gives direction and force to the light of the sky in the distance. The telephone mast and wires in *Field Verse I, Image # 3*

Figure 12.3. *Field Verse 1, Image # 5* – Nicholas Hughes.

seem to point to a higher, unseen dimension; the glowing traces – presumably reflected – make a worldly explanation of the spatial relations that seem hardly possible anymore. Hughes's semi-abstract worlds are sometimes soft and soothing, sometimes magical and threatening, but always full of intensely felt depth and luminous potential.

MIKE PERRY

Mike Perry's pictures of landscapes (see http://www.m-perry.com) appear at first glance cool and documentational. They are, however, governed by a visual imperative that draws us into rough, almost physically palpable spaces and then elevates us aesthetically. In *Rockface at Jennwand* (South Tyrol, 2010), we are relentlessly drawn upwards by the zig-zagging diagonal lines in the middle of the picture that lead the eye into the craggy, misty heights of a rock quarry; in *Loch Cluanie* (Western Highlands, Scotland, 2009), we are drawn across soggy, rough moorland into a foggy, light horizon. Although these are clearly ravaged, inhospitable landscapes, they are nonetheless not depicted as the mere objects of human depredation. In a certain sense, the fact that they can still draw us inward and upward with what is left of their natural beauty suggests a kind of root belief in the world itself without which ecological activism would not be possible.

Silver Birch 3 (North Rim, Grand Canyon, USA 2002) transforms natural depth relations (the thicket of birch trees) into an ambivalent image with an abstract, Jackson-Pollock-like quality: nature and culture converge here in spite of themselves. *Silver Birch 3* is interesting to compare with Ansel Adams's modernist and Lee Friedlander's postmodernist renditions of the same or similar trees. Thanks to Adams's exacting photographic method his famous trees stand out crisply and cleanly before a black background and exemplify a strikingly beautiful, overpowering quality that one might call birchiness – an essential, formally compelling trait revealed through the skill of the photographer. Friedlander's tree pictures are basically parodies of Adams's style: he photographs trees in broad daylight in a way that effectively flattens the depth of field and makes their branches into a tangled mess constantly competing with the backgrounds behind them (see Friedlander 2005: 390–432).

Perry's birches are neither one nor the other. They are not clearly delineated enough to convey modernist thingness and, although forming a tangled thicket, they are too aesthetically pleasing to block our identification with the order they create. Once more, I would ascribe this peculiar aesthetic positioning of the birches to what I have called double framing. The photographer in this case creates a secondary, rather than a primary, identification with the trees. Rather than being struck by their essence, we search for aesthetic order in the tangle of branches (this order can in fact be established in the circle of branches in the lower middle of the picture, which coincides with an area of high contrast allowing a small group of saplings to stand out more than the rest).

Môr Plastig, Flip Flop 13 (Saadani Beach, Tanzania, 2013) (figure 12.4), from the series *Môr Plastig* ('Sea of Plastic'), shows one of the many flip-flops Perry has collected and photographed after beachcombing. This image effectively reverses the ravaged-nature motif of the landscapes. We are now confronted by plastic that itself has been corroded by the ocean and been rendered hauntingly beautiful because of it. Here, too, there is a subtle message suggesting the workings of a kind of opaquely operating natural religion: if the ocean can thusly beautify the plastic junk we throw into it, then there is some hope somewhere. This attitude is not uncritical, but it reverses completely the postmodern attitude that recognises only one-sided perpetrator-victim relations and that sees its ethical purpose in preventing evil rather than in participating in positive truth processes. This counter-position has been formulated by Badiou (2001) programmatically in *Ethics: An Essay on the Understanding of Evil* and by myself from the perspective of

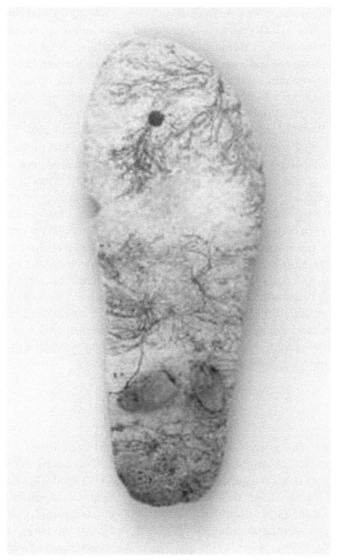

Figure 12.4. *Môr Plastig, Flip Flop 13* – Mike Perry.

performatist ethics (Eshelman 2011). The numinous beauty captured in *Môr Plastig, Flip Flop 13* has an ethical impetus to it that is derived from its ambivalent, oceanic origin. Only by addressing this ambivalent origin – the performative interaction of nature and culture – in a positive way can we arrive at constructive solutions to environmental problems.

In *Astral America: Arco Refinery* (California, USA, 2002), Perry's factory –
from the series *Astral America* – is not a flat, inert industrial object like that
depicted in the work of Bernd and Hilla Becher, whose serial photos of drab
industrial buildings had a great influence on both postmodern landscape and
portrait photography. Instead, the factory seems to reach upward before a
bright stripe on the horizon that gives it a three-dimensional, cathedral-like
quality. The crane, the central smokestack and the red street markers direct
our gaze first towards the centre, then onwards and upwards. This photo
strives, as do Perry's landscape pictures, to transcend the rough materiality of its visual givens and presents a robust, spiritualised, but ultimately
non-heroic vision of American industry (for this factory is too drab, the sky
too grey). Here, postmodernists will no doubt miss a scathing representation
of industrial capitalism as a menacing, destructive force. Perry's picture obviously does not do this, but at the same time it is not uncritical: it renders very
effectively the quasi-religious character of American industrial capitalism
without turning it into a hypercritical caricature. This attitude is comparable
to Andreas Gursky's large-scale photos of scenes resulting from globalisation, which capture the enormous scale and the aesthetic lure of globalisation
without crudely vilifying it. By contrast, the scathing postmodern critiques of
capitalism can offer no positive alternative (communism? back to nature?);
their endless critique is made possible by the endless irony that they do not
have to supply any kind of positive answer themselves.

KURT TONG

Kurt Tong's photos (see http://www.kurttong.co.uk) from the series *People's
Park* return to the amusement parks of his Chinese homeland that have
become increasingly neglected due to the modernisation of Chinese society.
Instead of documenting this process of decay in an ironic, distanced way,
Tong uses techniques of framing and centring to create spatial harmonies that
arise in spite of (and sometimes precisely because of) the parks' run-down
states. This metaphysical optimism, which is characteristic of performatist
art, does not deny decay or decline but manages to find dignified order and
beauty in it nonetheless.

My first image from *People's Park* uses the winding form of a miniature
train track to cause culture and nature to appear as a relaxed, gently collab-
orative unity; the glinting tracks seem to embrace the trees in a graceful loop.
Another *People's Park* picture (figure 12.5) captures a painting-like, illusory
surface in the former window of a wall, thus literally demonstrating the performatist act of double framing (the photo frames the frame in a centred, unified way that the eye cannot resist). A third picture initially disrupts the basic

Figure 12.5. From *People's Park* – Kurt Tong.

harmonic scheme of Tong's other pictures by juxtaposing the round figures of the amusement ride with the square ones of the bench; the blue colour of the chairs and of the uppermost unit of the ride restores that harmony once again.

The pictures of the amusement rides in *People's Park* are also juxtaposed with faded colour snapshots of Tong's family taken in these parks during his childhood. The contrasting of old and new evokes the genuine experience of a bygone childhood but avoids ironically presenting aesthetically trivial family photos as high art (the qualitative difference between the family snapshots and Tong's present-day photos is too marked). The two types of photography in fact complement one another effectively. The snapshots are elevated by their presentation together with actual art photography; high art, for its part, is shown to be rooted in real, visually documented human experience. The muted harmonies of Tong's carefully composed photos allow him (and us) to experience childhood memory places in a non-idealised way that takes into account the passage of time without sinking into irony or bathos.

The series *In Case It Rains in Heaven* documents a widespread Chinese burial practice. Relatives of the deceased person make or buy objects made of joss paper that represent consumer objects particularly dear to that person and then ritually burn these objects, which are thought to make possible a comfortable or even lavish life in heaven for the deceased. Superficially, these crude paper reproductions of consumer items are kitsch, and photographing them and presenting them in a high-art context would at first seem to be a characteristic act of postmodern irony. Tong's intent is, however, decidedly non-ironic: introducing the project on his website, Tong says that all the items depicted were 'burnt as offerings for my ancestors'. What he, in fact, achieves is an aesthetically and spiritually charged double framing of these offerings. By photographing them in a neutral way against a black background apart from any context he gives them an aesthetic dignity of their own; conversely, the spiritual charge of these objects is transferred back to the viewer through the aesthetic act, which totalises and intensifies the effect of the individual offerings.

It is perhaps just a coincidence that a similar procedure is employed in high art by the German photographer Thomas Demand, who makes skilfully constructed three-dimensional cardboard replicas of interiors and natural objects, photographs them with a large-format camera and then demolishes them (see Eshelman 2008). By constructing, documenting and destroying these objects, Demand acts as a kind of a photographer-God, performing his own sacral ritual of world-making in an aesthetic, secular mode. Tong, for his part, participates indirectly in a real sacral rite by elevating it to the level of art; instead of confronting us with flat, kitschy death he offers us three-dimensional (albeit clumsily constructed) objects of art that have a very real and important social function thanks to their connection with those who once lived. The material trace of the photo leads back into life, not death.

MIKE SINCLAIR

Mike Sinclair's photos (see http://www.mikesinclair.com) of the American Midwest (his hometown is Kansas City, Missouri) avoid the usual ironic send-ups of quotidian architecture and consumer society that we have come to expect since Lee Friedlander or William Eggleston. Instead, Sinclair depicts banal forms that evoke an upwardly directed feeling of transcendence (such as church-tower-like structures in the *Main Street* series) or create quiet harmonies between nature and culture. The winged pavilion in an image from the *City Beautiful* series is almost Buddhist in its harmonic, bird-like grace; the looping, tear-shaped gully pulls us sensually into the autumn landscape (figure 12.6), a bit like in a Grant Wood painting come to life. The irresistible feeling of being drawn into the warm, undulating depths of the park overrides the barrenness of the immediate theme.

In an untitled picture from the series *Popular Attractions*, the formal arrangement of the two telephone poles in the picture of a line at a fairground

Figure 12.6.   From *City Beautiful* – Mike Sinclair.

eatery creates an upward movement similar to that in the two pictures from the *Main Street* series; this is enhanced by the gently sloping telephone wires and the tilted lines of the booth and the surrounding objects. Through its form, the warm, brightly lit, inwardly directed lines of the steak sandwich stand acquires a sacral charge that transfers in a positive way to the mundane act of eating. Sinclair's pictures project an almost meditative calm and capture the unconscious striving for transcendence contained in humdrum situations and scenes. Sinclair's distinctive vision of Middle America avoids sentimental boosterism on the one hand and the snarky celebration of suburban ugliness on the other; it shows Middle America in a mode of quiet grace that eludes easy positive representation and disarms insincere mockery.

CONCLUSION

In my brief remarks on post-postmodern photography, I have tried to approach the subject in as direct a way as possible. The only way we can distinguish between historical epochs like the ones treated here is first to employ

categorical oppositions that offer clear distinctions between them (oppositions that are anathema to postmodernism itself). Second, I have defined
the new direction by isolating what the Russian Formalists called *priemy* or
devices – technical procedures that have certain functional effects that are
open to direct description.

The root device of performatism is double framing. In art photography, this
means that the photographer forces us to identify in a secondary or mediated
way with whatever he or she is showing us in the photographic image. This
makes no sense either to a modernist or to a postmodernist. The modernist wants us to be moved or shocked by images directly; the postmodernist
knows that all experience is mediated and that knowledge of this mediation
undercuts or poisons any sort of identification we might have with the image.
Performatism is a synthesis of these two ways of viewing the world (but also
not reducible anymore to either one). It recognises that images are mediated,
but it also realises that mediated images do not have to turn out to be disor-
dered, flat, dead or ironic.

In a certain sense, performatism turns the basic guiding principle of postmodernism against itself: where postmodernism wilfully created disorder and
irony, performatism wilfully creates order and unity. The main reason for this
turn, at least as far as I am concerned, is to be found in art itself rather than
in some sort of basal shift in globalised capitalism, politics or society as a
whole. The relentlessly receding, ironic critique of almost everything has its
aesthetic limits and with time grows as tiring and trite as anything else.

The turn to unity and order raises new opportunities and problems of its
own. On the one hand, it gives artists a chance to once more grasp the world
in positive visual terms, to once more convey to us uplifting experiences of
unity, depth, life, order, belief and beauty (within the confines of the double
frame, which never lets us forget that these experiences are constructed). This
sort of positive experience is basic to all human society and to all human
endeavours, and historically it certainly precedes the sort of Neo-Nietzschean
scepticism that informs postmodernism. No society has ever existed that is
not based on belief of some kind, and performatist art taps directly into belief
in a way that postmodernist irony cannot.

On the other hand, the performatist turn raises a variety of ethical questions
implicitly or explicitly relating to the capitalist, globalised world in which we
live. Postmodernists generally assume that any turn away from their critique
of power relations will result in a kind of neoconservative, or fundamental-
ist, or simply acquiescent attitude. At the moment, it is premature to say
just how the performatist approach to the world will develop in ethical and/
or political terms. However, it seems likely that this ethical concern will be
closely associated with aesthetic ones that show us new ways of coping with
the world rather than repeating old ways of criticising it. The artists treated

in this chapter are not directly agenda-driven, but through their art they do address ethical and political problems that will continue to be of great urgency in a globalised world. These include coping with globalisation itself (Kisina), with the destruction of the environment (Perry), with questions of national identity (Pirogov and Sinclair), with problems of time and personal identity (Tong) as well as with more abstract questions regarding the fabric of being itself (Hughes). Through double framing, performatism establishes numinously charged, ambivalent aesthetic unities from which these and other questions can be addressed.

A final note is in order on the relationship of metamodernism to performatism. Performatism was formulated programmatically ten years before metamodernism and has similar broad pretensions to explaining post-postmodernism in regard to literature, art, photography, architecture and theory. It resembles – but also differs from – metamodernism in its functional concept of double framing and in the way it defines history. Metamodernism explains the culture shift away from postmodernism in terms of a 'structure of feeling' arising out of the 'dialectical oscillation' between modernism and postmodernism ('metaxy'), it sees a 'romantic turn' in the newly aris-ing works of literature, art, media productions and so on, and it includes a sweeping cultural critique of politics (for a detailed discussion see the 'Introduction' to this collection). Performatism, by contrast, describes works of art, literature, architecture and so on, in terms of specific techniques and the implicit norms regulating their usage and does not apply these to politics or societal discourse, which demonstrably do not function like works of art. The key concepts of performatism are hence 'function' and 'double framing' and not 'structure of feeling'. Although performatist works are quite hetero-geneous in form and style, they tend more towards a 'classical' aesthetics of order than a 'romantic' aesthetics of disorder (the photographs discussed earlier are definitely closer to the former than the latter). Also, in describing the historical shift away from postmodernism I prefer the good old Hegelian term 'synthesis' to the figure of a 'dialectical oscillation' between modern-ism and postmodernism. Although performatism and metamodernism both agree that there really *is* something new going on, it seems to me here that metamodernism tries to straddle the fence too much on this particular issue. Either we are dealing with a dialectical synthesis resulting in a new stage of historical development, or we are dealing with a static, non-historical oscilla-tion, but not with a 'dialectical oscillation' that seems to accommodate both while being neither one nor the other (a 'both-neither dynamic'). Finally, performatism is based on a functional analysis of the formal features of works of art and not on an amorphous 'structure of feeling'. This is why perfor-matism avoids using concepts like the 'New Sincerity', which is helpful in describing how artists, critics, readers and audiences feel about developments after postmodernism but is not helpful in describing the works themselves (it would be futile, for example, to try to establish whether the photographs treated earlier are 'sincere' or not). These two approaches are, however, not entirely mutually exclusive; it would no doubt be possible to analyse how specific performatist visual or literary devices of blocking irony create the effect of a 'New Sincerity' in public discourse.

It is my hope that this chapter will help make readers aware that the present-day reactions to postmodernism are not random, arbitrary and particular, but follow a larger epochal logic that can be described in a conceptually coherent, systematic way.

EPILOGUE

Chapter 13

Thoughts on Writing about Art after Postmodernism

James Elkins

What tends to concern me these days isn't the art itself, but the writing about art: it seems to me that the writing is what needs to be written about. What bothers me is the lack of questioning and, of course, then, the lack of plausible theorisations and conceptualisations of the potential of writing, including experimental forms and styles.

It strikes me a number of contemporary art theorists, critics, visual studies scholars and art historians continue to write according to disciplinary models, within and to disciplinary audiences, but at the same time they build their work on poststructuralist foundations, including writers from Benjamin to Foucault and Butler. This creates a dissonance between the conceptualisation of writing in the theoretical sources – where writing is fundamental to sense, where it is unchained from disciplinary allegiances, where it cannot be funnelled into utilitarian expositions – and the well-mannered prose that continues to be produced by the art world. We are still good post-structuralists: no one has forgotten the lessons of the 1960s and 1970s, and no one is arguing with the Roland Barthes of, say 'The Death of the Author' (1977 [1968]) or *Camera Lucida* (1981 [1980]). Yet in the absence of those sorts of critiques, we still see an instrumentalisation of language, to the point where it is considered normative to construct a post-structuralist argument, of the kind that should, by its own logic, question disciplinarity, within the rigid stylistic and formal boundaries of one's own discipline.

It's also the case that theorists, historians or critics of art do not generally operate in full awareness of the spectrum of contemporary experimental fiction, from Kenneth Goldsmith and Christian Bök to Enrique Vila-Matas, Mark Leyner, Segio De La Pava, Sergio Chejfec, Lydia Davis and Mathias Enard. If you write, and you don't write in the imaginative light of the full range of contemporary writers, then you are working in a narrow domain, artificially constrained by disciplinary allegiances. A stimulating example would be Ali Smith. In *Artful*, Smith (2012) reproduces verbatim four lectures that she gave at Oxford interwoven with an autobiographical or memoiristic kind of narrative about the loss of a loved one. Here, fiction and non-fiction are blurred, enlarging the expressive range to address the lecture's theme of temporality. There is an astonishing lack in academic writing of attempts at those sorts of intersections. These frustrations have been pushing me further and further in the direction of experimental writing. I feel a kind of impatience, born from the lack of awareness of these issues. I like to think of my position as a series of questions that could be posed to academic or professional writers on art: 'How might you take writing seriously? What would be entailed, from your perspective, in engaging writing in a fuller sense? Is writing principally a matter of disciplinary models, clarity and usage, or are wider models of writing available?'

The question of writing has appeared in different guises, but it seems to me that you could specify various moments in which it has been seen as a problematic. During the first moment, in the 1960s and 1970s, a certain strand of feminist art history found it necessary to speak in an autobiographical mode, especially in Anglo-American writing. That moment is now part of history and is studied as historiography in graduate classes. It includes, for example, early essays by Griselda Pollock and autobiographical interventions by Linda Nochlin (see Boxer 2001). The second moment, in the early 1990s, is structured around debates about 'word and image', exemplified by, say Mieke Bal (1991) or early work by W.J.T. Mitchell (1980, 1986, 1995). The third moment can be observed, for instance, in the book Harper Montgomery and I co-edited, based on a seminar series of the same name, *Beyond the Aesthetic and the Anti-Aesthetic* (2013) in which the early 2000s appeared as part of this history of the problematisation of writing about art. Yet, here, a still contemporary problematic also surfaced in the work of Gavin Butt or Irit Rogoff in *Art After Criticism* (2004) in which the performative – as a time-based art that needs to find its proper form in writing – was seen as a potential challenge for writing. If there were a fourth moment, I guess it would consist of writing that is concerned, generally speaking, with the Internet. My favorite example is the Chinese American writer Tan Lin as his work has everything to do with contemporary forms of attention. We could, therefore, create a provisional narrative or sketch an intermittent history of the awareness of the problematic of writing, yet I don't think that these moments would necessarily connect. Maybe a better way to think about all of this is as an ongoing challenge issued from texts – French post-structuralist texts – written now a half century ago, and still very much unanswered.

This is a speculative essay on the state of writing about art, in three episodes. For me, it is important: (1) to take writing as seriously as the post-structural critique would imply; (2) to engage writing in the full aware-ness of its contemporary developments; and (3) to move outside of the limited conceptualisation of writing within the fields that produce art writing. As an art historian or a critic, what I produce is words, and if those words are lim-ited by my reticence to thoroughly adopt theoretical positions that I otherwise freely employ (point a), or by my ignorance of contemporary directions in writing (point b), or by my affiliation to disciplinary muteness about writing (point c), then I am not writing in a full sense.

HOW THE ACADEMY THINKS ABOUT
WRITING IN GENERAL

Ever since the reception of postmodernism in the 1970s, the academy has known that it cannot contain writing. The point of reference is Ronald Barthes, as the French post-structuralist who was most open and honest about what he was discovering in terms of writing. (Foucault, as a rather interest-ing aside, was not. On the one hand Foucault's machinery of language is unremitting; he is a juggernaut of argumentation. On the other hand, he is writing about the death of the author. This is an interesting polarity, which hasn't been teased out as much as it might be.) The essay, as a form, has become problematic because it is recognised that fiction bleeds into non-fiction, 'philosophy' into 'literature', the voiced into the unvoiced. The fact that the essay is impossible is the reason for the sudden drop in books about the essay; in English there are only the problematic anthologies by the anti-realist John d'Agata (2003, 2009, 2016) and the literary collection by Philip Lopate (1997).

There have been attempts to revive the essay form through 'Adorno', but to little effect. Yet the question is: What kind of model is this? Adorno's essay – i.e. the essay as form – is, as far as I'm concerned, *not* available as a model precisely because it is such a radical position in which writing has to find and undermine form at any moment in order to count as an essay. You can't use that as a template for writing on any subject. It's actually a way of thinking about how thought undermines structure.

In fact, Adorno doesn't need to be the touchstone. I can think of ten to fifteen potentially interesting theories of the essay (see Elkins 2013 for such a discussion). Everyone in the academy – art historians, critics, theorists – knows that it is impossible to continue to write nonfiction, but almost no one takes the consequences seriously. The exceptions are dis-unified and often of limited interest, and those two properties also show how little headway has been made (I am thinking of scattered figures like Jean-Louis Schefer, Jean-Claude Lebensztejn, Hélène Cixous, Griselda Pollock).

Meanwhile, there is an implicit notion about what a good academic style is. While re-reading three of the major surviving classical rhetorical texts by Quintillian, Cicero and Hermogenes, which I had not looked at since I was forced to read them in university, it struck me that the plain style or the clear style or the simple style, as it is variously translated, was never for any of them a writing degree zero on which you add ornamentation. It was always one of a palette of choices – the grand style, the ornate style and all the rest of it. Yet the plain style, at some point in the nineteenth-century academic codification of rhetoric, became the foundation on which you can then build. In the humanities, this enabled instructors to tell their students that they should first learn to write clearly and organise their thoughts and then – when they had become a professional or obtained a permanent job in the university – they could risk it: 'go ahead and add these ornaments to your words'.

However, the literary scholar Hugh Kenner called the plain style something like the most disorienting form of discourse precisely because of its ideology of clarity, which is so obviously false that in order to read a plain text as simply plain you need to be naïve in a literary and philosophical sense (1985). In the humanities I don't see any evidence of those sorts of critiques (even though Kenner was an academic). I see instead that students are referred to manuals of style, as well as various kinds of ephemeral grammar guides, to get them started and produce something which is nominally clear. If the prose achieves some kind of clarity, the next step – after an untheorised gap – is to help the student to write in the manner, mode or style of the professional journals in their field, so that they can go on and become successful. This is based on a misunderstanding of classical rhetoric. In contemporary rhetorical studies, the idea that the plain style is fundamental does not exist. One of the recent points of debate in classical rhetoric concerns, for instance, is the notion of *ekphrasis*. Some of these interpreters of first-century AD texts even discuss the notion in relation to W.J.T. Mitchell's essay 'Ekphrasis and the Other' (1992), resulting in points of intersection between a wider idea of ekphrasis and deconstruction. This is yet another case of the humanities lagging far behind their colleagues across the university campus.

HOW CONCEPTUAL WRITING UNDERSTANDS ITS RELATION TO ART

There is, therefore, a disconnect between the most interesting contemporary experimental and conceptual writing, on the one hand, and the writing that is done in the art world. Recently, several theorists of conceptual writing have proposed that writers like Vanessa Place, Caroline Bergvall and Christian Bök come out of conceptual art from the 1960s to the present. Vanessa Place (in Place and Fitterman, 2009) has argued that Hal Foster and others are pertinent for an understanding of her own and other practices. Craig Dworkin, a literary critic and theorist of conceptual writing, has produced an elaborate history tracing contemporary conceptual writing back to Duchamp, Warhol, Kosuth and others. Kenny Goldsmith has published an account that does the same, tracing his own practice back to Kosuth and others (see Dworkin and Goldsmith 2010).

These genealogies are only partly convincing from an art world point of view, not least because conceptual art began by giving up the medium, while conceptual writing consistently insists on the materiality – the non-referentiality – of its texts. If you were to give a seminar of art historians a text like Dworkin's and ask them whether this is a plausible history – that is, do you think that these contemporary practises in writing really go back to the 1960s and conceptual art in particular? – you might find that people wouldn't find it particularly persuasive. It's just that it's too general to have much purchase. They claim that literature and poetry have somehow lagged behind and are now catching up. In doing so, they put an odd kind of twist into existing histories in order to avoid existing parallels, ready to be taken up.

I would much rather that Kenny Goldsmith would speak or write more about the American writer Charles Reznikoff (1894–1976) who is really just a few microns distant from him. Conceptual poets, for various reasons, do not want to be the next iteration of that kind of constrained writing and need their conceptual projects to be different. However, historically speaking it's an implausible genealogy. It seems to me that to trace influence in a historically plausible way, you have to come to terms with some of your demons, as Carl Jung would say. For Dworkin, Goldsmith, Place, the more expected – and really, the more convincing – lineage goes to Malarmé, Bouvard and Pécuchet, Roussel, Oulipo and other experimental writing. In any case, such debates about contemporary experimental fiction, its lineages and its consequences for writing per se do not affect the discipline-bound writings of art historians, theorists and critics.

HOW WRITING IS UNDERSTOOD WITHIN ART HISTORY

Now that institutional critique has been – inevitably – absorbed into the system, the focus is shifting to the production of writing. That is the burden of Andrea Fraser's disconsolate essay for the 2012 Whitney Biennial, called 'There's No Place Like Home', and it is a common theme within art history. But what are the models for writing in the academy?

In North America, there has been a lot of talk about Alexander Nemerov, an art historian who works at Stanford. His style and his mode of argumentation are said to be models for an expanded sense of writing within the discipline. By literary standards, though, his work is belletristic: it has more in common with Walter Pater than with twentieth-century developments. Still, so far the appreciation of Nemerov has not included a literary appraisal, and I take that as a sign of the poverty of conceptualisation of writing in the field. T.J. Clark is also often mentioned as a model of engagement and writing, but the discourse about him is no less impoverished. He is either read as an art historian (i.e. his writerly voice is ignored in favour of his arguments), or he is praised as a writer but in the same unmodulated, inarticulate terms that Nemerov is praised.

This simple sense of 'good writing' has been a characteristic of art history from the beginning – Roberto Longhi was also praised in these terms – and it shows the disconnect between even elementary forms of literary criticism and art history. The academy's obsessive interest in W.G. Sebald requires an analysis in its own right: he is admired for his mixture of fiction, memoir and historical writing, but he is not emulated. This has also characterised the reception of other experimental historians and critics – from John Berger to Georges Didi-Huberman. They have both been models and inspirations for art critics and historians, but virtually no one attempts to emulate them, or even analyse their modes of writing. I co-organised a conference called Art Speech at MoMA in spring 2011 to address this (see MoMA 2011): we were interested in why art historians need to write out their texts when they are speaking in public (most scientists do not), and what the nuance of writing conveyed, especially if it was unremarked by the writer or the audience. We experimented: we played a videotape of one of T.J. Clark's talks, and we followed it by a PowerPoint reduction of his talk, to see what remained after the 'writerly' subtleties had been subtracted. Very little remained, which is a puzzle for art history.

The wider problem is the nature of the university. The large body of literature on the unity of the university has been written almost exclusively in the humanities, consisting of literature going back to Humboldt and including a text by Derrida. To my knowledge, there is no book on the nature or unity of the university written by someone outside the humanities – though perhaps E.O. Wilson's *Consilience* (1998) might be understood as a counter-example. The point is that it has always been an internal debate in which people in the humanities project their ideas of what a coherent education or university life might be like onto other fields. Still, one of the biggest gaps in the humanities is exactly this unity between its own disciplines. This is most glaring in the theorisation of writing. It is not acknowledged – except, of course, in literature and comparative literature – by and large in Art History, Theory and cultural criticism. It is as though it does not exist. Most of the people in, say, law, medicine, social sciences and so on know perfectly well that if they wanted to learn about their visual practices they could come over to the art departments or media departments. Yet the art scholars would never think of crossing the hall to the literature department. That, to me, is the larger issue here.

ENVOI

There is, as far as I am concerned, only one option: to take writing seriously enough so that it risks undermining my own intentions to write about art. That is Barthes's lesson – and that's how he was working in the last years of his life. My book *What Photography Is* (Elkins 2011) is already something other than history, criticism or theory: I suppose it is something like a memoir. In it, I have tried to see what would happen if art writing is given the freedom that everyone, since Barthes, has claimed for it. The result, *What Photography Is,* may end up being used even less than Fançois Laruelle's *The Concept of Non-Photography* (2011), a 'non-philosophy' book on 'non-photography'.

I was once at a conference in the United Kingdom and at the end, during the wrap-up speech, one of the people who convened it rhetorically said, 'Well, I'd just like to note the fact that over the last three days all of us have mentioned *Camera Lucida'*. Almost everyone indeed had; except for one person. 'I wonder why that is', he continued. 'I think it's because the book is so beautiful'. This was my starting point. It seemed to me to be a very inadequate thing to say for an academic. You would really want to define what you mean by that word beautiful as well as what you intend that word to be doing if you are using it that way. The more I looked into this the more it occurred to me that *Camera Lucida* has been read in two very polarised ways. It has been excavated for theories – and this is the normative way of reading it within the academy. Michael Fried (2008), for instance, went to section 20 and took one sentence from it. He has a couple of things to say in passing about how good the writing is – and he does not even mean it. He's really only interested in that one sentence, which helps him out with his own theories. That's an extreme – but typical – kind of excavation of Barthes's writing. *Camera Lucida* has also been understood as an experiment in writing – a jungle of overwrought French writing somehow hiding theories – and I think that's more or less what the speaker at the UK conference meant.

The persistence of *Camera Lucida* might be assignable to the fact that it has not been read in a synthetic fashion. It is either read as embedded theory or as experimental memoir, or else it is read first one way, and then the other. Batchen does this, for instance, in *Photography Degree Zero* (2011), an anthology about *Camera Lucida*. In his introduction, he lists all the critical literary terms that he likes from the late Barthes and, then, he proposes the exact opposite in his own contribution. There, he argues that *Camera Lucida* can be seen as a history of photography because it contains at least one photograph from every decade of the history of photography. In other words, *Camera Lucida* unaccountably becomes something that can be mined for a historiographic or positivistic purpose.

In *What Photography Is*, I was trying to take writing as seriously as I think Barthes took it so as to open up to the possibility that the writing would take me in a direction that would undermine my own theories – and it would cease to become a theory book. I am not the right person to judge whether my book can be mined for theories or managed to undermine them – but I have a feeling that it is a bit of both. I have some theories, of course. Yet the book is very badly behaved as theory. It is worse than badly behaved as history. And it's not really criticism. So it's an experiment in art writing. However, it doesn't make good on its own promise to let the writing behave as strangely as it would like, even if that means the subject is no longer photography. In the end, the subject is still photography and the conceptual framework is still analytic, critical and historical.

Hence my decision: aside from the stray essay, like this one, and aside from lecturing, I am giving up writing art criticism, theory and history. Instead I am, simply, writing. I have been doing that for two years, and I intend to continue another four years before I try to publish. It's a big leap, moving from the comfort of a neatly packaged disciplinary and conceptual home, out into the moving territory of writing itself: but if I didn't at least try, I would be playing false to the very conceptual and theoretical interests that inform my practice (that is point a); I would be provincial in relation to contemporary writing (point b); and I would be constrained by the narrow interests of the discipline that happens to pay my salary (point c).

References

Abramson, Seth. 2015a. 'The Metamodernist Manifesto'. *The Huffington Post*. 8 April 2015. Accessed 20 May 2015. http://www.huffingtonpost.com/seth-abramson/the-metamodernist-manifes_7_b_6995644.html

Abramson, Seth. 2015b. 'Metamodern Literature and the Metaverse'. *Huffington Post*. 15 April 2015. Accessed 20 May 2015. http://www.huffingtonpost.com/seth-abramson/metamodern-literature-and_b_7067708.html

Adorno, Theodor. 2003 [1967]. 'Art and the Arts'. In *Can One Live After Aushwitz?: A Philosophical Reader*, edited by Rolf Tiedemann, translated by Rodney Livingstone, 368–87. Stanford, CA: Stanford University Press.

van den Akker, Robin. 2013. 'Whatever Works'. Review of *NW*, by Zadie Smith. In *American Book Review, In Focus: Metamodernism*, edited by Christian Moraru. May/June 3–4. 15 and 30.

Allen, Stan and Marc McQuade, eds. 2011. *Landform Building: Architecture's New Terrain*. Zurich: Lars Muller.

al-Samad, Abdel Kafi. 2014. 'Lebanon's Islamists View Declaration of Caliphate as Heresy'. *Al-Akhbar English*. 1 July 2014. Accessed 15 August 2014. http://english.al-akhbar.com/content/lebanon's-islamists-view-declaration-caliphate-heresy

Améry, Jean. 1980. *At the Mind's Limits*. Bloomington: Indiana University Press.

The Andrew Marr Show. 2016. BBC 1, 10 July 2016.

Arquilla, John. 2011. 'The (B)end of History'. *Foreign Policy*. 27 December 2011. Accessed 15 January 2013. http://www.foreignpolicy.com/articles/2011/12/27/the_bend_of_history

Attridge, Derek. 2004. *The Singularity of Literature*. London: Routledge.

Avanessian, Armen. 2016a. 'Asynchronous Present Past'. In *Speculative Art Histories*, edited by Sjoerd van Tuinen. Edinburgh: Edinburgh University Press.

Avanessian, Arme. 2016b. *Der Zeitkomplex: Postcontemporary*. Berlin: Merwe.

Badiou, Alain. 2001. *Ethics. An Essay on the Understanding of Evil*. London: Verso.

Badiou, Alain. 2012. *The Rebirth of History: Times of Riots and Uprising*. London; New York: Verso.

Baker, Nicholson. 2010 [1988]. *The Mezzanine*. New York: Grove.

Bal, Mieke. 1991. *Reading 'Rembrandt': Beyond the Word – Image Opposition*. Cambridge: Cambridge University Press.

Barker, Chris and Emma A. Jane. 2016. *Cultural Studies: Theory and Practice*. Fifth Edition. London: Sage.

Barth, John. 1988 [1968]. 'Title'. In *Lost in the Funhouse*, 105–13. New York: Anchor.

Barthes, Roland. 1977 [1968]. 'The Death of the Author'. In *Image-Music-Text*, translated by Stephen Heath, 142–48. London: Fontana Press.

Barthes, Roland. 1981 [1980]. *Camera Lucida. Reflections on Photography*. Translated by Richard Howard. New York: Hill and Wang.

Basu, Laura. 2014. 'British Satire in *The Thick of It*'. *The International Journal of Media and Culture* 12(2): 89–103.

Batchen, Geoffrey. 2011. *Photography Degree Zero. Reflections on Roland Barthes's Camera Lucida*. MIT Press.

Baudrillard, Jean. 1993 [1976]. *Symbolic Exchange and Death*. Translated by Iain Hamilton Grant. London: Sage.

Baudrillard, Jean. 1983. *Simulations*. Cambridge, MA: MIT Press.

Baudrillard, Jean. 2003 [2002]. *The Spirit of Terrorism and Other Essays*. New Edition. Translated by Chris Turner. London; New York: Verso.

Beard, William. 2005. 'Maddin and Melodrama'. *Canadian Journal of Film Studies* 14(1): 2–17.

Beasley-Murray, Jon. 2010. *Posthegemony: Political Theory and Latin America*. Minneapolis; London: University of Minnesota Press.

Benn Michaels, Walter. 2013. 'Forgetting Auschwitz: Jonathan Littell and the Death of a Beautiful Woman'. *New Literary History* 25(4): 915–30.

Berg, Gretchen. 1989. 'Nothing to Lose: An Interview with Andy Warhol'. In *Andy Warhol: Film factory*, edited by Michael O'Pray, 54–61. London: BFI.

Bergthaller, Hannes. 2006/2007. 'Dis(re)memebering History's *Revenants*: Trauma, Writing, and Simulated Orality in Toni Morrison's *Beloved*'. *Connotations* 16(1–3): 116–36.

Berlant, Lauren. 2008. 'Thinking about Feeling Historical'. *Emotion, Space and Society* 1: 4–9.

Best, Steven and Douglas Kellner. 1999. *Postmodern Theory: Critical Interrogations*. Basingstoke: Macmillan.

Beigbeder, Frédéric. 2004. *Windows on the World*. London: Harper Perennial.

Bloch, Ernst. 1965. *Tübinger Einleitung in die Philosophie I*. Frankfurt a.M: Suhrkamp.

Bloch, Ernst. 1985 [1935]. *Erbschaft dieser Zeit*. Frankfurt a.M: Suhrkamp.

Boltanski, Luc and Ève Chiapello. 2007. *The New Spirit of Capitalism*. London: Verso.

Booth, Wayne C. 1961. 'Distance and Point-of-View: An Essay in Classification'. *Essays in Criticism* 11: 60–79.

Bourriaud, Nicolas. 2002 [1998]. *Relational Aesthetics*. Translated by Simon Pleasance, Fronza Woods and Mathieu Copeland. Les presses du reel.

Bourriaud, Nicolas. 2009. *The Radicant*. New York: Lucas & Sternberg.

Boxer, Sarah. 2001. 'Paintings Too Perfect? The Great Optics Debate'. *New York Times*. 4 December 2001. Accessed 16 October 2016. www.nytimes.com/2001/12/04/arts/paintings-too-perfect-the-great-optics-debate.html

Brandt, Jenn. 2015. '9/11, Hyperreality, and the Global Body Politic: Frédéric Beigbeder's *Windows on the World*. *Studies in 20th & 21st Century Literature* 39(1): 1–17. doi: 10.4148/2334-4415.1578

Brenner, Neil, Jamie Peck and Nik Theodore. 2010. 'Neoliberalism Resurgent? Market Rule After the Great Recession'. *The South Atlantic Quarterly* 111(2): 265–88.

Brenner, Neil, Jamie Peck and Nik Theodore. 2011. 'After Neoliberalization?' In *Global Ideologies and Urban Landscapes*, edited by Manfred B. Steger and Anne McNevin, 9–21. Abindon; New York: Routledge.

Brinkema, Eugenie. 2014. *The Forms of the Affects*. Durham, NC; London: Duke University Press.

Britton, Andrew. 2009. 'In Defense of Criticism'. In *Britton on Film: The Complete Film Criticism of Andrew Britton*, edited by Barry Keith Grant, 373–77. Detroit: Wayne State University Press.

Brouillette, Sarah. 2014. *Literature and the Creative Economy*. Stanford: Stanford University Press.

Browse, Sam. forthcoming. *Cognitive Rhetoric: The Cognitive Poetics of Political Discourse*. Amsterdam: John Benjamins.

Buchanan, Ian. 2006. *Fredric Jameson: Live Theory*. London; New York: Continuum.

Buchen, Stefan and Marie Delhaes. 2014. 'Die Katzen der Jeiligen Krieger'. *Süddeutsche Zeitung*. 2 August 2014. Accessed 15 August 2014. http://www.sueddeutsche.de/kultur/propaganda-zum-dschihad-die-katzen-der-heiligen-krieger-1.2072890

Butt, Gavin, ed. 2004. *After Criticism: New Responses to Art and Performance*. Wiley-Blackwell.

Caiani, Manuela and Linda Parenti. 2016 [2013]. *European and American Extreme Right Groups and the Internet*. London; New York: Routledge.

Cardoso, Rafael. 2010. 'Craft Versus Design: Moving Beyond a Tired Dichotomy'. In *The Craft Reader*, edited by Glenn Adamson, 321–32. Oxford; New York: Berg Publishers.

Carson, Tom. 2004. Gilligan's Wake. New York: Picador.

Castells, Manuel. 2012. *Networks of Outrage and Hope: Social Movements in the Internet Age*. Cambridge; Malden, MA: Polity.

Castells, Manuel, João Caraça and Gustavo Cardoso, eds. 2012. *Aftermath: The Cultures of the Economic Crisis*. Oxford: Oxford University Press.

Castro, Brian. 2008 [2003]. *Shanghai Dancing*. New York: Kaya Press.

Chaadaev, Peter. 1969. *The Major Works of Peter Chaadaev: A Translation and Commentary*. Notre Dame: University of Notre Dame Press.

Clough, Patricia Ticineto. 2007. 'Introduction'. In *The Affective Turn: Theorizing the Social*, edited by Patricia Ticineto Clough and Jean Halley, 1–33. Durham, NC; London: Duke University Press.

Colbert, Stephen. 2006. 'Stephen Colbert Roasts Bush at Whitehouse Correspondent's Dinner'. *YouTube*. Accessed 1 November 2016. https://www.youtube.com/watch?v=2X93u3anTco

Cole, Michael W. 2002. *Cellini and the Principles of Sculpture*. Cambridge: Cambridge University Press.

Cole, Teju. 2012. *Open City*. New York: Random House.

Cole, Teju. 2014 [2007]. *Every Day Is for the Thief*. London: Faber & Faber.

Collins, Suzanne. 2008–2010. 'A Conversation – Suzanne Collins, Author of *The Hunger Games* Trilogy: Questions and Answers'. *Scholastic*. Accessed 15 August 2015. http://www.scholastic.com/thehungergames/media/qanda.pdf

Coogan, Steve. 2011. 'Steve Coogan: I'm a Huge Fan of Top Gear. But This Time I've Had Enough'. *The Guardian*. Accessed 23 May 2016. http://www.theguardian.com/tv-and-radio/2011/feb/05/top-gear-offensive-steve-coogan

Corbyn, Jeremy. 2016. 'Jeremy Corbyn – A People-Powered Project'. *YouTube*. Accessed 1 November 2016. https://www.youtube.com/watch?v=3H-Jbu89etY

Cornell, Lauren. 2013. 'Beginnings + Ends'. *Frieze* 159. Accessed 15 August 2015. https://frieze.com/article/beginnings-ends/

Crawford, Alison. 2009. '"Oh Yeah!": Family Guy as Magical Realism?' *Journal of Film and Video* 61(2): 52–69.

Critchley, Simon. 2012. *Infinitely Demanding: Ethics of Commitment, Politics of Resistance*. London; New York: Verso.

Culler, Jonathan D. 1988. *Framing the Sign: Criticism and Its Institutions*. Oxford: Blackwell.

Cutter, Martha J. 2000. 'The Story Must Go On and On: The Fantastic, Narration, and Intertextuality in Toni Morrison's *Beloved* and *Jazz*'. *African American Review* 34(1): 61–75.

d'Agata, John. 2003. *The Next American Essay (A New History of the Essay)*. Graywolf Press.

d'Agata, John. 2009. *The Lost Origins of the Essay (A New History of the Essay)*. Graywolf Press.

d'Agata, John. 2016. *The Making of the American Essay (A New History of the Essay)*. Graywolf Press.

Dalrymple, William. 2014. 'The Isis Demand for a Caliphate Is About Power, Not Religion'. *The Guardian*. 13 July 2014. Accessed 15 August 2014. https://www.theguardian.com/commentisfree/2014/jul/13/isis-caliphate-abu-bakr-al-baghdadi-jihadi-islam

Danielewski, Mark Z. 2000. *House of Leaves*. New York: Pantheon.

Davis, Kimberly Chabot. 1998. '"Postmodern Blackness": Toni Morrison's *Beloved* and the End of History'. *Twentieth Century Literature* 44(2): 242–60.

De Landa, Manuel. 1997. 'The Machinic Phylum'. In *TechnoMorphica*, edited by Joke Brouwer and Carla Hoekendijk, 34–59. Rotterdam: V2_Publishers.

Deleuze, Gilles. 2002 [1981]. *Francis Bacon: The Logic of Sensation*. Translated by Daniel W. Smith. London; New York: Continuum.

Deleuze, Gilles and Félix Guattari. 1983. *Anti-Oedipus*. Minneapolis: University of Minnesota Press.

Deleuze, Gilles and Félix Guattari. 1987. *A Thousand Plateaus: Capitalism and Schizophrenia*. Translated by Brian Massumi. Minneapolis: University of Minnesota Press.

de Mul, Jos. 1999 [1990]. *Romantic Desire in (Post)modern Art and Philosophy*. Albany: State University of New York Press.

Derrida, Jacques. 1982. 'Signature Event Context'. In *Margins of Philosophy*, translated by Alan Bass, 309–30. Chicago, IL: Chicago University Press.

Derrida, Jacques. 1994. *Spectres of Marx: The State of the Debt, the Work of Mourning, and the New International*. Translated by Peggy Kamuf. New York: Routledge.

Derrida, Jacques. 2002. 'Force of Law: The "Mystical Foundation of Authority"'. In *Acts of Religion*, edited by Gil Anidjar, translated by Mary Quaintance, 228–98. New York: Routledge.

DeWitt, Helen and Ilya Gridneff. 2006. *Your Name Here*. Publisher: Author.

Donne, John (2012 [1624]) *'Meditation 17 ("For Whom the Bell Tolls" and "No Man is an Island")'*, *The Best of John Donne*. 45-7. Createspace Independent Publishing Platform.

Doubrovsky, Serge. 2013. 'Autofiction'. *Auto/Fiction* 1(1): 1–3.

Duménil, Gérard and Dominique Lévy. 2004. *Capital Resurgent. Roots of the Neoliberal Revolution*. Cambridge; London: Harvard University Press.

Duménil, Gérard and Dominique Lévy. 2011. *The Crisis of Neoliberalism*. Cambridge, MA; London: Harvard University Press.

Dupré, Sven, von Kerssenbrock-Krosigk, Dedo and Wismer, Beat. 2014. *Art and Alchemy*. The Mystery of Transformation. Hirmer.

Dumitrescu, Alexandra. 2007. 'Interconnections in Blakean and Metamodern Space'. *Double Dialogues* 7. Accessed 28 October 2016. http://www.doubledialogues. com/article/interconnections-in-blakean-and-metamodern-space/

Duncan, Pansy. 2016. *The Emotional Life of Postmodern Film: Affect Theory's Other*. New York; London: Routledge.

Dupré, Sven, Dedo von Kerssenbrock-Krosigk and Beat Wismer. 2014. *Art and Alchemy: The Mystery of Transformation*. Hirmer.

Dworkin, Graig and Kenneth Goldsmith. 2010. *Against Expression: An Anthology of Conceptual Writing*. Evanston, IL: Northwestern University Press.

Dyer, Geoff. 2009. *Jeff in Venice, Death in Varanasi*. Edinburgh: Canongate.

Eagleton, Terry. 2008 [1983]. *Literary Theory: An Introduction*. Anniversary edition. London: Blackwell.

Eco, Umberto. 1993. 'Postmodernism, Irony, the Enjoyable'. In *Modernism/Postmodernism*, edited by Peter Brooker, 225–28. London; New York: Longman.

Edelkoort, Li and Philip Fimmano, curators. 2014. 'For the Gathering: From Domestic Craft to Contemporary Process exhibition'. 28 May – 27 June 2014, Israel's Design Museum Holon.

Egan, Jennifer. 2011 [2010]. A Visit from the Goon Squad. New York: Anchor.

Egenhofer, Sebastian. 2010. *Produktionsästhetik*. Zürich; Berlin: Diaphanes.

Eggers, Dave. 2001. *A Heartbreaking Work of Staggering Genius: A Memoir Based on a True Story*. New York: Vintage Books.

Egginton, William. 2013. *How the World Became a Stage: Presence, Theatricality, and the Question of Modernity*. Albany: State University of New York Press.

Elias, Amy J. 2012. 'Postmodern Metafiction'. In *The Cambridge Companion to American Fiction After 1945*, edited by John N. Duvall, 15–29. Cambridge: Cambridge University Press.

Elkins, James. 2011. *What Photography Is*. New York: Routledge.

Elkins, James. 2013. 'Chapter 25: What Is an Essay? Eleven Theories'. *What Is Interesting Writing in Art History?* Accessed 5 September 2016. http://305737.blogspot. fr/2013/02/chapter-25.html

Elkins, James and Harper Montgomery. 2013. *Beyond the Aesthetic and the Anti-Aesthetic: The Stone Art Theory Institutes. Volume Four*. Penn State University Press.

Eshelman, Raoul. 2008. *Performatism, or the End of Postmodernism*. Aurora, CO: The Davies Group Publishers.

Eshelman, Raoul. 2010. 'Performatism in Contemporary Photograpy: Alina Kisina'. *Artmargins*. 29 May 2010. http://www.artmargins.com/index.php/2-articles/581-performatism-contemporary-photography-alina-kisina-article

Eshelman, Raoul. 2011. 'Performatism, *Dexter*, and the Ethics of Perpetration'. *Anthropoetics* 17(1). http://www.anthropoetics.ucla.edu/ap1701/1701Eshelman.htm

Eugenides, Jeffrey. 2011. *The Marriage Plot*. New York: Farrar, Straus and Giroux.

Eve, Martin Paul. 2012. 'Thomas Pynchon, David Foster Wallace and the Problems of "Metamodernism": Post-Millennial Post-Postmodernism?' *C21 Literature: Journal of 21st Century Writings* 1(1): 7–25.

Fairclough, Norman. 2000. *New Labour, New Language?* London: Routledge.

Falguières, Patricia. 2005. 'Afterword'. In *Ernst Kris, Le style rustique, translated by Christophe Jouanlanne & Ginette Morel*, 241–5. Paris: Éditions Macula.

Feigelfeld, Paul. 2015. 'Media Archeology Out of Nature: An Interview with Jussi Parikka'. *e-flux*. Accessed 23 July 2016. http://www.e-flux.com/journal/media-archaeology-out-of-nature-an-interview-with-jussi-parikka/

Fielding, Steven. 2014. *A State of Play: British Politics on Screen, Stage and Page, from Anthony Trollop to* The Thick of It. London: Bloomsbury.

Filmer, Paul. 2003. 'Structure of Feeling and Socio-Cultural Formation: The Significance of Literature and Experience to Raymond William's Sociology of Culture'. *The British Journal of Sociology* 54(2): 199–219.

Fish, William. 2016. '"Post-Truth" Politics and Illusory Democracy'. *Psychotherapy and Politics International*. doi: 10.1002/ppi.1387.

Fisher, Mark. 2009. *Capitalist Realism? Is There No Alternative?* Ripley: 0 Books.

Foster, Hal. 1996. *The Return of the Real: The Avant-Garde at the End of the Century*. Cambridge, MA: MIT Press.

Franklin, Bob. 1994. *Packaging Politics*. London: Arnold.

Franklin, Bob. 1998. *Tough on Sound Bites, Tough on the Causes of Sound Bites*. London: Catalyst Trust.

Franzen, Jonathan. 2001. *The Corrections*. New York: Farrar Straus and Giroux.

Franzen, Jonathan. 2003. 'Mr. Difficult'. In *How to Be Alone: Essays*, 238–69. New York: Picador.

Fraser, Andrea. 2012. 'There's No Place Like Home'. [Essay for the 2012 Whitney Biennial] Online: whitney.org/Exhibitions/2012Biennial/AndreaFraser

Fried, Michael. 1967. 'Art and Objecthood'. *Artforum International* 5: 12–23.

Fried, Michael. 2008. *Why Photography Matters as Art as Never Before*. Hartford: Yale University Press.

Friedlander, Lee. 2005. *Friedlander*. Text by Peter Galassi. Afterword by Richard Benson. New York: Museum of Modern Art.

Frye, Northrop. 1957. *Anatomy of Criticism: Four Essays*. Princeton, NJ: Princeton University Press.

Fukuyama, Francis. 1992. *The End of History and the Last Man*. London: Penguin.

Fukuyama, Francis. 2012. 'The Future of History'. *Foreign Affairs*. 1 January 2012. Accessed 16 January 2013. https://www.foreignaffairs.com/articles/2012-01-01/future-history

Funk, Wolfgang. 2015. *The Literature of Reconstruction: Authentic Fiction in the New Millennium*. London: Bloomsbury Academic.

Furlani, Andre. 2007. *Guy Davenport: Postmodernism and After*. Evanston, IL: Northwestern University Press.

Galgut, Damon. 2010. *In a Strange Room*. London: Atlantic Books.

Garber, Marjorie. 1996. 'Postmodernism and the Possibilities of Biography'. In *The Seductions of Biography*, edited by Mary Rhiel and David Schoff, 175–77. New York; London: Routledge.

Garcia, Angela. 2008. 'The Elegaic Addict: History, Chronicity, and the Melancholic Subject'. *Cultural Anthropology* 23(4): 718–46.

Gibbons, Alison. 2015. '"Take That You Intellectuals" and "KaPOW!": Adam Thirlwell and the Metamodernist Future of Style'. *Studia Neophilologica* 87(Supp 1): 29–43.

Gibbons, Alison. 2016. '"I Haven't Seen You Since (a Specific Date, a Time, the Weather)": Global Identity and the Reinscription of Subjectivity in Brian Castro's *Shanghai Dancing*'. *Ariel: A Journal of International English Literature* 47(1–2): 223–51.

Gillespie, Nick and Jesse Walker. 2006. 'South Park Libertarians'. *Reason*. December 2006. http://reason.com/archives/2006/12/05/south-park-libertarians

Gilmore, Leigh. 1994. 'The Mark of Autobiography: Postmodernism, Autobiography, and Genre'. In *Autobiography and Postmodernism*, edited by Ashley Kathleen, Leigh Gilmore and Gerald Peters, 3–21. Amherst: University of Massachusetts Press.

Goffman, Erving. 1959. *The Presentation of Self in Everyday Life*. London: Penguin.

Goldsmith, Kenneth. 2011. *Uncreative Writing: Managing Language in the Digital Age*. New York: Columbia University Press.

Goldstein, Jeffrey. 2005. 'Emergence, Creative Process, and Self-Transcending Constructions'. In *Managing Organizational Complexity: Philosophy, Theory, and Application*, edited by Kurt A. Richardson, 63–78. Greenwich, CT: Information Age Publishing.

Gorfinkel, Elena. 2005. 'The Future of Anachronism: Todd Haynes and the Magnificent Andersons'. In *Cinephilia: Movies, Love and Memory*, edited by Marijke de Valck and Malte Hagener, 153–68. Amsterdam: Amsterdam University Press.

Green, Jeremy. 2005. *Late Postmodernism: American Fiction at the Millennium*. New York: Palgrave.

Greven, Thomas. 2016. 'The Rise of Right-Wing Populism in Europe and the United States: A Comparative Perspective'. *Friedrich Ebery Stiftung*. May 2016. Accessed 1 November 2016. http://www.fesdc.org/fileadmin/user_upload/publications/RightwingPopulism.pdf

Grossberg, Lawrence. 1992. *We Gotta Get Out of This Place: Popular Conservatism and Postmodern Culture*. New York; London: Routledge.

Gudmundsdóttir, Gunnthórunn. 2003. *Borderlines: Autobiography and Fiction in Postmodern Life Writing*. Amsterdam; New York: Rodopi.

Hardt, Michael and Antonio Negri. 2001. *Empire*. Cambridge, MA: Harvard University Press.

Hardt, Michael and Antonio Negri. 2011. 'The Fight for "Real Democracy" at the Heart of Occupy Wall Street'. *Foreign Affairs*. 11 October 2011. Accessed 15 October 2016. https://www.foreignaffairs.com/articles/north-america/2011-10-11/fight-real-democracy-heart-occupy-wall-street

Harman, Graham. 2005. *Guerilla Metaphysics. Phenomenology and the Carpentry of Things*. Open Court.

Harsin, Jayson. 2015. 'Regimes of Posttruth, Post Politics and Attention Economics'. *Communication, Culture and Critique* 8: 327–33.

Hartog, Francois. 2016. *Regimes of Historicity: Presentism and Experiences of Time*. Columbia University Press.

Harvey, David. 1990. *The Condition of Postmodernity. An Enquiry into the Origins of Cultural Change*. Oxford/Cambridge: Blackwell Publishers.

Harvey, David. 2005. *A Brief History of Neoliberalism*. Oxford: Oxford University Press.

Hassan, Ihab. 2003. 'Beyond Postmodernism: Toward an Aesthetic of Trust'. *Angelaki: Journal of the Theoretical Humanities* 8(1): 3–11.

Hegel, G.W.F. 1971. *Philosophy of Mind. Part 3 of the Encyclopaedia of the Philosophical Sciences*. Translated by William Wallace and A.V. Miller. Oxford: Clarendon.

Hegel, G.W.F. 1977. *Phenomenology of Spirit*. Translated by A.V. Miller. Oxford: Oxford University Press.

Heise, Ursula K. 2008. *Sense of Planet and Sense of Place: The Environmental Imagination of the Global*. New York: Oxford University Press.

Heiser, Jörg. 2007. *Romantic Conceptualism*. Vienna: BAWAG Foundation.

Heiser, Jörg. 2010a. 'State of the Art: What Is "Super-Hybridity"?' *Frieze* 133. Accessed 15 August 2015. http://www.frieze.com/issue/article/pick-mix/

Heiser, Jörg. 2010b. 'Analyze This: A Round Table Discussion Led by Jörg Heiser on "Super-Hybridity": What Is It and Should We Be Worried? With Ronald Jones, Nina Power, Seth Price, Sukhdev Sandhu and Hito Steyerl'. *Frieze*. Accessed 15 August 2015. https://frieze.com/article/analyze

Heiser, Jörg. 2012. *Super-Hybridity. A Brief Genealogy of a Method, and a State of Being*. West: The Hague. Accessed 15 August 2015. http://issuu.com/galeriewest/docs/west_presents_j_rg_heiser

Heti, Sheila. 2013. *How Should a Person Be?* London: Harvill Secker.

Holland, Mary. 2012. 'A Lamb in Wolf's Clothing: Postmodern Realism in A. M. Homes's *Music for Torching* and *This Book Will Save Your Life*'. *Critique* 53(3): 214–37.

Holland, Mary. 2013. *Succeeding Postmodernism: Language and Humanism in Contemporary American Literature*. London, New York: Bloomsbury.

Huber, Irmtraud. 2014. *Literature After Postmodernism: Reconstructive Fantasies*. Houndmills: Palgrave Macmillan.

Huehls, Mitchum. 2016. *After Critique: Twenty-First-Century Fiction in a Neoliberal Age*. Oxford: Oxford University Press.

Huffer, Lynne. 2013. *Are the Lips a Grave?: A Queer Feminist on the Ethics of Sex*. New York: Columbia University Press.

Hurd, Robert. 2007. 'Taking Seinfeld Seriously: Modernism in Popular Culture'. *New Literary History* 37(4): 761–76.

Hutcheon, Linda. 1988. *A Poetics of Postmodernism: History, Theory, Fiction.* New York: Routledge.

Hutcheon, Linda. 2002 [1995]. *The Politics of Postmodernism.* Second Edition. New York: Routledge.

Huyssen, Andreas. 1986. *After the Great Divide.* London. The Macmillan Press Ltd.

Iser, Wolfgang. 1993. *The Fictive and the Imaginary: Charting Literary Anthropology.* Baltimore, MD: Johns Hopkins University Press.

Jagoda, Patrick. 2016. *Network Aesthetics.* Chicago: University of Chicago Press.

James, David. 2012. *Modernist Futures: Innovation and Inheritance in the Contemporary Novel.* New York: Cambridge University Press.

James, David and Urmila Seshagiri. 2014. 'Metamodernism: Narratives of Continuity and Revolution'. *PMLA* 129(1): 87–100.

Jameson, A. D. 2012. 'Theory of Prose & Better Writing (ctd): The New Sincerity, Tao Lin, & "Differential Perceptions"'. *HTMLGIANT.* 28 May 2012. Accessed 12 September 2016. http://htmlgiant.com/craft-notes/theory-of-prose-better-writing-ctd-the-new-sincerity-differential-perceptions/

Jameson, Fredric. 1984. 'Periodizing the 60s'. *Social Text* 9/10: 178–209.

Jameson, Fredric. 1991 [1984]. 'The Cultural Logic of Late Capitalism'. In *Postmodernism, or, The Cultural Logic of Late Capitalism*, 1–54. London; Brooklyn: Verso.

Jameson, Fredric. 1992 [1988]. 'Postmodernism and Consumer Society'. In *Modernism/Postmodernism*, edited by Peter Brooker, 163–79. London: Longman.

Jameson, Fredric. 1998. *The Cultural Turn: Selected Writings on the Postmodern, 1983–1998.* London; New York: Verso.

Jones, Owen. 2015. 'Let's Do Hope Not Despair: Owen Jones Meets Jeremy Corbyn'. *YouTube.* Accessed 1 November 2016. https://www.youtube.com/watch?v=qBbsU9VkRvQ

Johnson, Merri Lisa. 2008. 'Dismembering the Heterosexual Imaginary: A Feminist Cultural Anatomy of the Infidelity Narrative in Nancy Mair's *Remembering the Bone House*'. *Tulsa Studies in Women's Literature* 27(2): 327–52.

Johnston, Lucy. 2015. *Digital Handmade: Craftsmanship and the New Industrial Revolution.* New York: Thames and Hudson.

Kagan, Robert. 2008. *The Return of History and the End of Dreams.* New York: Vintage Books.

Kaletsky, Anatole. 2011 [2010]. *Capitalism 4.0: The Birth of a New Economy.* London: Bloomsbury.

Kashin, Olen. 2014. 'The Most Dangerous Man in Ukraine Is an Obsessive War Reenactor Playing Now with Real Weapons'. *New Republic.* 23 July 2014. Accessed 15 August 2014. https://newrepublic.com/article/118813/igor-strelkov-russian-war-reenactor-fights-real-war-ukraine

Kaufman, Charlie, writer. Dir. Spike Jones. 2002. *Adaptation.* Los Angeles: Columbia Pictures.

Kelly, Adam. 2010. 'David Foster Wallace and the New Sincerity in American Fiction'. In *Consider David Foster Wallace: Critical Essays*, edited by David Hering, 131–46. Los Angeles: Sideshow.

Kelsey, Robin. 2009. 'Eye of the Beholder: Robin Kelsey on Michael Fried's *Why Photography Matters . . .' Artforum International* 47(5): 53–54, 57–58.

Kenner, Hugh. 1985. 'The Politics of the Plain Style'. *New York Times*. 15 September 1985. Accessed 1 November 2016. http://www.nytimes.com/1985/09/15/books/the-politics-of-the-plain.html?pagewanted=all

Keyes, Ralph. 2004. *The Post-Truth Era: Dishonesty and Deception in Contemporary Life*. New York: St Martins Press.

Kirby, Alan. 2009. *Digimodernism: How New Technologies Dismantle the Postmodern and Reconfigure Our Culture*. New York; London: Continuum.

Kjellman-Chapin, M. 2009. 'Fake Identity, Real Work: Authenticity, Autofiction, and Outsider Art'. *SPECS Journal of Art and Culture* 2: 148–58. http://scholarship.rollins.edu/cgi/viewcontent.cgi?article=1151&context=specs

Knausgaard, Karl Ove. 2013 [2009]. *A Death in the Family [My Struggle:1]*. Trans. Don Bartlett. London: Vintage Books.

Konstantinou, Lee. 2009. 'Wipe That Smirk Off Your Face: Postironic Literature and the Politics of Character'. PhD diss., Stanford University.

Konstantinou, Lee. 2016a. *Cool Characters: Irony and American Fiction*. Cambridge, MA: Harvard University Press.

Konstantinou, Lee. 2016b. 'Barack Obama's Postironic Bildungsroman'. In *Barack Obama's Literary Legacy: Readings of Dreams from My Father*, edited by Richard Purcell and Henry Veggian, 119–40. New York: Palgrave MacMillan.

Konstantinou, Lee. 2017. 'Neorealist Fiction'. In *American Literature in Transition: 2000–2010*, edited by Rachel Greenwald Smith. Cambridge: Cambridge University Press.

Kotsko, Adam. 2010. *Awkwardness*. Winchester, UK: Zero Books.

Kraus, Chris. 2006 [1998]. I Love Dick. Los Angeles, CA: Semiotext(e).

Krauthammer, Charles. 2003. 'Holiday From History'. 14 February 2003. The Washington Post. Accessed 14 August 2017. https://www.washingtonpost.com/archive/opinions/2003/02/14/holiday-from-history/05dd0d16-b653-47bd-baab-06794e7291ec/?utm_term=.5419be56155f

Kushner, Rachael. 2014 [2013]. *The Flamethrowers*. New York: Scribner.

Lacan, Jacques. 1991. *The Seminar of Jacques Lacan, Book II: The Ego in Freud's Theory and in the Technique of Psychoanalysis 1954–1955*. Edited by Jacques-Alain Miller. Translated by Sylvana Tomaselli. New York: Norton.

Landy, Joshua. 2011. 'Still Life in a Narrative Age: Charlie Kaufman's *Adaptation*'. *Critical Inquiry* 37(3): 497–514.

Lapoujade, David. 2000. 'From Transcendental Empiricism to Worker Nomadism'. *Pli: Warwick Journal of Philosophy* 9: 190–99.

Laruelle, Fançois. 2011. *The Concept of Non-Photography*. Second Revised edition. Urbanomic.

Latour, Bruno. 2010. 'An Attempt at a "Compositionist Manifesto"'. *New Literary History* 41: 471–90.

Leighton, Angela. 2007. *On Form: Poetry, Aestheticism, and the Legacy of the Word*. Oxford: Oxford University Press.

Lee, Stewart. 2007. 'Stewart Lee – Taxi Driver Argument'. *YouTube*. Accessed 1 November 2016. https://www.youtube.com/watch?v=4n-UGQcG3Jw&list=RD4n-UGQcG3Jw#t=11

Lerner, Ben. 2011. *Leaving the Atocha Station*. Minneapolis, MN: Coffee House Press.

Lerner Ben. 2014. *10:04*. London: Granta.

Lethem, Jonathan. 2003. *The Fortress of Solitude*. New York: Doubleday.

Lethem, Jonathan. 2013. *Dissident Garden*. New York: Doubleday.

Levinas, Emmanuel. 1998 [1981]. *Otherwise Than Being or Beyond Essence*. Pittsburgh, PA: Duquesne University Press.

LeWitt, Sol. 1969. 'Sentences on Conceptual Art'. Accessed 20 September 2016. http://www.altx.com/vizarts/conceptual.html

Leyner, Mark. 2012. *The Sugar-Frosted Nutsack*. New York: Little, Brown.

Lin, Tao. 2009. *Shoplifting from American Apparel*. New York: Melville House.

Lipovetsky, Gilles. 2005. *Hypermodern Times*. Cambridge; Malden, MA: Polity.

Lippert, Leopold. 2010. 'Negotiating Postmodernity and Queer Utopianism in *Shortbus*'. In *Landscapes of Postmodernity: Concepts and Paradigms of Critical Theory*, edited by Petra Eckhard, Michael Fuchs and Walter Höbling, 195–205. London: Transaction Publishers.

Loader, Reina-Marie. 2010. 'The Fountain – A Call to Discussion'. *Notes on Metamodernism*. 5 September 2010. Accessed 6 September 2016. http://www. metamodernism.com/2010/09/05/the-fountain-a-call-to-discussion

Lopate, Philip. 1997. *The Art of the Personal Essay: An Anthology from the Classical Era to the Present*. Anchor.

Luckhurst, Roger. 1996. '"Impossible Mourning" in Toni Morrison's *Beloved* and Michèle Roberts's *Daughters of the House*'. *Critique* 37(4): 243–60.

Lueg, Konrad and Gerhard Richter. 1963. *Leben mit Pop: eine Demonstration für den kapitalistischen Realismus*. Düsseldorf: Möbelhaus Berges.

Luhmann, Niklas. 1999. 'The Paradox of Form'. In *Problems of Form*, edited by Dirk Baecker, 15–26. Stanford, CA: Stanford University Press.

Lyotard, Jean-François. 1988 [1983]. *The Differend: Phrases in Dispute*. Manchester: Manchester University Press.

MacDowell, James. 2010. 'Notes on Quirky'. *Movie: A Journal of Film Criticism* 1. http://www2.warwick.ac.uk/fac/arts/film/movie/contents/notes_on_quirky.pdf

MacDowell, James. 2012. 'Wes Anderson, Tone and the Quirky Sensibility'. *New Review of Film and Television Studies* 10(1): 6–27.

MacDowell, James. 2014. 'The Andersonian, the Quirky, and "Innocence"'. In *The Films of Wes Anderson: Critical Essays on an Indiewood Icon*, edited by Peter Kunze, 153–70. London: Palgrave Macmillan.

MacDowell, James. 2016. 'Quirky Culture: Tone, Sensibility, and Structure of Feeling'. In *A Companion to American Indie Film*, edited by Geoff King, 83–105. London: Blackwell.

Mack, Michael. 2014. *Philosophy and Literature in Times of Crisis: Challenging Our Infatuation with Numbers*. New York; London: Bloomsbury.

MacKenzie, Scott. 2003. 'Manifest Destinies: Dogma 95 and the Future of the Film Manifesto'. In *Purity and Provocation: Dogma 95*, edited by Mette Hjort and Scott MacKenzie, 48–57. London: British Film Institute.

Malabou, Catherine. 2005. *The Future of Hegel: Plasticity. Temporality and Dialectic*. Translated by Lisbeth During. New York: Routledge.

Malabou, Catherine. 2007. 'Again: "The Wounds of the Spirit Heal, and Leave No Scars Behind"'. *Mosaic* 40(2): 27–37.

Marcus, Ben. 1998 [1995]. *The Age of Wire and String*. Champaign, IL: Dalkey Archive Press.

Marples, David. 2014. 'Igor Strelkov – Moscow Agent or Military Romantic?' *ODR: Russia and Beyond*. 13 June 2014. Accessed 15 August 2014. https://www.open democracy.net/od-russia/david-marples/igor-strelkov-moscow-agent-or-military-romantic

Masschelein, Anneleen. 2007. 'Foreword'. *Image [&] Narrative* 19. http://www.imageandnarrative.be/inarchive/autofiction/foreword.htm

Massumi, Brian. 2002. *Parables for the Virtual: Movement, Affect, Sensation*. Durham, NC; London: Duke University Press.

Mayshark, Jesse Fox. 2007. *Post-Pop Cinema: The Search for Meaning in New American Film*. Westport: Praeger Publishers.

McCaffery, Larry. 2012. 'An Expanded Interview with David Foster Wallace'. In *Conversations with David Foster Wallace*, edited by Stephen J. Burn, 21–52. Jackson: University Press of Mississippi.

McDonough, William and Michael Braungart. 2002. *Cradle to Cradle: Remaking the Way We Make Things*. New York: North Point Press.

McGurl, Mark. 2009. *The Program Era: Postwar Fiction and the Rise of Creative Writing*. Cambridge, MA: Harvard University Press.

McHugh, Gene. 2011. *Post Internet*. Brescia: Link Editions. http://www.linkartcenter.eu/public/editions/Gene_McHugh_Post_Internet_Link_Editions_2011.pdf

McLaughlin, Robert L. 2004. 'Post-Postmodern Discontent: Contemporary Fiction and the Social World'. *Symploke* 12(1/2): 53–69.

McLaughlin, Robert. 2007. 'Postmodernism in the Age of Distracting Discourses'. In *The Mourning After: Attending the Wake of Postmodernism*, edited by Neil Brooks and Josh Toth, 53–64. Amsterdam: Rodopi.

McLaughlin, Robert L. 2012. 'Post-Postmodernism'. In *The Routledge Companion to Experimental Literature*, edited by Joe Bray, Alison Gibbons and Brian McHale, 212–23. London; New York: Routledge.

Mezzofiore, Gianluca. 2014a. 'Syrian Civil War Videos Used for Online Propaganda in Israel-Gaza Conflict'. *International Business Times*. 21 July 2014. Accessed 15 August 2014. http://www.ibtimes.co.uk/syrian-civil-war-videos-used-online-propaganda-israel-gaza-conflict-1457571

Mezzofiore, Gianluca. 2014b. 'Igor Strelkov: Key MH17 Crash Suspect Linked to Massacre of 3,000 Bosnian Muslims in 1992'. *International Business Times*. 25 July 2014. Accessed 15 August 2014. http://www.ibtimes.co.uk/igor-strelkov-key-mh17-crash-suspect-linked-massacre-3000-bosnian-muslims-1992-1458304

Milne, Seumas. 2012. *The Revenge of History: The Battle for the Twenty First Century*. London; Brooklyn: Verso.

Mills, Brett. 2005. *Television Sitcom*. London: Palgrave Macmillan.

Mills, Brett. 2009. *The Sitcom*. Edinburgh: Edinburgh University Press.

Mitchell, W.J.T. 1980. *The Language of Images*. Chicago, IL: University of Chicago Press.

Mitchell, W.J.T. 1986. *Iconology: Image, Text, Ideology*. Chicago, IL: University of Chicago Press.

Mitchell, W.J.T. 1992. 'Ekphrasis and the Other'. *South Atlantic Quarterly* 91(3): 695–719.

Mitchell, W.J.T. 1995. *Picture Theory: Essays on Verbal and Visual Representation.* Chicago, IL: University of Chicago Press.

Mohanty, Satya P. 2000 [1993]. 'The Epistemic Status of Cultural Identity: On *Beloved* and the Postcolonial Condition'. In *Reclaiming Identity: Realist Theory and the Predicament of the Postmodern*, edited by Paula M. L. Moya and Michael R. Hames-Garcia, 29–66. Berkeley: University of California Press.

MoMA. 2011. 'Art Speech: A Symposium on Symposia, Day 1'. *MoMA*. 20 May 2011. Accessed 1 November 2016. www.moma.org/explore/multimedia/audios/248/3067

Moraru, Christian. 2011. *Cosmodernism: American Narrative, Late Globalization, and the New Cultural Imaginary*. Ann Arbor: University of Michigan Press.

Moraru, Christian. 2013. 'Introduction to Focus: Thirteen Ways of Passing Postmodernism'. *American Book Review, In Focus: Metamodernism* May/June: 3–4.

Moretti, Franco. 2000 [1987]. *The Way of the World: The* Bildungsroman *in European Culture*. London: Verso.

Morrison, Toni. 1988 [1987]. *Beloved*. New York: Plume.

Mortimer, A. K. 2009. 'Autofiction as Allofiction: Doubrovsky's *L'Après-vivre'*. *L'Espirit Créateur* 49(3): 22–35.

Moya, Paula M. L. 2000a. 'Introduction: Reclaiming Identity'. In *Reclaiming Identity: Realist Theory and the Predicament of the Postmodern*, edited by Paula M. L. Moya and Michael R. Hames-Garcia, 1–26. Berkeley: University of California Press.

Moya, Paula M. L. 2000b. 'Postmodernism, "Realism," and the Politics of Identity'. In *Reclaiming Identity: Realist Theory and the Predicament of the Postmodern*, edited by Paula M. L. Moya and Michael R. Hames-Garcia, 67–101. Berkeley: University of California Press.

Nealon, Jeffrey T. 2012. *Post-Postmodernism; or, The Cultural Logic of Just-in-Time Capitalism*. Stanford, CA: Stanford University Press.

Nelson, A. 2011. 'Completely Average in Every Way'. *Amazon.com*. 28 March 2011. Accessed 6 September 2016. http://www.amazon.com/review/R6S1WMRYAGVD7/ref=cm_srch_res_rtr_alt_59

Ngai, Sianne. 2012. 'Network Aesthetics: Juliana Spahr's *The Transformation* and Bruno Latour's *Reassembling the Social'*. In *American Literature's Aesthetic Dimensions*, edited by Cindy Weinstein and Christopher Looby, 367–92. New York: Columbia University Press.

Nicholson, Linda. 1999. *The Play of Reason: From the Modern to the Postmodern*. Buckingham: Open University Press.

O'Brien, Geoffrey. 1997. 'Sein of the Times'. *The New York Review of Books*, 12 August 1997. 12–14.

O'Connor, Alan. 2006. *Raymond Williams*. Oxford: Rowman and Littlefield Publishers, Inc.

O'Reilly, Tim. 2005. 'What Is Web 2.0? Design Patterns and Business Models for the Next Generation of Software'. Accessed 6 May 2016. http://www.oreilly.com/pub/a/web2/archive/what-is-web-20.html

Orlean, Susan. 2000 [1998]. *The Orchid Thief: A True Story of Beauty and Obsession*. New York: Ballantine Books.

Osborne, Peter. 2011. 'The Fiction of the Contemporary: Speculative Collectivity and Transnationality in the Átlas Group'. In *Aesthetics and Contemporary Art*, edited by Armen Avanessian and Luke Skrebowski, 101–23. Berlin: Sternberg Press.

Ozeki, Ruth. 2013. A Tale for the Time Being. Edinburgh: Canongate.

Palissy, Bernard. 1996. *Œuvres Complètes*, 2 vols. Edited by Marie-Madeleine Fragonard, Keith Cameron, Jean Céard, Marie-Dominique Legrand, Frank Lestringant and Gilbert Shrenck. Mont-de-Marsan, France: Éditions InterUniversitaires.

Parisi, Luciana. 2013. *Contagious Architecture: Computation, Aesthetics, and Space*. Cambridge MA; London: MIT Press.

Paterson, Richard. 1998. 'Drama and Entertainment'. In *Television: An International History*. Second edition, edited by Anthony Smith, 57–68. Oxford: Oxford University Press.

Pearce, Michael. 2001. ' "Getting behind the image": Personality Politics in a Labour Party Election Broadcast'. *Language and Literature* 10(3): 211–20.

Pellegrini, Ann and Jasbir Puar. 2009. 'Affect'. *Social Text* 27(3): 35–38.

Perez, Carlota. 2009. 'The Double Bubble at the Turn of the Century: Technological Roots and Structural Implications'. *Cambridge Journal of Economics* 22: 779–805.

Pfeil, Fred. 1988. 'Postmodernism as a "Structure of Feeling" '. In *Marxism and the Interpretation of Culture*, edited by Cary Nelson and Lawrence Grossberg, 381–403. Chicago: University of Illinois Press.

Pine, B. Joseph and James H. Gilmore. 2011 [1999]. *The Experience Economy: Work Is Theatre and Every Business Is a Stage*. Updated edition. Boston: Harvard Business School.

Place, Vanessa and Robert Fitterman. 2009. *Notes on Conceptualisms*. Ugly Duckling Presse.

Plascencia, Salvador. 2005. *The People of Paper*. New York: Mariner Books.

Poe, Edgar Allan. 1998 [1844]. 'The Purloined Letter'. In *Selected Tales*, edited by David Van Leer, 249–65. Oxford: Oxford University Press.

Poecke, Niels van. 2014. 'De ballast van vernieuwing: Over metamodernisme in de popmuziek'. *Gonzo Circus* 122. Accessed 29 July 2014. http://www.gonzocircus. com/essay-de-ballast-van-vernieuwing-over-metamoder- *nisme-in-de-popmuziek*

Pollock, Griselda and Fred Orton. 1978. *Vincent Van Gogh: Artist of His Time*. Phaidon.

Poniewozik, James. 2011. 'Louie Watch: Self, Love'. *Time*. 12 August 2011. Accessed 1 November 2016. http://entertainment.time.com/2011/08/12/louie-watch-self-love/

Pressman, Jessica. 2014. *Digital Modernism: Making It New in New Media*. Oxford; New York: Oxford University Press.

Purdy, Jedediah. 1999. *For Common Things: Irony, Trust, and Commitment in America Today*. New York: Knopf.

Pye, Douglas. 2007. 'Movies and Tone'. In *Close-Up 02*, edited by John Gibbs and Douglas Pye, 1–80. London: Wallflower Press.

Rak, Julie. 2013. *Boom! Manufacturing Memoir for the Popular Market*. Waterloo, ON: Wilfrid Laurier University Press.

'R_byass'. 2001. 'The Book I Wish I'd Written'. *Amazon.co.uk*. 22 August 2001. Accessed 6 September 2016. http://www.amazon.co.uk/review/RYQWNXQ YGB0AS

Rapoport, David C. 2002. 'The Four Waves of Rebel Terror and September 11'. *Anthropoetics* 8(1). Accessed 28 October 2016. http://www.anthropoetics.ucla.edu/ap0801/terror.htm

Rhee, Michelle Young-Mee. 2011. ' "Greater Lore": Metafiction in Chang-rae Lee's *Native Speaker'. MELUS* 36(1): 157–76.

Roberts, David. 2010. 'Post-Truth Politics'. *Grist.* Accessed 1 November 2016. http://grist.org/article/2010-03-30-post-truth-politics/

Roiland, Josh. 2012. 'Getting Away from It All: The Literary Journalism of David Foster Wallace and Nietzsche's Concept of Oblivion'. In *The Legacy of David Foster Wallace*, edited by Samuel Cohen and Lee Konstantinou, 25–52. Iowa City, IA: University of Iowa Press.

Rombes, Nicholas. 2005. 'Irony and Sincerity'. In *New Punk Cinema,* edited by Nicholas Rombes, 72–85. Edinburgh: Edinburgh University Press.

Rosenberg, Alyssa. 2012. 'How "The Wire" Influenced "Parks and Recreation" '. *ThinkProgress.* http://thinkprogress.org/alyssa/2012/04/26/471789/the-wire-parks-and-recreation/

Rosenblatt, Roger. 2001. 'The Age of Irony Comes to an End'. *Time.* 24 September 2001. Accessed 8 September 2016. http://content.time.com/time/magazine/article/0,9171,1000893,00.html

Roth, Marco. 2009. 'Rise of the Neuronovel'. *n+1.* 14 September 2009. Accessed 24 June 2016. https://nplusonemag.com/issue-8/essays/the-rise-of-the-neuronovel

Rudnick, Paul and Kurt Andersen. 1989. 'The Irony Epidemic'. *Spy* (Mar): 92–98.

Rustad, Gry. 2012. 'Metamodernism, Quirky and Feminism'. *Notes on Metamodernism.* 29 February 2012. Accessed 6 September 2016. http://www.metamodernism.com/2012/02/29/metamodernism-quirky-and-feminism/#_edn3

Sadoux, Marion. 2002. 'Christine Angot's *Autofictions*: Literature and/or Reality?' In *Women's Writing in Contemporary France: New Writers, New Literatures in the 1990s*, edited by Gill Rye and Michael Worton, 171–81. Manchester; New York: Manchester University Press.

Saldívar, Ramón. 2011. 'Historical Fantasy, Speculative Realism, and Postrace Aesthetics in Contemporary American Fiction'. *ALH* 23(3): 574–99.

Saunders, Max. 2010. *Self Impression: Life-Writing, Autobiografiction, and the Forms of Modern Literature*. Oxford: Oxford University Press.

Savorelli, Antonio. 2010. *Beyond Sitcom – New Directions in American Television Comedy*. Jefferson, MO: McFarland.

Scarry, Elaine. 1987. *The Body in Pain*. London: Oxford University Press.

Schwarz, Henry and Anne Balsamo. 1996. 'Under the Sign of Semiotext(e): The Story According to Sylvere Lotringer and Chris Kraus'. *Critique* 37(3): 205–20.

Sconce, Jeffrey. 2002. 'Irony, Nihilism and the New American 'Smart' Film'. *Screen* 43(4): 349–69.

Scorsese, Martin, dir. 2013. *The Wolf of Wall Street*. Los Angles: Paramount.

Searle, Adrian. 2009. 'The Richest and Most Generous Tate Triennial Yet'. *The Guardian.* 3 February 2009. Accessed 13 May 2012. http://www.guardian.co.uk/artanddesign/2009/feb/02/altermodern-tate-triennial?intcmp=239.

Sebald, W. G. 1999 [1995]. *The Rings of Saturn*. New York: New Directions.

Self, Will. 2010. *Walking to Hollywood*. London: Bloomsbury.

Sennett, Richard. 2009. *The Craftsman*. London: Penguin books.

Shachar, Hila. 2011. 'Seeking Substance in Historical Costume Films'. *Notes on Metamodernism*. 24 October 2011. Accessed 6 September 2016. http://www.metamodernism.com/2011/10/24/seeking-substance-in-historical-costume-films/

Shotter, John. 1996. '"Now I Can Go On": Wittgenstein and Our Embodied Embeddedness in the "Hurly-Burly" of Life'. *Human Studies* 19: 385–407.

Simondon, Gilbert. 2012. *Du mode d'existence des objects techniques*. Paris: Aubier.

Simpson, David. 1995. 'Raymond Williams: Feeling for Structures, Voicing "History"'. In *Cultural Materialism: On Raymond Williams*, edited by Christopher Prendergast, 29–50. Minneapolis: University of Minnesota Press.

Smith, Ali. 2012. *Artful*. Penguin Books.

Smith, Ali. 2014. *How to Be Both*. London: Hamish Hamilton.

Smith, Pamela. 2004. *The Body of the Artisan. Art and Experience in the Scientific Revolution*. Chicago/London: The University of Chicago Press.

Smith, Rachel Greenwald. 2015. *Affect and American Literature in the Age of Neoliberalism*. Cambridge: Cambridge University Press.

Smith, Zadie. 2006 [2005]. *On Beauty*. New York: Penguin Books.

Smith, Zadie. 2007. 'Fail Better'. *The Guardian*. 13 January 2007. Accessed 24 June 2016. http://faculty.sunydutchess.edu/oneill/failbetter.htm

Sontag, Susan. 1990. *On Photography*. New York: Picador.

Sorkin, Michael, ed. 1992. *Variations on a Theme Park: The New American City and the End of Public Space*. New York: Hill and Wang.

Spahr, Juliana. 2005. *This Connection of Everyone with Lungs*. Berkeley: University of California Press.

Spuybroek, Lars. 2012. *The Sympathy of Things: Ruskin and the Ecology of Design*. Rotterdam: V2_Institute for Unstable Media.

Stengers, Isabelle and Despret, Vinciane. 2014. *Women Who Make a Fuss: The Unfaithful Daughters of Virginia Woolf*, translated by April Knutson. Minneapolis: Univocal.

Stephanson, Anders. 1988. 'Regarding Postmodernism – A Conversation with Fredric Jameson'. In *Universal Abandon? The Politics of Postmodernism*, edited by Andrew Ross, 3–30. Minneapolis: University of Minnesota Press.

Stephenson, Neal. 2000 [1995]. *The Diamond Age: Or, a Young Lady's Illustrated Primer*. New York: Bantam Spectra Books.

Sterling, Bruce. 2012. 'An Essay on the New Aesthetic'. *Wired*. 2 April 2012. Accessed 29 July 2014. http://www.wired.com/ 2012/04/an-essay-on-the-new-aesthetic

Stiegler, Bernard. 2010. *For a New Critique of Political Economy*. Translated by Daniel Ross. Cambridge/Malden MA: Polity Press.

Sturgeon, Jonathon. 2014. '2014: The Death of the Postmodern Novel and the Rise of Autofiction'. *Flavorwire*. 31 December 2014. Accessed 3 February 2015. http://flavorwire.com/496570/2014-the-death-of-the-postmodern-novel-and-the-rise-of-autofiction

Tallis, Benjamin. 2016. 'Living in Post-Truth: Power/knowledge/responsibility'. *New Perspectives* 24(1): 7–18.

Tarantino, Quentin, dir. 2009. *Inglourious Basterds*. New York: Weinstein Company.

Taylor, Charles. 1989. *Sources of the Self: The Making of Modern Identity*. Cambridge, MA: Harvard University Press.

Theweleit, Klaus. 1987. *Male Fantasies*. Minneapolis: University of Minnesota Press.

Thirlwell, Adam. 2012. *Kapow!* London: Visual Editions.

Timmer, Nicoline. 2010. *Do You Feel It Too? The Post-Postmodern Syndrome in American Fiction at the Turn of the Millennium*. Amsterdam; New York: Rodopi.

Toth, Josh. 2010. *The Passing of Postmodernism: A Spectroanalysis of the Contemporary*. Albany: State University of New York Press.

Toth, Josh. 2013. 'Healing Postmodern America: Plasticity and Renewal in Danielewski's *House of Leaves*'. *Critique* 54(2): 181–97.

Turner, Luke. 2011. 'Metamodernist // Manifesto'. *Metamodernism.org*. Accessed 1 November 2016. http://www.metamodernism.org

Tyrone X, Vaman. 2012. 'Book Review: Tao Lin's Richard Yates, Shoplifting at American Apparel, and Bed'. *AALR*. 23 April 2012. Accessed 24 June 2016. https://archive.is/WtqlG

Vaessens, Thomas and Yra van Dijk. 2011. 'Introduction: European Writers Reconsidering the Postmodern Heritage'. In *Reconsidering the Postmodern*, edited by Thomas Vaessens and Yra van Dijk, 7–24. Amsterdam University Press.

Vermeulen, Pieter. 2015. *Contemporary Literature and the End of the Novel: Creature, Affect, Form*. Basingstoke: Palgrave Macmillan.

Vermeulen, Timotheus. 2013. 'Review: Christoph Knecht'. *Frieze*. 7 September 2013. Accessed 6 September 2016. https://frieze.com/article/christoph-knecht

Vermeulen, Timotheus. 2015. 'The New "Depthiness"'. *e-flux* 61(1): n.p. http://www.e-flux.com/journal/the-new-depthiness/

Vermeulen, Timotheus and Gry Rustad. 2013. 'Watching Television with Jacques Rancière: US "Quality Television', Mad Men and the "late cut"'. *Screen* 53(3): 341–54.

Vermeulen, Timotheus and Robin van den Akker. 2010. 'Notes on Metamodernism'. *Journal of Aesthetics and Culture* 2: 1–14. http://www.aestheticsandculture.net/index.php/jac/article/view/5677/6304

Vermeulen, Timotheus and Robin van den Akker. 2015. 'Utopia, Sort Of: A Case Study in Metamodernism'. *Studia Neophiliogica* 18(Supp 1): 55–67.

Voegelin, Eric. 1989. 'Equivalences of Experience and Symbolization in History'. In *The Collected Works of Eric Voegelin*, edited by E. Sandoz, Volume 12, 115–33. Baton Rouge: Louisiana State University Press.

Wallace, David Foster. 1989. 'Westward the Course of Empire Takes Its Way'. In *Girl with Curious Hair*, 231–373. New York: Norton.

Wallace, David Foster. 1997. 'E Unibus Pluram: Television and U.S. Fiction'. In *A Supposedly Fun Thing I'll Never Do Again*, 21–82. London: Abacus.

Wallace, David Foster. 1999. 'Octet'. In *Brief Interviews with Hideous Men*, 131–60. New York: Little, Brown and Company.

Wallace, David Foster. 2001 [1996]. *Infinite Jest*. London: Abacus.

Wallace, David Foster. 2001 [1999]. 'Octet'. In *Brief Interviews with Hideous Men*, 111–36. London: Abacus.

Wallace, David Foster. 2004. 'Good Old Neon'. In *Oblivion: Stories*, 141–81. London: Abacus.

Wallace, David Foster. 2004 [1987]. *The Broom of the System*. New York: Penguin.

Wallace, David Foster. 2011. *The Pale King: An Unfinished Novel*. London: Hamish Hamilton.

Wampole, Christy. 2012. 'How to Live Without Irony'. *New York Times*. 17 November 2012. Accessed 24 June 2016. http://opinionator.blogs.nytimes.com/2012/11/17/how-to-live-without-irony/

Warwick, A. R. 2012. 'Falling Very Slowly: The Metamodernism of Terry Gilliam's *Tideland*. *Artwrit*. Accessed 6 September 2016. http://www.artwrit.com/article/falling-very-slowly-the-metamodernism-of-terry-gilliams-tideland

Wegner, Phillip E. 2014. *Periodizing Jameson: Dialectics, the University, and the Desire for Narrative*. Evanston, IL: Northwestern University Press.

Whyte, William H. 2002. *The Organization Man*. Foreword by Joseph Nocera. Philadelphia: University of Pennsylvania Press.

Will, George F. 2001. 'The End of Our Holiday from History'. *The Washington Post*. 12 September 2001. Accessed 1 November 2016. https://www.washingtonpost.com/archive/opinions/2001/09/12/the-end-of-our-holiday-from-history/9da607fd-8fdc-4f33-b7c9-e6cda00453bb/

Williams, Raymond. 2001 [1954]. 'Film and the Dramatic Tradition'. In *The Raymond Williams Reader*, edited by John Higgins, 25–41. Oxford; Malden, MA: Blackwell Publishers.

Williams, Raymond. 1965. *The Long Revolution*. Harmondsworth: Penguin.

Williams, Raymond. 1977. *Marxism and Literature*. Oxford: Oxford University Press

Williams, Raymond. 1979. *Politics and Letters: Interviews with New Left Review*. London: New Left Books.

Williams, Raymond and Michael Orrom. 1954. *Preface to Film*. London: Film Drama.

Wilson, E. O. 1998. *Consilience: The Unity of Knowledge*. Random House. www.wtf.tw/ref/wilson.pdf.

Wittgenstein, Ludwig. 1929. 'Lecture on Ethics'. Ts-207, normalized transcription. Transcriptions can be found on: www.wittgensteinsource.org.

Wittgenstein, Ludwig. 2001 [1922]. *Tractatus Logico Philosophicus*. New York: Routledge.

Wodak, Ruth. 2009. *The Discourse of Politics in Action: Politics as Usual*. Basingstoke: Palgrave.

Wolfendale, Peter. 2014. *Object-Orientated Philosophy: The Noumenon's New Clothes*. Falmouth: Urbanomic.

Woodward, Kathleen. 1996. 'Global Cooling and Academic Warming: Long-Term Shifts in Emotional Weather'. *American Literary History* 8(4): 759–79.

Woodward, Kathleen. 2009. *Statistical Panic: Cultural Politics and Poetics of the Emotions*. Durham, NC; London: Duke University Press.

Wu, Yung-Hsing. 2003. 'Doing Things with Ethics: *Beloved*, *Sula*, and the Reading of Judgment'. *MFS* 49(4): 780–805.

Zavarzadeh, Mas'ud. 1975. 'The Apocolyptic Fact and the Eclipse of Fiction in Recent American Prose Narratives'. *Journal of American Studies* 9(1): 69–83.

Zeller, Christoph. 2010. *Ästhetik des Authentischen: Literatur und Kunst um 1970*. Berlin: de Gruyter.

Zinc, Nell. 2014. *The Wallcreeper*. London: Harper Collins.

Žižek, Slavoj. 2000. *The Art of the Ridiculous Sublime: On David Lynch's* Lost Highway. Seattle: University of Washington Press.

Žižek, Slavoj. 2002. *Welcome to the Desert of the Real! Five Essays on September 11 and Related Dates*. London; New York: Verso.

Index

About the Contributors

Robin van den Akker is lecturer of philosophy and cultural studies in, and academic programme coordinator of, the Humanities Department at Erasmus University College Rotterdam (NL) and co-founding editor of the research platform *Notes on Metamodernism*. His research on contemporary aesthetics and culture and the digitisation of everyday life has been published in the *Journal of Aesthetics and Culture, Frieze, ArtPulse, Monu, The American Book Review* and various other journals, magazines and collections. As a member of 'Filosofisch Elftal' ('Team Philosophy'), he has a regular column on current affairs in the Dutch national daily newspaper *Trouw*.

Sam Browse is lecturer in the Department of Humanities at Sheffield Hallam University. His research uses ideas from cognitive linguistics, classical rhetoric and cognitive and social psychology to examine persuasion in political discourse. He is the author of *Cognitive Rhetoric: The Cognitive Poetics of Political Discourse* (forthcoming). His teaching has spanned a wide range of subject areas, including stylistics, critical theory, discourse analysis, grammar and narrative theory.

James Elkins's writing focuses on the history and theory of images in art, science and nature. Some of his books are exclusively on fine art (*What Painting Is, Why Are Our Pictures Puzzles?*). Others include scientific and non-art images, writing systems and archaeology (*The Domain of Images, On Pictures and the Words That Fail Them*), and some are about natural history (*How to Use Your Eyes*). Recent books include *What Photography Is*, written against Roland Barthes's *Camera Lucida; Artists with PhDs,* second edition; and *Art Critiques: A Guide*, third edition.

Raoul Eshelman is professor of Slavic literature at the Ludwig-Maximilians-Universität in Munich. He received his doctorate in Slavic literature from the University of Konstanz in 1988. He has taught, among other places, at the University of Hamburg, Berkeley, Rutgers (Newark), Heidelberg and Konstanz and is the author of numerous studies on Russian and Czech modernism and postmodernism. His present concentration is on performatism, or the epoch after postmodernism. In this regard, he is the author of some twenty articles on the subject as well as of the book *Performatism, or the End of Postmodernism* (2008).

Wolfgang Funk is assistant professor of English literature and culture at Johannes Gutenberg-Universität Mainz, where he is currently working on a post-doc project on late Victorian women poets and their use of evolutionary imagery. He has published articles on Bryony Lavery (2007), Jasper Fforde (2010), Martin McDonagh (2010), Dave Eggers (2011), Jez Butterworth (2011), Hilary Mantel (2013), Peter the Wild Boy (2015), May Kendall (2015) and Max Müller (2016). He is the co-editor of *Fiktionen von Wirklichkeit: Authentizität zwischen Materialität und Konstruktion* (2011) and *The Aesthetics of Authenticity: Medial Constructions of the Real* (2012). His Ph.D. thesis, *The Literature of Reconstruction: Authentic Fiction in the New Millennium*, was published in 2015.

Alison Gibbons is reader in contemporary stylistics at Sheffield Hallam University, United Kingdom. Her research consistently pursues a stylistic approach to innovative and contemporary narrative. Alison is the author of *Multimodality, Cognition, and Experimental Literature* (2012, pbk 2014, Chinese Trans. 2016). As well as being an editor of *Metamodernism: Historicity, Affect, and Depth after Postmodernism*, she is editor of *Mark Z. Danielewski* (2011, pbk 2015; with Joe Bray), the *Routledge Companion to Experimental Literature* (2012, pbk 2014; with Joe Bray and Brian McHale), and *Pronouns in Literature: Positions and Perspectives in Language* (2018; with Andrea Macrae). Her central research interests currently focus on multimodal fiction, metamodernism, contemporary autofiction, fiction on the Arab Spring and the reception of contemporary narratives through empirical study.

Jörg Heiser is professor and director of the Institute Art in Context, at the University of Arts in Berlin. He was associate editor of *frieze* magazine from 1998 to 2003, and co-editor from 2003 to 2016, and has been a critic for *Süddeutsche Zeitung* since 1997. As a curator, among other projects, he realised *Funky Lessons* (BüroFriedrich Berlin, Bawag Foundation Vienna, 2004–2005) and *Romantic Conceptualism* (Kunsthalle Nuremberg and Bawag Foundation Vienna, 2007). His books include *All of a Sudden. Things*

That Matter in Contemporary Art (2008), and *Double Lives in Art and Pop Music* (forthcoming 2017).

Irmtraud Huber studied comparative literature, English and theatre studies in Munich. She worked as a lecturer at the English department of the Universität Bern, where she completed her PhD with a thesis on 'Reconstructive Dreams: A Pragmatic Fantastic After Postmodernism'. Her thesis was awarded with the Helene-Richter Prize of the Deutscher Anglistenverband. With support from the Swiss National Science Foundation, she has held a visiting fellowship at Columbia University, New York, and is about to pursue her research as a visiting fellow of the University of Cambridge and Queen Mary College, University of London. She is an affiliated postdoctoral member of Clare Hall, Cambridge, and an associated postdoctoral fellow of the Walter Benjamin Kolleg, Universität Bern. Her current research focuses on perceptions and representations of time in Victorian poetry.

Lee Konstantinou is assistant professor of English at the University of Maryland, College Park. He wrote the novel *Pop Apocalypse* (2009) and the critical monograph *Cool Characters: Irony and American Fiction* (2016). He co-edited the collection *The Legacy of David Foster Wallace* (2012) with Samuel Cohen. He is writing a monograph on Helen DeWitt's novel *The Last Samurai* and is beginning research on a history of art comics in the United States. He is a Humanities section editor with the *Los Angeles Review of Books*.

James MacDowell is assistant professor in film and television studies at the University of Warwick. He is the author of the monographs *Irony in Film* (2016) and *Happy Endings in Hollywood Cinema: Cliché, Convention and the Final Couple* (2013). He sits on the board of the open access journal *Movie: A Journal of Film Criticism*.

Gry C. Rustad (PhD) is post-doctoral fellow at the University of Oslo at the Department of Media and Communication and a visiting scholar at Northwestern University's Screen Cultures Program. Her main interests are television aesthetics and television as cultural form, and she is currently working on a research project about aesthetic innovation in web television. She has co-published on television aesthetics in among other places Screen and has forthcoming publications on Reality-TV aesthetics.

Kai Hanno Schwind holds a position as associate professor at Westerdals Oslo School of Arts, Communications and Technology. He holds a PhD in media studies from the University of Oslo with a dissertation on the adaptation of situation comedy formats in different countries (2015: 'Found in Translation: The Office – a hybrid sitcom as blueprint for successful trans-national television format adaptation') and a master's degree in film- and television studies from Johann Wolfgang Goethe University in Frankfurt, Germany (2004: 'The Most Beautiful Lies – Aspects of the Australian Leg-end in Contemporary Australian Cinema'). His recent research interest has a focus on socio-cultural aspects of humour and political satire, and the dynam-ics of media and nostalgia. He has recently published articles in *HUMOR – International Journal of Humor Research*, *Comedy Studies*, as well as in various German and Norwegian journalistic publications.

Nicoline Timmer is a visual artist and autonomous researcher. She was awarded her PhD in 2008 by the University of Utrecht for her dissertation on post-postmodern American fiction. Her book *Do You Feel It Too? The Post-Postmodern Syndrome in American Fiction at the Turn of the Millen-nium* was published in 2010. She combined her Ph.D. research with a fine arts education at the Gerrit Rietveld Academy in Amsterdam. After graduating from this academy she did a two-year artist residency at the Rijksakademie van Beeldende Kunsten (2012–2013). Over the years she has lectured at several universities and art academies. Currently, she is working on an opera, called *Once upon a particular occasion*, combining sound, visual philosophy, movement and writing. Her main interests are new approaches of the self, relationality, presence and enchantment. In February 2017 her first novel *En toen aten we zeehond* was published.

Josh Toth is associate professor of English at MacEwan University. He is co-editor of *The Mourning After: Attending the Wake of Postmodernism* (2007) and author of *The Passing of Postmodernism: A Spectroanalysis of the Contemporary* (2010) and *Stranger America: A Narrative Ethics of Exclusion* (2018).

Sjoerd van Tuinen is assistant professor in philosophy at Erasmus Uni-versity Rotterdam and holds a PhD (on Deleuze and Leibniz) from Ghent University. He is editor of several books, including *Deleuze and The Fold. A Critical Reader* (2010), *De nieuwe Franse filosofie* (2011), *Speculative Art Histories* (2017) and *The Polemics of Resentment* (2018), and has authored *Sloterdijk. Binnenstebuiten denken* (2004).

Timotheus Vermeulen is associate professor in media, culture and society at the University of Oslo and co-founding editor of the research platform *Notes on Metamodernism*. Tim has written on contemporary aesthetics, art, film and television for numerous journals and magazines, including *Journal of Aesthetics and Culture*, *E-Flux*, *Monu* and *Screen* as well as *Frieze* and *Frieze D/E* where he is a regular contributor. He is the author of *Scenes from the Suburbs* (Edinburgh University Press 2014) and co-editor of *New Suburban Stories* (2013; with Martin Dines).